NORTH CAROLINA
STATE BOARD OF COMMUNITY COLLEGES
LIBRARIES
SAMPSON TECHNICAL COLLEGE

P9-EIE-433

THE AMERICAN PERCEPTION OF CLASS

LABOR AND SOCIAL CHANGE

A SERIES EDITED BY PAULA RAYMAN
AND CARMEN SIRIANNI

HN
90
S6
V36
1987

1-22-88

24,532

T H E
AMERICAN PERCEPTION OF CLASS

REEVE VANNEMAN
LYNN WEBER CANNON

TEMPLE UNIVERSITY PRESS
PHILADELPHIA

Temple University Press, Philadelphia 19122
Copyright © 1987 by Temple University. All rights reserved
Published 1987
Printed in the United States of America

The paper used in this publication meets the minimum
requirements of American National Standard for Information
Sciences—Permanence of Paper for Printed Library Materials,
ANSI Z39.48-1984

Library of Congress Cataloging-in-Publication Data

Vanneman, Reeve, 1945–
The American perception of class.

(Labor and social change)
Bibliography: p. 311
Includes index.
1. Social classes—United States. 2. Labor and
laboring classes—United States. 3. Class consciousness
—United States. 4. Social conflict—United States.
I. Cannon, Lynn Weber, 1949–   . II. Title.
III. Series.
HN90.S6V36   1987   305.5′0973   86-14349
ISBN 0-87722-436-6 (alk. paper)

To Jane

R.V.

To John Robert Cannon, Jr.

L.W.C.

Contents

vii

TABLES

ix

Tables

FIGURES

ACKNOWLEDGMENTS

This book will annoy many of the scholars in its field. Preliminary versions of our argument that we presented in conference papers and journal articles provoked immediate hostility. The consistent support of our friends has enabled us to continue our work despite these reactions. We owe them a great deal and hope that the final product meets their expectations.

Several people worked with us on various parts of the research. Fred Pampel and Steve McNamee joined us in the early stages of the research that are reported in Chapter 4 and coauthored the first publications from the project. Steve has continued to provide assistance as we worked our way through several conceptual problems. Marcia Kirkpatrick helped direct the survey reported in Chapter 5. Benjamin To first developed the cross-national data reported in Chapter 6. Michelle Moore provided library research and Julie Wallace assisted with the references. Their contributions have made our work not only better but more enjoyable.

Many people read part or all of the manuscript. Dan Clawson, Marci DePeters, Jerry Hage, Richard Kraus, Roger Reitman, Michael Shalev, Carmen Sirianni, David Stark, and Wlodek Wesolowski offered many helpful suggestions. They deserve our thanks but none of the responsibility for the final version. Our editors, Michael Ames and Mary Capouya, gave us just the right mix of enthusiasm and careful criticism to keep the project moving. Derek Thompson and the crew at the Maryland Computer Cartography Lab provided resources and patient guidance that made the graphics possible. Ken Kammeyer added helpful evaluations in revising and selecting the final figures. Gerry Todd labored with most of the word processing and patiently endured all our revisions.

Earlier versions of parts of this manuscript appeared in *The American*

Journal of Sociology, *The American Sociological Review*, *Social Indicators Research*, *Social Science Quarterly*, and *Work and Occupations*. We are grateful to these journals for their many reviews and suggestions.

Financial support was provided by grants from the National Science Foundation and the Department of Labor. The computer centers of the University of Illinois, the University of Maryland, and Memphis State University provided the computer time for the hundreds of statistical analyses that this research required. The data were made available in part by the Interuniversity Consortium for Political and Social Research and were originally collected for the National Data Program for the Social Sciences at the National Opinion Research Center, the Center for Political Studies of the Institute for Social Research at the University of Michigan, ABC News and the Washington Post, and David Butler and Donald Stokes's "Study of Political Change in Britain." The data reported in Chapter 5 were collected by the Survey Research Laboratory of the University of Illinois. The granting agencies, the universities, the consortium, and the collectors of the original data bear no responsibility for the analyses and interpretations presented here.

To all these people who made our research possible and encouraged us to continue, I extend my deepest thanks.

Bethesda, Maryland   REEVE VANNEMAN

Over the twelve years that I have worked on this project, many colleagues, friends, students, and family members have provided support, encouragement, and reassurance. Early on at the University of Illinois, Steve McNamee and Marcia Kirkpatrick shared many long days and late nights in the Green Room Lounge working on different aspects of the project. The words of Dolly Parton, Tammy Wynette, and others, which clad our office walls and filled the air, were a continuous source of reassurance. And when things got tough, we would steal away, rest, listen to music, and have fun.

In recent years, support has come from a variety of sources, most important, from Elizabeth Higginbotham and Bonnie Thornton Dill. For many years, Elizabeth and Bonnie have played the full range of supportive roles on this project—good colleagues, best friends, and even sponsors. They read portions of the manuscript at each of its stages and gave critical feedback that especially enhanced our treatment of Blacks and women. They contributed resources from the Center for Research on Women at Memphis State University to support completion of the book. More important, as best friends, they encouraged me to continue at many difficult junctures over the years. By their example as brilliant, productive, proud, and committed Black women, as well as by their teachings, they showed me how to survive and even to thrive while challenging the basic assumptions of the discipline. For these and many other contributions too extensive to name, I am deeply grateful.

Other colleagues have also encouraged us and critiqued individual chapters. They include: Harold Benenson, Maxine Baca Zinn, Tina U. Howard, Robert Newby, Sandi Morgen, Michael F. Timberlake, and Kirk Williams.

Since 1976, many people at Memphis State University have contributed to the project. I am grateful to the many graduate students who have worked on data analysis and/or given feedback on the ideas. They include: Mary Ann Carpenter, William Chan, Sally High, Marianne L. A. Leung, Yvonne Newsome, Peggy Plass, Carol Risher, and Stella Warren. In addition, I appreciate the assistance of Boyce Elmore and others at the Memphis State University Computer Center, and of JoAnn Ammons, Marie Santucci, and other staff at the Center for Research on Women.

Special thanks go to our editor, Michael Ames for his enthusiasm and encouragement and to Mary Capouya, the production editor, for her patience and assistance in coordinating a publication with two authors who are miles apart.

My perspective on this research was derived in part from my working-class roots. My family has always taken pride in me and my accomplishments and has been encouraging throughout the process.

My deepest gratitude goes to John Robert Cannon, Jr., to whom I dedicate this book. He has shared fully in the excitement as well as the disappointments of this project. Over the years, he brought home the bacon, cooked it, and made sure we had some fun. His steadfast support for me and my work made this book possible.

Memphis, Tennessee   LYNN WEBER CANNON

THE AMERICAN PERCEPTION OF CLASS

CHAPTER 1
AMERICAN EXCEPTIONALISM

Conventional wisdom tells us that Americans are not class conscious. America's workers seem to lack the desire for class struggle that motivates socialist movements around the world. France and Italy have large Communist parties that capture much of the working-class vote; Austria, Germany, and the Scandinavian countries have worker-based Social Democratic parties; England and Australia have Labour parties that have won elections and governed during some if not most of the post–World War II period. Throughout Europe, workers' unions have sought not an accommodation to industrial capitalism but its replacement by a system of collective ownership. Working-class revolutions were fought in Paris in 1871, in Germany in 1918, and, of course, in Russia in 1917. And the newly formed working classes of Latin America, Africa, and Asia have looked to Marx, Lenin, and Mao for guidance in their struggles for national liberation and economic emancipation.

In comparison, the accomplishments of the American working class appear meager indeed: a mild, accommodation-oriented union movement that is losing membership; a reformist Democratic Party that, even when successful, fails to deliver much of consequence for the working class.

The seeming conservatism of the American working class has long confronted our best theories of industrial society with the enigma of "American exceptionalism." In Europe, nineteenth-century industrialization provoked a working-class resistance that developed into a "specter" haunting the world economy. It was assumed that America would soon follow this pattern and might even become its outstanding example. But the historical signs were often ambiguous. European radicals rejoiced at signs of American working-class militance, then despaired at the weakness of its socialist movement. American business celebrated the glories of "triumphant capitalism" but worried whether the radicalism abroad would invade these

1

shores. By the turn of the twentieth century, America remained a paradox of industrial strength and working-class weakness.

In 1906 the German sociologist Werner Sombart asked the now familiar question, "Why is there no socialism in the United States?" Although Sombart's question was premature in 1906 (the Socialist Party of America enjoyed its fastest growth right after the publication of his essay; see Weinstein, 1967; Aronowitz, 1983:17), it was perhaps prescient; unlike the industrialized countries of Europe, the United States never sustained a socialist movement. By the mid-1920s the American Left was in disarray.

The failure of American socialism and the weakness of the American labor movement have intrigued social scientists since Sombart; their explanations have become an entire academic industry.[1] Every facet of American life has been singled out and examined as a possible cause. For the popular press (see Thernstrom, 1964:57), American workers are not revolutionary because America is the land of *opportunity*: the "American Dream" directs workers' energies toward individual mobility rather than collective protest. For Sombart (1906), the main difference is that *prosperity* showers American workers with material abundance; in contrast, the greater deprivation of European workers fuels their demands for revolutionary change. For Louis Hartz (1955), it is America's *lack of a feudal past* that has obscured class lines and promoted instead an individualistic ("Lockian") ethos. For several recent Marxist interpreters (e.g., Jerome Karabel, 1979; Mike Davis, 1986), America's working class is weak because of *racial and ethnic divisions*: the more homogeneous populations of European nations present fewer natural barriers to working-class solidarity. For Seymour Martin Lipset (1960:73; 1983:2), *political suffrage* is a key: male American workers won the right to vote earlier than European workers, so their economic demands were not combined with a political movement into a revolutionary ideology. For C. T. Husbands (1976) the main obstacle is the *two-party system*. For Frederick Jackson Turner (1920), the *American frontier* drained the discontent that was bottled up in the teeming urban centers of Europe.

The debate over American exceptionalism continues to generate contro-

---

1. Some summaries can be found in Bottomore, 1966:48–55; Lipset, 1977; Karabel, 1979; Shalev and Korpi, 1980; Katznelson, 1981:10. Our list, which follows, cannot do justice to the complexities of the theories cited. Karabel notes that most of the factors discussed today had already been cited by Sombart in his 1906 essay. We explore each explanation in greater detail at the appropriate point.

versy because American conditions provide a test case for Marx's theory of socialist revolution (see Sweezy, 1967:26). Over a century after his death, Marx still sets the terms of the debate. It is as if the gods of social theory constructed an experiment with all the necessary ingredients and waited to see whether the predicted reaction would occur.

Marx and Engels identified the working class as the revolutionary element within modern capitalism. The proletariat was both the unique product of capitalist society and the agent of its destruction. This irony gave the historical process a grand inevitability: "The development of Modern Industry, therefore, cuts from under its feet the very foundation on which the bourgeoisie produces and appropriates products. What the bourgeoisie, therefore, produces, above all, is its own grave-diggers" (Marx and Engels [1848], 1976:496). The gravediggers were to be the modern working class.[2]

If capitalism produces its own destroyers, the progression toward working-class revolution should be clearest where capitalism is most advanced. As Marx ([1867] 1976:8–9) declared in his preface to *Capital*, "The country that is more developed industrially only shows, to the less developed, the image of its own future."

For much of the twentieth century, the United States has boasted the most advanced capitalist economy. By Marx's logic, therefore, the United States should harbor the most militant working class.[3] Instead, socialist movements are weaker here than in other capitalist countries, and workers least revolutionary.[4] The image of the future appears to be class accommodation, not class struggle. Critics of Marx quickly cited the failure of this

---

2. See also Engels ([1880] 1972:58–59): "Socialism: Utopian and scientific."

3. This was still part of the Marxist orthodoxy at the turn of the century. The leading European Marxists, Karl Kautsky, August Bebel, Eduard Bernstein, and Paul Lefargue, all endorsed the view that socialism would come to the United States first (see Moore, 1970; Lipset, 1977:49).

4. It is precisely this paradox that attracted Sombart's interest: "If, as I have myself always maintained and often stated, modern Socialism follows as a necessary reaction to capitalism, the country with the most advanced capitalist development, namely the United States, would at the same time be the one providing the classic case of Socialism, and its working class would be supporters of the most radical of Socialist movements. However, one hears just the opposite. . . . In fact, an assertion of this kind cannot fail to awaken our most active interest, for here at last is a country with no Socialism, despite its having the most advanced capitalist development. The doctrine of the inevitable Socialist future is refuted by the facts" (1906:15–16).

"test case" as conclusive evidence against the entire opus of Marxian theory.[5]

Today, the problem has taken a new twist. Many now think of the working class as only a nineteenth-century problem. The shift to a "postindustrial" economy has relegated the class struggle to the background as the labor force has become less industrial and more white collar, and as nineteenth-century robber barons were replaced by bureaucratic managers (Wattenberg, 1974; Naisbitt, 1982). From this new, postindustrial perspective, not only was Marx wrong; he is now irrelevant.

As in all such ideologically loaded subjects, it is important to get the facts straight first. America has indeed been exceptional but not always to the extent that our mythology would have us suppose. The evidence that American exceptionalism *exists*, much less what causes it, is not unequivocal. As Ira Katznelson (1981:9) points out, it is not just America that has been exceptional in failing to fulfill Marx's prediction of a revolutionary working class. The fact is that *no* advanced industrial society has transformed itself into a socialist state. We need to be careful, therefore, to specify precisely what it is about American society that is exceptional. The problem requires a carefully balanced appreciation of seemingly contradictory facts. Our contention is that the American working class is neither small nor passive. It is, however, *weak*, and it is this combination of size and militance with political and economic weakness that demands explanation.

American Class Conflicts

American exceptionalism does not mean that class conflicts have been absent in this country but rather that these conflicts never escalated to a point where they became a permanent battle line dividing society into well-entrenched encampments. In particular, it is *unions* and *parties* that have pro-

---

5. In fact, the opposite theory soon proved popular: revolutions are more likely during the early phases of industrialization and in economically backward areas of the world (Moore, 1954:226; Bendix, 1956:437; Mills, 1963:256; Sweezy, 1967:43; Lipset, 1979:14; Gouldner, 1980:50; Katznelson, 1981:9). Even Engels once seems to have subscribed to this theory: "The class struggles here in England, too, were more turbulent during the *period of development* of large-scale industry and died down just in the period of England's undisputed industrial domination of the world. In Germany, too, the development of large-scale industry since

vided European workers enduring bases for their class protest, and it is these institutions that, in the United States, have consistently failed radicals' expectations. Moreover, it is a joint failure, the failure of both parties and unions, that marks American society as exceptional. Elsewhere there are union movements as weak as the American, and political systems where the Left is equally excluded, but the United States stands alone in the extent to which neither institution provides an outlet for working-class protest (Korpi and Shalev, 1980).[6]

Unions

The union movement in the United States is relatively small: in 1985 only 18 percent of employed Americans were union members (U.S. Bureau of Labor Statistics, 1986). American unionization rates are near the bottom of international statistics (see Figure 1.1).[7] Swedish workers are the most thoroughly organized, 90 percent of them now reporting union membership. Many other countries report approximately 50 percent: Austria, Aus-

---

1850 coincides with the rise of the Socialist movement, and it will be no different, probably, in America. It is the revolutionizing of all traditional relations by industry *as it develops* that also revolutionizes people's minds" (Marx and Engels [1892], 1953:244). Lenin ([1920] 1975 [vol. 3]:326) acknowledged that it was easier to begin a revolution in Russia than in the more developed nations of Europe.

6. Not recognizing the joint failure of unions and parties is the main flaw in Ira Katznelson's (1981) otherwise insightful study of American exceptionalism. Katznelson argues that American workers are militant at the workplace but have been diverted by ethnic antagonisms in a community-based politics. This analysis overlooks the fact that workplace militance has been as frustrated as socialist politics: despite the militance, the principal outcomes have been low unionization rates and conservative unions.

7. International statistics on union membership rates are sometimes unreliable and often not comparable. The percentages reported here should be interpreted cautiously, although all sources agree that U.S. rates are exceptionally low. The numbers for Sweden, Denmark, Norway, Australia, Great Britain, West Germany, Canada, and the United States are from Bain and Price (1980) and are probably the most reliable. The Belgian, Austrian, Japanese, and French rates are from Coldrick and Jones (1979) and are best interpreted as rough estimates. Barkan (1984) cites an Italian rate of 36 percent. All these estimates are roughly similar to Stephens's (1980) estimates for 1970 nonagricultural wage and salary workers in 16 countries. Korpi and Shalev (1980) aggregate unionization rates for 18 countries across 1946–1976; in this longer perspective U.S. rates are still low (27 percent) but are not so dissimilar from five other countries with rates below 30 percent—Japan, Canada, France, Switzerland, and Italy.

American Exceptionalism

FIGURE 1.1. Unionization rates of industrial countries, c. 1975

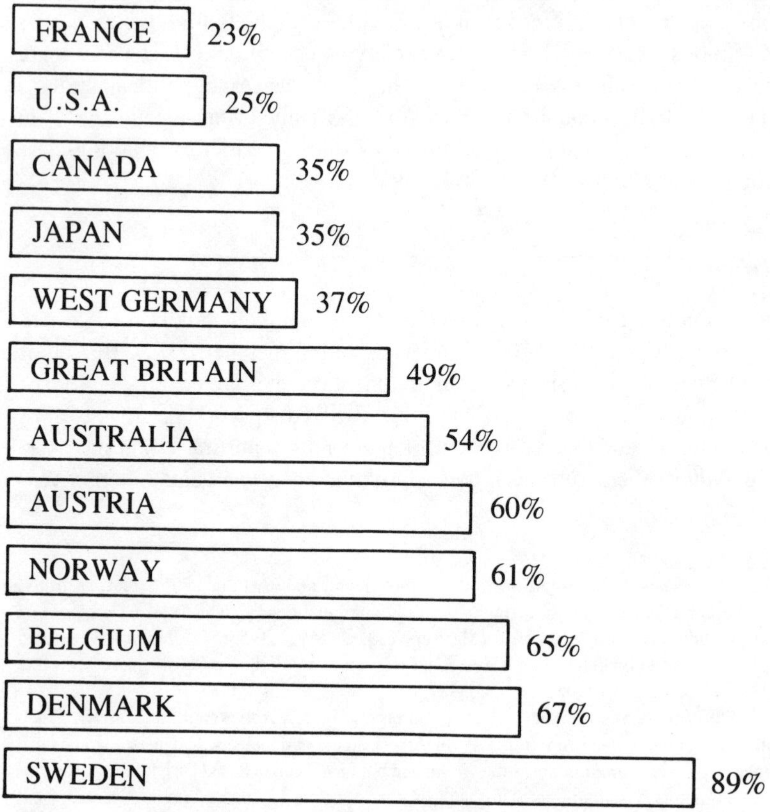

FRANCE	23%
U.S.A.	25%
CANADA	35%
JAPAN	35%
WEST GERMANY	37%
GREAT BRITAIN	49%
AUSTRALIA	54%
AUSTRIA	60%
NORWAY	61%
BELGIUM	65%
DENMARK	67%
SWEDEN	89%

SOURCES: Coldrick and Jones (1979); Bain and Price (1980).

tralia, Belgium, Great Britain, Denmark, and Norway all have unionization rates at least double the U.S. rate. Nevertheless, the low French rate
(23 percent) reminds us that low unionization, like each facet of American
exceptionalism, is shared with some other industrial societies.[8]

But these bare statistics belie the complexity of the American labor

---

8. The low U.S. membership levels can be excused to some extent by the low (and
declining) U.S. levels of blue-collar manufacturing employment, the traditional stronghold of

movement. As we will observe throughout this study, American labor conflicts have generated as much sustained violence as has working-class protest anywhere in the world.[9] It is well to remember that the May Day celebrated in Moscow's Red Square and throughout the world as a day of labor solidarity commemorates events that occurred not in Paris, Berlin, or St. Petersburg, but in Chicago.[10]

Political system

The absence of a viable socialist or Social Democratic party makes the U.S. political system almost unique among advanced industrial nations. A political program that in the U.S. context would seem mindlessly radical is, in every other advanced industrial country, one of the alternatives regularly offered to voters.

Government ownership of industry. In the United States, former Senator Adlai Stevenson's proposal to create a government-owned oil company never received serious consideration. But a nationalized oil corporation is hardly a radical proposal. Nationalized telephone, electric power, airline, and railway industries are the norm in most "capitalist" economies (see Table 1.1). There is also significant government ownership of the automobile, steel, and shipbuilding industries in many of these countries. The United States stands at the bottom of the distribution of government ownership. American private capital enjoys unchallenged control in almost every sector of the economy.

---

union movements. The United States has more white-collar workers (52 percent of its work force) and a larger service and retail sector (66 percent) than most other countries (ILO, 1982; OECD, 1983). Everywhere, the service-sector and white-collar workers are the most difficult to organize, so the American labor movement begins with a serious handicap.

9. Philip Taft and Philip Ross (1969:270) begin their report to the National Commission on Violence by claiming: "The United States has had the bloodiest and most violent labor history of any industrial nation in the world." Only occasionally do studies of American exceptionalism acknowledge this violence (see Dubofsky, 1975:12, and Katznelson, 1981:9, for useful attempts to develop theories that incorporate the paradox of extraordinary violence and a weak Left; also Lipset, 1963:202–5, for a less successful attempt).

10. In fact, our long history of labor militance has led some European Marxists to reinterpret the American working class as the true vanguard working class (e.g., Tronti, 1976: 104). See also Michel Crozier's recollections (1984) of his enthusiasm for the American labor movement of the 1940s.

TABLE 1.1. Government ownership of basic industry in nine countries

	Approximate Percentage					
	Railways	Telecommu- nications	Electricity	Airlines	Steel	Autos
Austria	100	100	100	100	100	100
England	100	100	100	75	75	50
France	100	100	100	75	75	50
Italy	100	100	75	100	75	25
W. Germany	100	100	75	100	0	25
Sweden	100	100	50	50	75	0
Canada	75	25	100	75	0	0
Japan	75	100	0	25	0	0
United States	25	0	25	0	0	0

SOURCE: Kerbo (1983:170; from *The Economist*, Dec. 30, 1978).

Much, but not all, government ownership is the result of pressure from working-class parties to remove the key sectors of the economy from the direct control of private capital.[11] The Democratic Party in the United States does not dare to suggest such an alternative. Yet what is unthinkable in the U.S. context is routine for French Socialists and British Labourites. One international study of political party programs (Janda, 1970; see also Monsen and Walters, 1983:30–33) found government ownership of industry to be the single most consistent element of leftist politics around the

---

11. Nationalization may not be an unambiguous defeat for capital. Often it is the "sick" but necessary industries that are taken over by the government and run at the expense of the taxpayer—to the benefit of the rest of the capitalist economy. These complexities, however, do not contradict the overall associations between government ownership and the strength of working-class parties.

world. Its virtual absence in U.S. political programs is an apt indicator of
the atrophy of working-class politics in this country.[12]

Class divisions in party support. Because the *output* of the U.S. political system has not much affected class interests, the *input* is not organized
along class divisions either. Neither voting nor finances are determined by
class appeals. The bulk of Democratic money comes from the same source
as Republican money—business (Domhoff, 1972). Elizabeth Drew (1983)
reports that Democrats appeal to business for campaign funds by citing the
"danger" of a political system in which one party represents business and
the other labor. Such a "dangerous" arrangement is, of course, precisely
how most other industrial democracies have been politically organized
throughout this century.

One of the favorite topics of political sociology in the opinion poll era
has been the analysis of the class complexion of Democratic and Republican voting. In the usual course of American politics, labor supports, and
the working class votes for, Democrats; business supports, and the middle
class votes for, Republicans. Many factors interfere to confuse this relationship: among voters, regional, racial, ethnic, and now gender loyalties
often override class sympathies; and in given elections, candidate popularity or foreign policy traumas may mask domestic economic concerns as a
basis for voting. But the working-class-Democrat and middle-class-
Republican affinities are quite resilient and constitute the drone against
which the individual notes of contemporary politics are played.

What is startling in international perspective is how weak this class-to-
party relationship is in the United States. In virtually every other democracy in the world, class membership is more closely aligned with party
vote than in the United States. One 1970–71 study compared seven European countries with the United States (see Inglehart, 1977:199). Britain
had the largest class cleavage: the British working class was 34 percent
more likely to vote Labour than was the British middle class. Other international studies (e.g., Lipset, 1981:21) report Swedish voting to be even
more class divided than British. In the remaining European countries (see
Table 1.2), the class difference varies between 13 percent (West Germany)
and 21 percent (Switzerland). But again, the United States has the smallest
difference, only 8 percent—about half that of the other democracies. Of

---

12. The Democrats' lack of any program of nationalization disputes Michael Harrington's
(1972:250–69) contention, endorsed by Lipset (1974:40), that the U.S. Democratic Party is
the equivalent of Europe's Social Democratic parties.

TABLE 1.2. Class support (voting) for Left parties in
            eight democracies

	Percentage Left Voting		Difference
	Manual Occupation	*Nonmanual Occupation*	
Sweden	73	29	− 44
Britain	67	32	− 35
Netherlands	64	43	− 21
France	72	53	− 19
Italy	60	46	− 14
W. Germany	65	51	− 14
Belgium	45	35	− 10
United States	41	33	− 8

SOURCE: Inglehart (1977:205); Stephens (1981).
NOTE: Occupation is head of household. Left parties are defined as in Inglehart.

course, the 1972 comparison may be unfair, since class voting was particularly obscured in the McGovern–Nixon confrontation. But other studies
using different time frames (e.g., Alford, 1967; Lipset, 1981) report similar conclusions: American political parties simply do not draw on class-
based support to anything like the same extent as parties elsewhere around
the globe.[13]

Again, however, we must warn the reader that these frequently cited
data are in fact more complicated than most interpreters have realized.
Most cross-national studies omit the voting category that is, in the United

13. Alford (1967) reports even weaker class voting in Canada, but subsequent reanalyses
(Ogmundson, 1975) suggest that a recoding of Canada's four parties reveals a greater class division than Alford discovered. It turns out that Canada's Liberals, like the U.S. Democrats,
are not truly the party of the working class.

States, most distinctively working class: the nonvoting category. The thing American workers are most likely to do on election day is stay home. And no wonder, given that the output of the political system provides them with so little to excite their class loyalty. Nonvoting is not the usual working-class option in elections elsewhere. As Walter Dean Burnham (1974) has pointed out so well, precisely that type of voter who in Europe votes for socialist and Social Democratic parties, is the one who, in the United States, doesn't vote at all. As we elaborate in Chapter 7, it is party structure, not the voters' psychology, that explains America's distinctive voting patterns. The lack of a genuine Left alternative fosters both the high rates of nonvoting and the low relationship between class and party.

The size of the working class

Postindustrial theorists have long engaged in a statistical shell game that shuffles workers according to varying classification schemes to support the claim of a decline in the American working class. One such scheme, for example, banishes janitors and waitresses to nonworking (middle-class?) status (Galbraith, 1967:276; Naisbitt, 1982:2). Andrew Levison's (1974) *Working-Class Majority* exposed many of these efforts a decade ago (see also Blumberg, 1980).

Our own classification, which we defend in Chapter 4, limits the middle class to the self-employed (that is, the "old" middle class of storekeepers and independent farmers) and professionals and managers (the "new" middle class whose members share the responsibilities of managing the lives of other workers). Additional workers who have sometimes been counted as middle class (e.g., white-collar clerical workers, technicians, salespersons, and even the more affluent craftsworkers) do not attain the control over other workers or even over their own lives that sets the middle class apart from Marx's proletariat.[14]

In this accounting scheme the working class has not shrunk at all; it has, in fact, expanded during much of this century. Our estimate of the working class in 1980 totals almost 70,000,000 workers; in 1900 it was only

14. We justify our more inclusive definition of the working class in Chapter 4, where we analyze the respective roles of working-class and middle-class jobs in the functioning of advanced capitalism. Measuring the size of the working class is a by-product of this more important need to understand the nature of working-class positions and what separates them from middle-class positions.

18,000,000 strong. Relative size has grown, as well: the 1980 working class was 70 percent of all working Americans; in 1900 it was only 61 percent (see Figure 1.2).

What has happened is not so much a change of the class structure itself as a change within the class categories. The growth of the "new" middle class of managers and professionals has almost exactly offset the decline of the "old" middle class of self-employed storekeepers and farmers. The middle class as a whole remains about the same size. Similarly, within the working class the decline in unskilled blue-collar labor has been matched by a growth in white-collar clerical and sales work.

Class Consciousness

The failure of the American Left is usually blamed on its inability to win support from a conservative working class (see especially Sombart, 1906; Perlman, 1928; Hartz, 1955; Lipset, 1963; Hochschild, 1981). According to their analyses, U.S. workers do not even think in the usual class categories; they see no sharp division separating capital and labor, but instead blur economic differences into a gradual hierarchy of status ranks. The workers' individual efforts to climb the status ladder leave them with little enthusiasm for collective action to change the hierarchy itself. Like middle-class Americans, workers are more concerned with individually getting ahead than with collectively organizing for class action.[15] Accord-

---

15. Louis Hartz (1955) explained American exceptionalism by the individualism of its liberal Lockian tradition. It is also a major theme running through Lipset's many inquiries (see esp. 1963:194,202; 1977). Ironically, radical theorists now echo the same individualistic note. For instance, Michael Parenti: "When one looks horizontally, that is, towards one's own peers and coworkers, it is usually not for solidarity but for cues as to how one's intraclass competitors are doing. Most often one's gaze is fixed vertically on those above and the goal is to fight one's way up the greasy pole. In contrast, class consciousness is essentially a lateral perception, the ability to make common cause with others who are normally defined as one's competitors" (1978:96). Parenti's comments are especially puzzling because they immediately follow the claim that capitalists are the most class-conscious group in America—yet capitalists are at least as individualistic as Parenti's description of workers. We explain this paradox (in Chapter 3) by arguing that individualism and class consciousness are not as mutually exclusive as usually presumed (see also Katznelson, 1981:16). Others who emphasize individualistic values are John Commons, 1908:758; Robert and Helen Lynd, 1937:453; Walter Dean Burnham, 1974:654; and Michael Burawoy, 1979:106–7.

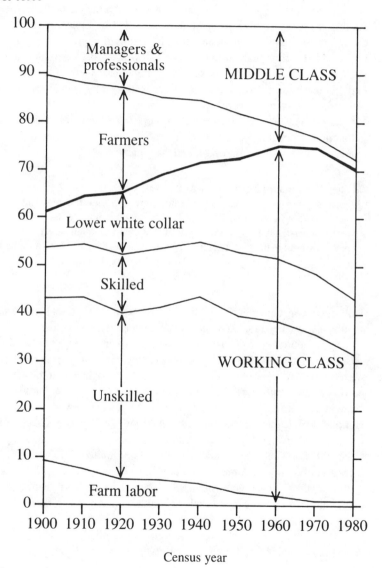

FIGURE 1.2. Changes in the class structure of the U.S. labor force

Percentage of labor force

Managers & professionals

MIDDLE CLASS

Farmers

Lower white collar

Skilled

WORKING CLASS

Unskilled

Farm labor

1900 1910 1920 1930 1940 1950 1960 1970 1980

Census year

SOURCE: U.S. Census, 1973a, 1983.

ing to this familiar reasoning, the American Dream has effectively tranquil-
ized American class consciousness.

The data we have gathered tell a very different story. Our central proposition is that Americans do perceive classes in American society—true
classes: not just vague status distinctions between the elegant and the un-
couth but actual conflict groups that are divided by opposing interests in
the capitalist organization of society. The vision of opposing classes is not
limited to the European proletariat or a few wishful American radicals.
Rather, class divisions are widely held popular perceptions. Americans
may not use a radical vocabulary to describe these class divisions, but they
fully recognize the categories being described.

Americans who know the country's working class readily testify to this
instinctual if not fully articulated class consciousness. Ed Sadlowski, the
maverick steelworkers' union official, is typical:

> There's a certain instinct that a worker has, much more so than some candy-
> assed storeowner. He understands who's screwing him, but he doesn't under-
> stand how to get unscrewed. The little chamber of commerce storefront man, he
> never understands he's gettin' screwed. He's part of Main Street, America. I
> place my faith in the working stiff, regardless of his hangups. He's still the most
> reliable guy on the street when push comes to shove. (Quoted in Terkel,
> 1980:267)

This class consciousness is ineffectual, however, because mental states
cannot always be translated into observed behavior, much less into any
successful outcome of class conflict. Workers may choose not to
act—either because they are too poorly organized to express their true
wishes effectively, or because they realistically recognize that they face too
powerful an opponent. In Sadlowski's language, they know who's
screwing them but don't understand how to get unscrewed. And even if
workers do act, there is no guarantee that they will succeed. Class conflict
is a contest between *two* parties, and even the most class-conscious proletariat will not easily overcome a vigorous and united dominant class. In
fact, it is often not possible to get "unscrewed."

Our analysis throughout this book depends on a crucial distinction for
explaining American exceptionalism: studies of American workers must
distinguish the opinions of the workers themselves (their class consciousness) from the forms that the class conflict eventually takes (such social
structures as unions and political parties). These structures have multiple

causes beyond the volition of American workers. We do not dispute the facts of American exceptionalism; at least within broad outlines, it is true that working-class movements have not had the impact on the United States that they have had on other industrialized countries. What we do dispute are the views that locate the explanation for these facts in the consciousness of the American worker. Most such explanations, even those that are sympathetic to workers and their plight, only *blame the victims* for their own oppression (Ryan, 1971).

This is not a new problem. Failure to maintain the distinction between workers' consciousness and the results of class conflict is an example of the fallacy of *psychological reductionism*—the assumption that the structure of any society can be reduced to the wishes and motivations of its members. Society is much more than a straightforward embodiment of the wills of the people within that society. Working-class movements fail for many reasons: workers' economic hardships, police repression, political co-optation, and ineffective leadership, to name a few. Many of these conditions are largely outside the control of workers. It is logically incorrect, therefore, to single out weak working-class consciousness as the main reason for the failure of the American Left. Instead, we must investigate that consciousness independently from the structural outcomes and then test whether the consciousness actually explains the results of the conflict.

Throughout this book we will see how often explanations of American exceptionalism have fallen into this simple trap of inferring levels of class consciousness from the outcomes of class conflict, rather than investigating the class consciousness itself. For the most part, our "knowledge" of working-class consciousness is little more than a set of "unproved assumptions" (Dubofsky, 1975:12). Evidence of American exceptionalism becomes confused with evidence for weak class consciousness. The collapse of Eugene Debs's 1894 Pullman strike, the electoral decline of the Socialist Party after 1912, and the conservative character of contemporary unions have all been accepted as evidence of the lack of working-class consciousness. In fact, these events demonstrate only the repeated failures of the American Left. That failure cannot be doubted. But the failure of working-class protest is not equivalent to the failure of working-class consciousness.

Of all the structural factors explaining the failure of the American Left, the most important is the strength of the opposition. This would seem to be the most obvious, as well, but it is surprising how many discussions of American exceptionalism neglect the dominant class. It is as if all that matters in political conflict is the strength of *one* of the parties, and the subordinate party, at that. Labor historian Melvyn Dubofsky has been one of the few to recognize that the *other* party to the conflict may have determined working-class failures in the United States. "The Wobblies and socialists failed not because American society was exceptional, but because they reached their respective peaks when the nation's rulers were most confident [and] united" (Dubofsky, 1974:298; see also Brecher, 1972:258; Dawley, 1976:188).

In contrast, successful socialist revolutions have all capitalized on the internal weakness of the ruling class (see Skocpol, 1979). Surely it is no accident that the two crucial revolutions of the twentieth century, the Russian and Chinese, both followed world wars that devastated the Russian and Chinese ruling classes. And it cannot be insignificant that throughout its industrial history the United States has not been invaded or even suffered major military defeat.

It is not our purpose yet to develop in detail an alternative theory of American exceptionalism based on the strength of its capitalist class. We merely want to suggest now that alternative explanations do exist— explanations that need not rely on working-class consciousness: explanations are more clearly structural because they are based on the situation in which workers find themselves rather than on the attitudes or desires of the workers themselves.

The Plan of the Book

Our thesis of a class-conscious U.S. proletariat contradicts conventional wisdom and several generations of social research. We suffer no illusions about the difficulties of breaking down this consensus. Fortunately, there are some well-accepted guidelines for conducting such an enterprise. First, the past conclusions must be examined and their logical errors exposed. Then new evidence must be presented, consistent with the new thesis. Finally, a new theory must be constructed that not only incorporates the new evidence but also accounts for the old facts that the accepted wisdom was designed to explain. By and large, this is the agenda for our work. We follow it more or less in the order outlined, although we do not resist the temptation to mix the various steps when we think that doing so clarifies the direction of our argument.

We begin by sampling several different lines of work that have been cited as evidence of weak class consciousness. We argue that each has fallen prey to the fallacy of inferring psychological states (the absence of class consciousness) from objective social structures (the failure of the U.S. Left). We concentrate most of this critique in Chapter 2 but scatter reminders throughout the text. Our strategy is to demonstrate the tantalizing ease with which so many diverse analyses have slipped into psychological reductionism.

Next, we introduce our new evidence, most of which is based on sample surveys, liberally balanced with appropriate selections from personal interviews and relevant histories of labor unrest. These new analyses constitute the bulk of the text. Unlike much earlier research on American exceptionalism, we focus directly on workers' attitudes and perceptions. We believe that the evidence demonstrates that Americans do recognize divisions within their society, divisions based on the control of production, divisions that the recent class scholarship identifies as the basis of modern capitalist class conflict. The analysis also shows that Americans have perceived these divisions for some time, and there is little indication that awareness of them is diminishing. Other tests question whether factors such as mobility, ethnic identification, and the frontier ideology—the traditional explanations of American exceptionalism—do in fact interfere with class perceptions. Cross-national tests cast doubt on American uniqueness.

It is the *consistency* of these many results that we find most convincing. Together they add up to a coherent statement about the perception of class divisions in the United States. One might dismiss a single test by itself as an aberrant deviation from the accepted wisdom, but it does not seem reasonable to reject the entire series.

The final chapter concentrates on the task of making sense of both the old and new evidence. As has already been suggested, our explanation of American exceptionalism focuses on U.S. capital, the dominant antagonist in class conflict. We venture the idea that the outcome of most class conflict is determined by the strength of the dominant class, that in most circumstances the dominant groups can control the extent and violence of the conflict. That is the nature of dominance, after all.

CHAPTER 2
BLAMING THE VICTIM

Psychological Reductionism in Class Theory

Our conclusions contradict most earlier research on working-class consciousness. How can we reconcile our research with the earlier results? Our first answer is that the earlier research offered surprisingly little true evidence denying class perceptions; its conclusions are often mere inferences based on the failure of socialist movements. In this chapter we review several examples of how readily past work has drawn these inferences without any direct evidence of the workers' actual states of mind. Our second answer, which we take up in the next chapter, is that the research which did actually investigate workers' consciousness has often been misinterpreted.

The error of inferring the absence of class consciousness from the failure of American socialism is so widespread and so easily committed that it has almost single-handedly wrecked the study of class consciousness. But conflict and consciousness exist at separate levels of social reality: socialism, unions, and protest movements (or their absence) are structural characteristics of a social system; class consciousness (or its absence) is a psychological attribute of individuals. The attempt to explain structural phenomena solely in terms of psychological attributes has been justifiably derided in social science as psychological reductionism. Movements such as working-class protest depend on many causes besides the workers' own ideas, they require access to resources and opportunities that are entirely unrelated to the motivation or commitment of the actors themselves. Socialist movements can fail when structural opportunities are missing, no matter how class conscious the workers have become.

Despite the universal warnings against it, psychological reductionism is rampant throughout the literature on workers' protest movements. From the flimsiest of evidence, firm conclusions are drawn about the workers' psychological states. The readily available structural explanations for working-class defeats are often neglected. In many instances, no plausible level of class consciousness could have overcome the inherent weaknesses of the workers' political and economic position, but these structural hand-icaps—even when acknowledged in telling the history—are glossed over in the construction of psychological explanations for the eventual failures.

We will review some examples to illustrate how easily, even with the best of intentions, investigators end up by blaming the workers for their own exploitation: "If only the workers were sufficiently class conscious, they would create the socialist movement that could transform the capital-ist system."[1] In selecting examples for scrutiny, we have deliberately cho-sen works by scholars who are most sensitive to the exploitation of Ameri-can workers. For example, a statement by the executive editor of *Socialist Review* is typical:

> We have no objective guarantee that the American working class recognizes capitalism as the cause of the injustice and inequalities of American life. The re-cent history of the American working class clearly shows that it lacks the or-ganizational and political capacity to struggle effectively for the fundamental transformation of society. (Escoffier, 1986:117)

In fact, not only does Escoffier blame workers for the failure of socialism, he tells how disturbing this conclusion is to American socialists today:

> Profound disappointments and doubts have shattered our faith in the objective and strategic possibilities implied by Marxist interpretations of history. Many of us are now adrift. Is socialism a meaningful political stance? If so, how is it? How can we maintain our commitment and seek to realize our hopes politically? Our political crisis is experienced as deeply personal and demoralizing. (1986:117)

Critics of the capitalist status quo have little reason to portray workers as passive believers in the American Dream; indeed, for some, such a conclu-

---

1. Blaming the victim of any form of oppression usually begins with some recognition of the oppression (although it avoids such harsh words as "oppression," "exploitation," "classism," "racism," using instead less direct terms such as "inequality," or "discrimina-tion") and acknowledging its consequences (e.g., "low status" or "low income"). Explana-tions for the oppression focus on hypothetical traits that are considered inherent to the groups biologically (e.g., low mental capacity) or due to inappropriate socialization (e.g., poor role models, "culture of poverty") or to improper mental states, over which people are deemed to have some control (e.g., a lack of motivation, interest, imagination, commitment, self-es-teem, or—in this case—"class consciousness").

sion is "deeply personal and demoralizing." But Escoffier only follows a long tradition of American radicals who have despaired of the working class ever acting as the agent of change (see Mills, 1963:237, 254–56; Marcuse, 1964; Sweezy [1967], 1972; and Wachtel, 1974). The fact that even these critics have still recited the litany of workers' conservatism attests to the strength of the prevailing myths and the temptations of reductionist inferences.

The Middletown Studies

Robert and Helen Lynd's (1929; 1937) classic studies of Muncie, Indiana, begun in the 1920s, provide our first example of unsupported conclusions about American class consciousness. This work is an especially useful example because the Lynds were well aware of the problems faced by "Middletown" workers. They took the time to listen to the workers and to their frustrated union organizers, and the stories they recount document the human meaning of the workers' deprivations. The Middletown studies have both shaped and reflected our beliefs about American class consciousness. They are an important part of the intellectual history of American sociology.

In 1935, the Lynds returned to the site of their previous research to examine the impact of the Depression on the Middle American optimism they had observed a decade earlier. The Depression had closed in on the town belatedly but inexorably. The big General Motors plant closed; the largest department store failed; and employment was cut in half. Wages were low throughout the town, even by Depression standards. Surely these were the conditions to incite radical protest. Instead, the Lynds found an enduring conservative culture: class conflict was stifled, and workers withdrew to cope as best they could. The Lynds took the opportunity to investigate firsthand the failure of American working-class protest.

Middletown's history is revealing because working-class quiescence was not always a foregone conclusion there. In the first year of Roosevelt's New Deal, a wave of union organization had swept over the town. Ten new unions were organized in 1933–34, and membership rose from 700 to 2,800. In the words of a local labor leader, "Men were coming in faster than we could handle them" (Lynd and Lynd, 1937:28). In January 1934 a drive was begun to organize the glass factory owned by the locally dominant Ball family. By March, 900 of the plant's 960 workingmen had joined the union.

Yet within a year, this promising start had collapsed. None of the big plants had been organized; workers abandoned the unions already set up, and total membership fell to 1,000. In 1935, General Motors returned to the town but only after getting assurances of an open shop and official co-operation in resisting union organization. What had happened? Where did the causes of this failure lie?

The evidence assembled by the Lynds points directly at the effective op-position rallied by Middletown's cohesive "business class." The Depres-sion itself gave employers an upper hand. The labor surplus encouraged dismissals and intimidated those workers fortunate enough to have jobs. As one worker put it:

> Our people are nervous about their jobs and don't dare kick about working con-ditions; I've been working fairly steadily at the D—— plant for seven years, but I have been and still am afraid to let out my belt and buy anything beyond immediate necessities, for I might get canned any day. (Lynd and Lynd, 1937:40)

Suspected union sympathizers were replaced. Blacklisting was easy in a town of 50,000. Seriously threatened plants responded with plans to move to a new city. A work force made up of people who had often experienced recent unemployment themselves, surrounded by thousands of impover-ished unemployed, responded with the intended emotion: fear. A local la-bor leader described the impact of this fear on attempts to organize the work force:

> The men were pretty well scared to begin with, since General Motors had moved out of town and another auto-parts plant had closed. We tackled them anyway. We organized a bunch of men at the A—— plant, where they paid their machinists as low as twenty cents an hour before N.R.A. And then hell cut loose in the plant! The ax was swung right and left by the company and those who weren't dismissed were scared to death. Finally, the men appealed to the Regional Labor Board for an election in 1934. The company fought against an election, carried the fight up to the top Labor Board through all kinds of ap-peals, until when the vote came in the spring of 1935, N.R.A. was so weak and the men so intimidated that they were afraid to vote. They're still unorganized out there, and the plant remains a lousy place where men work only to keep from having to go on relief. (Lynd and Lynd, 1937:33)

Newspapers, police, clergy, and local politicians closed ranks behind the counterattacking businesses. Four days before an announced meeting to begin organization of automotive workers, the afternoon newspaper ran photographs of violent labor arrests in Oregon. The radio station scheduled, then canceled, the broadcast of a union speech. Police arrested a worker distributing handbills, trailed union organizers, and scared off incoming "undesirables." The Lynds provide no evidence that any segment of the town's elite split off to support the workers' attempts to overcome their well-recognized deprivations.

As if the opposition weren't sufficiently formidable, labor faced its own leadership problems. Middletown's local labor leadership was inexperienced; the national unions sent incompetent organizers; and government patronage co-opted the few labor leaders who had risen to positions of influence. In these circumstances, the workers never stood much of a chance. Perhaps some extraordinary working-class leadership could have salvaged the situation, but in general, structural changes are engineered by ordinary people. Middletown proved to be an ordinary case: working-class opposition was overwhelmed. It is a wonder that workers risked any collective action at all in such a hostile climate. By 1935 the prevailing mood was a resigned but realistic hopelessness.

The Lynds, after documenting the initial enthusiasm for labor resistance and reviewing the effectiveness of a solidly united business class, only return to the tired theme of the failure of working-class *consciousness*: "Middletown labor in characteristic American fashion lacks any driving sense of class consciousness" (Lynd and Lynd, 1937:454). Their explanations are the familiar preconceptions:

He is an individualist in an individualist culture. (Lynd and Lynd, 1937:453)

He lives on a Middle Western farm, has moved in from the farm, or his father's family moved to town from a farm. He is thus close to the network of habits of thought engendered by the isolated, self-contained enterprise of farming. (Lynd and Lynd, 1937:453—an obvious echo of Marx's observations on the isolation of the French peasantry)

Car ownership stands to them for a large share of the "American Dream." (Lynd and Lynd, 1937:26)

He is apt to want quick action, or his union becomes just another thing that bothers him needlessly. (Lynd and Lynd, 1937:454)

Having documented the impossible situation the workers faced, why should the Lynds attribute the result to a failure of class consciousness?

Not only does their own evidence identify the structural obstacles; they also record many workers' comments that are excellent examples of class consciousness.

At times, the Lynds misinterpret the quotations so dramatically that the reader is left wondering if something has been misplaced. For example, upon learning of the return of General Motors, one worker remarked:

> *We auto workers* aren't getting too excited about the return of General Motors. It means a job, and that's important—for the months in the year *they're willing to hire you*. Only the *Chamber of Commerce crowd* are optimistic, and *they're* trying to fool *us workers*.

Not two sentences later, the Lynds conclude:

> And yet, as noted above, this fear, resentment, insecurity, and disillusionment has been to Middletown's workers largely an *individual* experience for each worker, and not a thing generalized by him into a *"class"* experience. (Lynd and Lynd, 1937:40–41; emphasis added)

Where, in the words of that worker, is there any evidence of an individualistic interpretation of his experience?

Perhaps the Lynds believe that an aroused class consciousness can triumph in any situation. But a belief in the irresistible power of class consciousness is just a radical inversion of the bourgeois belief in hard work and determination. Instead of hard work and determination, the radical inserts class consciousness; instead of an individualized bourgeois attainment, proletarian revolution. The social psychological emphasis remains the same. But success, whether bourgeois or proletarian, is a socially structured outcome and depends on the opportunities available. The Middletown described by the Lynds provides one of the worst imaginable situations for working-class protest. What is remarkable is that the workers attempted organized resistance at all.

Even as the Lynds were finishing their research, fresh attempts were underway to organize the automotive industry. Rather than a failure of class consciousness, such an attempt would appear to be a folly of unrestrained adventurism. Surely a new organizing drive would lead only to more dismissals of the potential leaders, more police harassment, and an even more cohesive and defensive ruling class. How could workers living on the margin of subsistence risk their families' one chance for a stable livelihood in return for such a small probability of success? Weak class consciousness could hardly have been their problem.

The History of American Mobility

Stephan Thernstrom (1964) makes the same mistake in his widely praised study of social mobility in nineteenth-century Newburyport, Massachusetts. Acknowledging that the historian has a difficult task in studying the consciousness of nineteenth-century workers ("dead men cannot be interviewed"), he opts instead to study actual rates of mobility and infer from them "lower class attitudes about mobility opportunities" (1964:58–59). He then feels comfortable in concluding that "Newburyport residents in 1880 were still persuaded of the uniqueness of American social arrangements, which they regarded as the prime cause of the progress they gloried in. They saw a stark contrast between the Old World and the New" (1964: 186).

In fact, Thernstrom knows no more about working-class attitudes than when he began his research. He can only speculate about what Newburyport workers "gloried in." His specific citations are from the conservative, middle-class newspaper—which Thernstrom himself admits had every reason to accept this self-serving ideology. What Newburyport workers believed is still hidden. Alan Dawley (1976:219) has correctly attacked Thernstrom's conclusions about workers' mobility beliefs as "one part pure speculation, one part consensus historiography, and no part of the actual ideas of Newburyport's laborers."

Thernstrom does turn up one record of working-class opinion. An irate worker in 1880 wrote the local newspaper in reply to editorials slurring the Democratic Party as based in the "slums, penitentiaries, and cock-pits." Here is the worker's story in his own words:

I was born in poverty and . . . have never known anything else. My radicalism and my democracy have been starved into me by long months of privation, by long hours of miserably paid work. . . . My feelings are bitter and my words are fierce on the subject of the non-producing class which lives on the earnings of productive labor in insolent superiority and keeps it in silent slavery. (Thernstrom, 1964:180)

One must applaud Thernstrom for his scholarly evenhandedness in preserving such a quotation, but one must also wonder what is left of his thesis. His only piece of *direct* evidence completely contradicts all his own conclusions on working-class consciousness. "Long months of privation" and "long hours of miserably paid work" hardly sound like the kind of progress Newburyport residents "gloried in." What more class-conscious, even Marxian, attitude could the historian ask for? Here is a worker, bitter toward the "non-producing class which lives on the earnings of productive labor in insolent superiority." The words defy us to maintain our belief in working-class acceptance of the American Dream.

What does Thernstrom make of all this? "It would be folly," he warns us, "to consider [these fierce words] proof of the depth and sharpness of actual political conflict." Instead, he advises, "a case for the opposite assumption might be made—that the extraordinary verbal violence of American politics in the post–Civil War period grew out of and served to conceal the relative absence of genuine issues, and that political contests were as much as anything else an elaborate game." This is disingenuous and contemptuous of his historical material. We cannot believe that the "long months of privation" and "long hours of miserably paid work" was, for the worker, just a part of some elaborate game.

In fact, Thernstrom's dodge of his own evidence is a telling reversal of Seymour Martin Lipset's dodge of the evidence on the violence of the American labor movement. He, too, maintains a thesis of weak class consciousness; he attributes the failure of American socialism to the American values of individualistic achievement and egalitarianism (Lipset, 1963: 204). What disturbs his thesis is the extraordinary violence of the American labor movement—fierce *action* even beyond Thernstrom's fierce *words*, violence that would seem to suggest a militant class consciousness. But Lipset tries to explain away the violence by arguing that such violent actions somehow actually confirm the American workers' acceptance of individual achievement and egalitarianism and rejection of class solidarity:

> Just as ideological conservatism and pursuit of narrow self-interests may be derived from the value system, so may the use of violent and militant tactics. . . .
> An open-class system leads workers to resent inequalities in income and status between themselves and others more frequently than does an ascriptively stratified system, where the only inequalities that count are class inequalities. (Lipset, 1963:204–5)

This line of reasoning would require us to reinterpret the violence of the labor movement not as an expression of class conflict but as a series of indi-

vidualistic and even random outbreaks of personal frustration—but that is
hardly consistent with the historical record.

What is most disturbing in both the Thernstrom and Lipset accounts is
the dogged determination to maintain a belief in weak class consciousness
despite obvious contradictory evidence. For Thernstrom, verbal violence is
evidence against actual violence; for Lipset, actual violence is evidence
against a violent class consciousness. Is there no fact and no opinion that
they cannot assimilate to their theories?

U.S. Labor History

In a column written during the 1980 Republican convention, journalist David Broder (1980) sought to explain Ronald Reagan's appeal to the voters
of small-town America. Broder had been corresponding with Ruth Johnson, an especially ardent Reagan supporter and Republican party stalwart
from Coeur d'Alene, Idaho.

> Coeur d'Alene, from what I know of it, is a good deal closer in spirit to the
> small town of Dixon, Illinois, where Reagan spent his boyhood in the second
> decade of this century, than it is to, say, the Detroit of 1980.
>
> Reagan's values—like Ruth Johnson's—were shaped in a community
> where families were strong and unions were weak. It was a community where
> wives stayed home and took care of the kids, and teachers stayed in the class-
> room and didn't worry about lobbying in Washington. It was a world where em-
> ployers looked out for their employees! (Broder, 1980)

Coeur d'Alene, Mr. Broder has forgotten, was the site of two of the
most violent labor conflicts in U.S. history. In 1892 armed miners attacked
a struck mine defended by private guards hired to protect imported strikebreakers. The miners succeeded in dropping 100 pounds of dynamite into
an operating mill, destroying it, and killing one strikebreaker while wounding 20 others. At another mill, company guards opened fire on the striking
miners, killing 5 and wounding 14. The miners fought back, captured the
mill, and sent the guards out of the county. This victory was followed by
the capture of another operating mine, where the miners again forced the
nonunion workers to flee the county.

As was to happen so consistently in American labor history, once class-
conscious workers had achieved some success, the U.S. Army stepped in

with overpowering force to reinstate the rule of capital. Martial law was declared, and the soldiers rounded up several hundred miners into outdoor "bullpens." The union leadership was charged with contempt of court and sent to jail outside the county. Local police officials, elected by the votes of union miners, had been sympathetic to or neutral in the strikes; they were replaced with appointees who would appropriately knuckle under to the invading force. The army even engaged in some strikebreaking of its own when capitalists proved too timid: in one mine where owners had actually reached a working agreement with the union, the army forced the dismissal of all known union men.

The most class conscious of revolutionaries must recognize reality when faced with overwhelming force. The 1892 strike was broken by such a force. But even in jail, the miners organized a new and yet more militant union, the Western Federation of Miners. The WFM was to become the foundation for the radical Industrial Workers of the World (IWW)—the syndicalist "Wobblies"—who sought to overthrow American capitalism two decades later. And in Coeur d'Alene in 1899, only seven years after the first battle, the miners again struck to force the one remaining nonunion mine to accept union organization and union-scale wages. In a virtual repeat of the earlier conflict, 300 miners attacked and overran the nonunion mine, evicted the guards and scabs, and dynamited the mill. Two men died, one union and one nonunion. Five days later martial law was declared, and the acting secretary of war in Washington sent the needed troops. The army was even more thorough this time, remaining for two years and outlawing the employment of union members. The bullpens were resurrected; union leaders were sentenced to prison terms of up to 17 years; and the union, in Coeur d'Alene at least, was crushed (Perlman and Taft, 1935:169–88; Jensen, 1950).

Americans have a collective amnesia about their history of labor conflict. Coeur d'Alene is hardly Broder's idyllic community where "families were strong and unions were weak," where "employers looked out for their employees." The actual history does not fit comfortably in the portrait of a complacent working class, so the history is often ignored.

Nor have labor historians succeeded in correcting the image of complacency; for many years, the dominant school of labor history helped perpetuate the conservative stereotype. According to this interpretation, American workers desired only the larger share of the pie that conservative trade unions promised them; workers were not willing to demand new socialist recipes to reorganize the control of production (see, e.g., Perlman, 1928:

169). But the only evidence these historians offer about workers' actual desires is the outcome of the labor conflicts themselves—another example of reductionism. In most of the cases, it is easy to identify situational causes that explain the failure of labor radicalism without any resort to inferences about workers' consciousness.

The consistent reappearance of the radical impulse in the labor movement belies the conservative interpretation. The president of the Western Federation of Miners, the union that arose from the Coeur d'Alene debacle, demanded "a complete revolution of present social and economic conditions." The WFM's goal was "to abolish the wage system which is more destructive than any other slave system devised" (Dubofsky, 1969:69). Eugene Debs, in leading the nationwide Pullman strike of 1894, called for nationalization of the railroads (a position endorsed by a new union in the strike wave of 1919–20). The International Workers of the World arose at the turn of the century as the radical alternative to the American Federation of Labor (AFL). Seeking to unite all workers in "One Big Union," the Wobblies were so radical that they refused to sign binding contracts with employers because such contracts compromised future labor militancy. After the IWW was crushed during World War I, a new wave of union militance culminated in the Great Steel Strike of 1919. And as in Middletown, the Great Depression and some New Deal protection brought yet another wave of union organization and strikes in the 1930s.

These recurrent waves of militant union activity testify to the existence of a large reservoir of working-class consciousness, biding its time, waiting for the opportunity to break out. On each occasion when labor protest was incited by wage cuts or work redefinition, militant workers stood ready to guard their traditional rights or past economic gains.

What is used to bolster the conservative interpretation is the frequency with which workers lost these battles. The Pullman strike of 1894, like the Coeur d'Alene strikes, was defeated by an army of federal troops. Eugene Debs and the Socialist Party were crushed during World War I by Debs's imprisonment and the Post Office's confiscation of all Socialist Party mail. The most radical of American unions, the IWW, was subjected to vigilante justice and judicial hysteria, commemorated now in the ballad of Joe Hill. In 1917 the U.S. Department of Justice raided IWW offices across the country and arrested "almost the entire first- and second-line leadership" (Dubofsky, 1975:125). But these failures were not the failures of working-class consciousness; instead, they represent the successful application of political repression (Goldstein, 1978).

A second fact used to sustain the conservative interpretation of the American labor movement is that not only did the socialist and radical alternatives repeatedly fail, but the collaborationist non-political AFL succeeded. In the success of Samuel Gompers and the AFL, some labor historians have seen the embodiment of true working-class sentiments. In this view, the radicals and political reformers were only middle-class utopians or alienated intellectuals; real workers wanted only to protect their jobs and wages from employers' greed; it was because the AFL trade unions limited themselves to these more modest goals that they were supported by the majority of workers.

Gompers and the AFL unions did deliberately modify their previously Marxist views in order to ensure their success. But that moderation was designed not to create greater appeal to the working class but to achieve greater toleration from business and the government (Dick, 1972:104). Gompers watched the suppression of more class-conscious movements and was appropriately intimidated. The decision to fashion a more limited trade unionist movement was a strategy calculated to minimize the probability of destruction at the hands of the ruling class (Gompers, 1925:97). It proved to be the safest course: Gompers stood aside and watched the organized power of a thriving capitalist class crush his more radical opposition. But that opposition was eliminated not because it did not appeal to the working class but because it aroused the unbridled wrath of American capital.

Selig Perlman, a major figure in the conservative interpretation of labor history, once described how he came to his belief in the weak class consciousness of American workers.[2] Perlman had set out, under John Commons's tutelage at the University of Wisconsin, to study the socialist movements of immigrant workers in the 1860s and 1870s. He discovered that these radical working-class movements were eventually transformed into the conservative AFL—exactly the reverse of the Marxist thesis that class consciousness would arise out of pure-and-simple trade unionism. From this "topsy-turvy order of things," Perlman concluded, "Obviously,

---

2. To be fair, we should note that Perlman acknowledged capitalist strength as a factor in the failure of working-class movements: his list of the causes of the AFL's success accords capitalist strength equal position with the lack of working-class consciousness and the moderating effects of a widespread property-owning middle class. But he does not develop this explanation, nor have later commentators picked it up. It is the lack of working-class consciousness that Perlman dwells on and, by implication, promotes as the decisive factor (1928: 154–55, 162).

working people in the real felt an urge towards collective control of their employment opportunities, but hardly towards similar control of industry" (Perlman, 1928: viii). Obviously? Here is an apt illustration of the trap of reductionist reasoning. The inference about working people's "urge" does not at all follow from the historical outcome he is describing. In fact, Perlman knew of Gompers's fear of capitalist repression, but the alternative explanation is ignored for the simplicity of the reductionist approach.

The logic becomes even more convoluted in Perlman's discussion of the suppression of "dual unions" and "outlaw" strikes. In America, the AFL itself ruthlessly fought radical splinter groups, at times even providing scabs to break the radicals' strikes. The leadership of European unions, on the other hand, tolerated radical splinter groups and permitted dual membership. On the face of it, this divergence of the European and American labor movements should be attributed to different leadership strategies. But to Perlman, the difference in the behavior of trade union *leaders* is evidence of differences in the consciousness of *workers*. American trade union leaders suppressed radical alternatives, according to Perlman, because they feared the weakness of American class consciousness; British trade union leaders could afford toleration because they were confident that underneath the dual unions and outlaw strikes was a solid working-class cohesiveness. Perlman reinterprets the strategy of union leaders as evidence of working-class consciousness. When inferences such as this contaminate the theory, no amount of data will dislodge the conclusion.

It is important to realize why Gompers's success does not per se establish the conservatism of American workers. Equally plausible structural explanations fit the same historical data. Given governmental repression of all radical working-class movements, the mass of workers were left with a choice between a class-conscious but thoroughly defeated radical movement and a conservative AFL that promised much less but at least was permitted some successes.[3] In this environment, the workers' decisions to align themselves with the more successful AFL says little about their lack of class consciousness; it reflects only a simple rationality in the face of given historical alternatives. Moreover, the terms of that choice were dic-

---

3. Indeed, because of Gompers's support of World War I, he enjoyed access to President Wilson and could win some basic improvements in working-class life. Government-sponsored mediation boards promoted recognition of AFL unions, partly to avoid the threat of the more radical IWW. The state-sanctioned unions at that time succeeded in winning the eight-hour day, equal pay for women, better working conditions, and higher wages.

tated by business, not by workers; workers never had a choice between the conservative AFL and a *successful* radical working-class movement. The radical alternative was crushed, while the conservative option flourished under governmental nurturance.[4] In fact, even the AFL's conservatism can be interpreted as a response to the governmental repression. Earlier socialist tendencies within the AFL and in Gompers himself were stifled when it became clear that radicalism entailed arrest and certain failure.

The Commons–Perlman portrait of a conservative working class has been challenged by contemporary labor historians. Dubofsky (1974), we noted, comes closest to resolving the puzzle by blaming the failure of the IWW and the Socialist Party on the strength of American capitalism rather than the weakness of the working class. Historians of the American Left should transfer their attention, Dubofsky recommends, from socialists and labor leaders to corporate magnates and their political allies.

But even Dubofsky fails to follow the logic through to a clear break with the concept of weak consciousness. What is it about American capitalists that Dubofsky asks historians to study? Their "hegemony" over the "values, attitudes and actions of the working-class masses." Here Dubofsky falls back into the old habit: he *assumes* a hegemony over working-class consciousness that is nowhere demonstrated by the facts he has assembled. Where is the evidence that the values and attitudes of workers were so overwhelmed by the "preeminently business culture?" Evidence on cultural hegemony is, of course, harder to find for the labor historian of the first quarter of the twentieth century than for survey researchers of the third and fourth quarters. But the lack of evidence on attitudes counsels scholarly caution rather than a reaffirmation of conservative myths. The Coeur d'Alene miners, Dubofsky's own beloved Wobblies, and thousands of other rebellious American workers have provided a lasting testament that their economic and political subordination was never consolidated into ideological surrender.[5]

---

4. Repression is never a faultless tool; often it boomerangs to provoke greater protest. Without the AFL alternative, governmental repression would have appeared to be straightforward class warfare with the state unmistakeably hostile to labor. But the simultaneous encouragement of the AFL made the repression more ambiguous and permitted the state to define the issue as one of "responsible" unionism versus "violent" and "anarchic" Bolshevism. This openness to conservative unions helped solidify elite and middle-class opinion against the more radical unions.

5. But Dubofsky's advice may sense something truly distinctive in American culture, even if he locates it incorrectly in the working class. What may be exceptional in U.S. ideology is

Poor People's Movements,

In their widely influential book *Poor People's Movements*, Frances Fox Piven and Richard Cloward (1977) have assembled a persuasive case documenting the structural constraints on working-class defiance. They recognize the inherent weakness of workers and the poor in any political conflict as a consequence of social position: workers and poor people have less wealth, less influence, less access to the media—in short, less control over almost every resource that is important for success in a political conflict. Their lack of resources has exposed workers to the single most important cause of their failure: physical and economic coercion by the ruling class. "Those for whom the rewards are most meager, who are the most oppressed by inequality, are also acquiescent. Sometimes they are the most acquiescent, for *they have little defense against the penalties that can be imposed for defiance*" (Piven and Cloward, 1977:6; emphasis added).

Here is a straightforward and eminently reasonable *structural* explanation of working-class acquiescence. There is a wealth of research to support the vulnerability of the poor to coercion; Piven and Cloward compile some of the best evidence themselves. The structural explanation is also *logically sufficient*. We need devise no other causes of working-class acquiescence to understand the paucity of class protests.

Nevertheless, even these authors soon lapse into a careless confusion of structural and psychological explanations:

> Moreover at most times and in most places, *and especially in the United States*, the poor are led to believe their destitution is deserved. . . . In more modern societies, such as the United States, riches and power are ascribed to personal qualities of industry and talent; it follows that those who have little or nothing have only what they deserve. (Piven and Cloward, 1977:6; emphasis added)

They go on to quote approvingly the statement that "the *guilt* and *self-concepts* of the poor have kept them docile" (Edelman, 1971:56; emphasis

---

not the capitalists' hegemony over working-class ideas but the actual *uniformity* within the ruling class. Because recorded culture is typically ruling-class culture, what appears as interclass hegemony may be only intraclass conformity. What historians should study is the development of a remarkable consensus within the capitalist class, a consensus that was never achieved among European elites.

added). Now it makes a great deal of difference whether one attributes the acquiescence of the poor to their "guilt and self-concepts" or to their vulnerability to coercion. The two should not be lightly mixed together in the same theoretical stew. Especially in an essay that so convincingly demonstrates the inherent structural weakness of working-class movements, why resort to psychological explanations? Is there any empirical evidence that guilt and self-concepts are significant inhibitions to working-class protest? To be sure, the poor are "led to believe" many things—the question is, do they follow meekly along? Dominant classes may *assume* that the poor have accepted the official line, but the scholar should seek sufficient evidence. Yet not a single quote, not even a haphazard and unscientifically sampled remark, is offered to document any "guilt and negative self-concepts."

On the contrary, the four protest movements studied by Piven and Cloward suggest a large reservoir of class hostility. The unemployed during the Depression, industrial workers struggling to unionize, Blacks in the civil rights movement, and welfare recipients in the 1960s all demonstrated a readiness to take to the streets to demand redress. It was only when these movements tried to transform themselves into legitimate institutions that they slipped into ineffectiveness. Piven and Cloward's insight is that formal organizations of the poor are *necessarily* weak; they are attempting to play a political game in which the dominant class holds most of the cards. Organizational work becomes a tactical disaster for the poor because it concentrates energy where the poor are most disadvantaged and ignores those resources that the poor *do* have—the most important of which is their ability to disrupt the smooth functioning of the exploitative system. Historically, the poor have been most successful when they have been most disruptive. Mobilization to demand justice requires only a commitment to social change, and this commitment was not lacking in any of the movements reviewed. So long as the movements relied on the workers and the unemployed themselves—that is, on their willingness to take to the streets—the movements won concessions from the authorities. But the impulse to create permanent, established organizations within "the system" is a shift toward weakness.

It is the irony of the Piven and Cloward thesis, an irony repeated again and again in the literature of the Left, that they have built a superb case *against* the class-consciousness explanations of American exceptionalism and yet repeat the same lack-of-class-consciousness homilies. Like the Lynds, they assemble evidence that documents a remarkable (alas, almost foolhardy) readiness among American workers to challenge the existing system. Unlike the Lynds, Piven and Cloward conclude quite explicitly that workers' weaknesses are largely structural, not psychological. Still they do not take the logical next step of expunging the tired psychological explanations from the catalogue of working-class handicaps. Guilt and negative self-concepts are still cited, almost ritualistically. The issue is never confronted, and the received wisdom is left unchallenged.

The "New Left" in the 1960s

So far, we have reviewed examples of psychological reductionism in the social science literature. At least brief attention must also be directed to political activists. The "New Left" that flourished in the 1960s and 1970s has been as guilty as academe of blaming the failure of U.S. class conflict on American workers' weak class consciousness. Interestingly, the leaders of the "Old Left," who first organized the working class in massive and often violent resistance to U.S. capitalism, rarely fell into this trap. There are few laments about workers' false consciousness in the writings of Eugene Debs (1948), "Big Bill" Haywood (1929), or William Z. Foster (1920).

The American New Left viewed the working class from a social distance that obscured its perception of working-class realities. The New Left had middle-class, often professional, origins (Flacks, 1971). It was largely a college student movement. The leading chapters of Students for a Democratic Society (SDS) were organized at the nation's elite private universities (such as Columbia) or top state universities (like Berkeley). At first, the students viewed the working class with ambivalence. They recognized the historic role that Marx had allocated to the working class but did not see in American workers a potential for radical change. The establishment media were quick to reinforce this ambivalence by publicizing fights between "hard hats" and student protesters.

The New Left eventually adopted two attitudes toward the working class (see John Welch, 1979, for an excellent discussion of this history). Some decided that students were working class themselves. After all, they were not capitalists; most were preparing for wage-labor positions, and they too suffered from a lack of control over their lives. This "new working class" analysis allowed the students to maintain their comfortable position as a revolutionary vanguard without ever having to deal with the mass of

American workers. A second approach insisted on organizing working-class communities. Workers had to be educated to abandon their false consciousness, and it was up to the students to show them how they were exploited by capitalism and oppressed by the state. This approach was transparently condescending.[6] As one group of critics put it, "Nowhere do they speak of learning from the people they hope to work with" (quoted in Welch, 1979:181). The possibility that workers were already conscious of the class divisions in the United States seems never to have been seriously considered. And the theory that education was all that was necessary to make the revolution was naive at best.

But the errors are common errors. Americans are taught to believe in a conservative working class; foreign observers and middle-class radicals, people who have no access to working-class communities, cannot check these beliefs against daily realities. And so the myth is perpetuated.

"Restraining Myths"

In questioning the validity of mainstream social science research, we share the frustrations of Richard Hamilton (1975), who has worked some of these same fields ahead of us. Hamilton identifies several social and intellectual processes that reinforce what he calls the "restraining myths" and protect them against careful scrutiny. Some of these processes are endemic to scholarly work.

1. The conventional wisdom is so widely held that investigators are loath to undertake fresh research to test it; doing so would only "prove the obvious." Thus, cross-national tests of working-class consciousness have hardly ever been attempted, despite everybody's assurance of American exceptionalism.

---

6. Again, the comparison with the Old Left is illuminating. Note Eugene Debs's very different attitude toward leadership of the working class: "Too long have the workers of the world waited for some Moses to lead them out of bondage. He has not come; he never will come. I would not lead you out if I could; for if you could be led out, you could be led back again. I would have you make up your minds that there is nothing that you cannot do for yourself" (speech on "Industrial Unionism," December 10, 1905, in Debs, 1970:124). However, some of the AFL hostility to the Knights of Labor and to later socialists derived from the class division separating Gompers from these middle-class reformers (see Gompers, 1925:97, 262).

2. Scholars have a "selective memory," often citing the few but widely known studies that support the conventional wisdom, regardless of their scientific merit. Disconfirming studies, if they get published at all, are buried in the literature and written off as flukes. Thus, while most scholars recognize Richard Centers (1949) as the originator of class identification research, he is rarely studied today because he argued that U.S. workers were indeed class conscious. Instead, less radical treatments (for instance, Hodge and Treiman, 1968; Jackman and Jackman, 1983) are more widely cited now.

3. The organizations that claim to represent the views of some social group are invariably closer to the positions of the prevailing stereotype than is the actual population of group members. The high visibility of national labor unions distorts our impressions of the workers they represent. Americans have read about Samuel Gompers in their history books and have seen George Meany or Jimmy Hoffa on their television screens, whereas rank-and-file radicals are often known only to their work mates.

4. Hamilton notes that even if originally fallacious, the "restraining myths" can become self-fulfilling prophecy. Because U.S. workers are "known" to be complacent, progressives may never attempt to mobilize workers for radical change.

5. In studies supposedly confirming the conventional wisdom, enormous gaps can separate the data cited in the study and the conclusions the authors draw. This is exactly what we found in the Lynds' study of Muncie and in Thernstrom's study of Newburyport. In each case, the evidence collected from the workers' own words mocks the conclusions about a passive and individualistic working class.

We find Hamilton's analysis of "restraining myths" reassuring. He reinforces our view that something new can be said about "American exceptionalism" despite the decades of work already devoted to it. But if we are to get past the old restraints, we must keep distinct the observations of workers' psychology and workers' behavior, and we must demand *independent* evidence of each before we draw any conclusions about the link between them. To do this, we must next study workers' psychology directly, even though the relevant literature is more limited than data on workers' behavior.

CHAPTER 3
CLASS DIVISIONS AND STATUS RANKINGS

The Social Psychology of American Stratification

None of the studies we have reviewed can justify the conclusion that American workers lack class consciousness. On the contrary, past studies have consistently overlooked available evidence that Americans are indeed class conscious but that this consciousness is not translated into successful protest because of the opposition of a healthy and vigilant capitalist class. Past explanations of working-class protest failed not because they included social psychological explanations but because they did so without any independent evidence of the workers' actual psychology. The lack of class consciousness was inferred from the behavior; class consciousness itself was never studied.

Since we cannot infer class consciousness from the outcome of class conflict, we must study workers' ideas directly. Two images of class are found in the research literature on class perceptions (Ossowski, 1963). In the radical vision, class divides society into two conflicting camps that contend for control: workers and bosses, labor and capital, proletariat and bourgeoisie; in this dichotomous image, classes are bounded, identifiable collectivities, each one having a common interest in the struggle over control of society. In the conservative vision, class sorts out positions in society along a many-runged ladder of economic success and social prestige; in this continuous image, classes are merely relative rankings along the ladder: upper class, lower class, upper-middle class, "the Toyota set," "the BMW set," "Brahmins," and the dregs "from the other side of the tracks." People are busy climbing up (or slipping down) these social class ladders, but there is no collective conflict organized around the control of society.

The dichotomous image of class best accounts for conflicts.[1] Conflict,

1. This discussion (and much of this chapter) draws on the work of the Polish sociologist Stanislaw Ossowski, *Class Structure in the Social Consciousness*: "The dichotomic presenta-

as our parents all taught us, requires at least two parties. Just as there can be no conflict in social isolation, there can be no class in isolation; in our view, a class exists only insofar as it enters into antagonistic relations with another class. Masters and slaves, lords and serfs, bourgeoisie and proletariat (Marx and Engels [1848], 1976: 482–85) are defined by the *social* relations of domination and subordination. The very concept of slaves as a social category cannot exist unless there are masters; similarly, feudal lords are defined by the existence of serfs; and, at least in Marx's original meaning, the bourgeoisie and the proletariat exist only as an interrelated system. E. P. Thompson (1963:10–11) reminds us in a deservedly famous statement from his classic *The Making of the English Working Class*:

> There is today an ever-present temptation to suppose that class is a thing. This was not Marx's meaning, in his own historical writing, yet the error vitiates much latter-day "Marxist" writing. "It," the working class, is assumed to have a real existence, whith can be defined almost mathematically—so many men who stand in a certain relation to the means of production. . . . If we remember that class is a relationship and not a thing, we cannot think in this way.

In recent years, new classes have been added to neo-Marxist analyses in order to explain better the conflicts in twentieth-century capitalism. For example, the division between supervisors and subordinates has been added to Marx's original distinction between owners of capital and wage laborers. We discuss this and other neo-Marxist analyses in some detail in Chapter 4, but the important point now is that the new analyses retain the concept of class as a social relation between dominant and subordinate groups. Supervisors control subordinates: it is this power relation that puts them in different classes. Supervisors also tend to have higher incomes and more social prestige than subordinates, but it is not these status distinctions that separate them into different classes. Class requires a power relation.

Continuous rankings, in contrast, minimize the awareness of class conflict.[2] The ladder image is essentially classless; while economic and so-

---

tion may serve to underline the antagonistic relations existing in the society, relations where one side is "on top," the other "at the bottom," where one exploits the other, where one rules and the other obeys" (1963:30).

2. Again, from Ossowski: "It is possible to reduce the sharpness of the class stratification in a social-status system, not by trying to weaken the picture of social inequalities, but by stressing the continuity in the system . . . the conception of a continuum of social statuses does away with the classes themselves, without heeding the scale of inequalities" (1963:96).

cial differences persist and are widely recognized, no sharp division separates workers from their bosses. Inequality is described by degree of access to socially valued resources, typically income or prestige. People can be ranked in such a hierarchy—sociologists even assign quantitative scores indicating precise social standing[3]—but there is no class relation between positions on the scale.

We will, following Dahrendorf, call all such distinctions based on continuous rankings *status* distinctions to keep them separate from *class* divisions based on the social relations of production.

> *Class* is always a category for the purposes of the analysis of the dynamics of social conflict. . . . [But] wherever classes are defined by factors which permit the construction of a hierarchical continuum, they are wrongly defined; i.e., the term has been applied wrongly. Status, ranking by others, self-ranking, style of life, similar social conditions, and income level are all factors which define social strata but not social classes. (1959:76)

The class versus status distinction is basic to an understanding of the social psychology literature on the American working class: ours is a study of *class* perceptions.

Occupational Prestige

In the United States, the ladder of success is the more widely accepted image. It is found in both popular usage and academic inquiry (Ossowski, 1963). Schools and mass media use the ladder image as if it were the only appropriate picture of American society. "Making it" has been a cultural preoccupation, and "making it" has always been evaluated by a detailed scale of social success. Horatio Alger provided a common fantasy of sud-

---

3. Even the fashionable statistics in American social science during the 1960s and 1970s reinforced the use of the status-ranking model. The more sophisticated research methods at that time required interval-level or at least ordinal-level scales. Statistics based on the general linear model are neatly congruent with a conception of the stratification system as a continuous, linear hierarchy. Methodologists' dislike of categorical concepts was well expressed in a remark of George Bohrnstedt (1974:130): "Most of the variables of interest in the social sciences are continuous and *measurable* in theory at least at the interval level." So much for Marx.

den leaps up the economic scale, but most versions of the message were concerned with the finer distinctions of a one- or two-car garage or a "title on the door."

Academic research in the United States (but not, for the most part, else-where) adopted this same status-ranking model. Robert Nisbet, for in-stance, is typical in arguing that "the very forces which dissolved the class lines of pre-industrial society acted, in the long run, to prevent any new classes from becoming fixed. . . . The differences between the extremes of wealth and poverty is very great, today as always, but the scale is more *continuous*" (Nisbet, 1959:14; emphasis added).

The U.S. government allocated substantial resources to develop the status-ranking model. The 1947 NORC (National Opinion Research Cen-ter) prestige study (Reiss et al., 1961) made the first ambitious attempt to calculate exact occupational prestige scores based on the evaluations of a national sample of Americans.[4] Later studies followed (Hodge, Siegel, and Rossi, 1964; Siegel, 1971; and, in England, Goldthorpe and Hope, 1969), even more ambitious in scope and coverage. These occupational ratings and the generalization of their results to other occupations by Dun-can (1961) and Featherman et al. (1975) have provided us with an occupa-tional scale of appropriately detailed gradation (see Figure 3.1). In theory, no gaps exist in these prestige scales. Since the scores were based on the subjective judgments of the American people, the continuous status ladder appeared to be the universal American image.

Prestige rankings proved to enjoy an impressive consensus. Blacks and whites, college graduates and high school dropouts, men and women: all rank occupations in approximately the same order. Between 1947 and 1961, occupational prestige rankings changed very little, despite years of rapid economic growth (Hodge, Siegel, and Rossi, 1964).

In fact, prestige rankings appear to be similar in all industrial societies (Inkeles and Rossi, 1956; Hodge, Treiman, and Rossi, 1966; Treiman, 1977).[5] Both the supposedly class-conscious Europeans and the more indi-

---

4. The NORC study and its successors asked large national samples to rate dozens, and eventually hundreds, of occupations on their "general standing." The respondents had to choose a rating from five possible levels: "excellent," "good," "average," "below average," and "poor." National prestige scores were calculated from the average responses for each oc-cupation being rated.

5. However, Parkin (1971), Penn (1975), and Yanowitch (1977) present evidence that so-cialist societies rank the industrial working class higher in prestige than do capitalist societies.

FIGURE 3.1. Prestige score of selected occupations

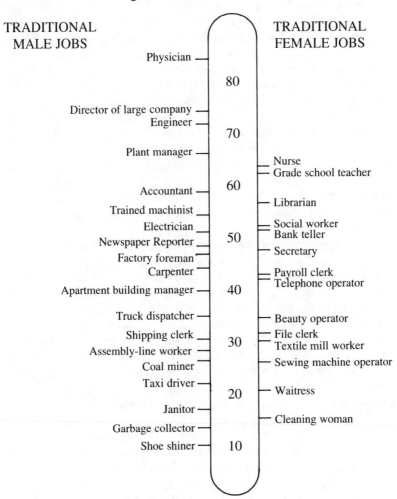

TRADITIONAL MALE JOBS

TRADITIONAL FEMALE JOBS

- Physician — 80
- Director of large company —
- Engineer — 70
- Plant manager —
  - Nurse
  - Grade school teacher
- Accountant — 60
  - Librarian
- Trained machinist —
- Electrician —
  - Social worker
- Newspaper Reporter — 50
  - Bank teller
- Factory foreman —
  - Secretary
- Carpenter —
- Apartment building manager — 40
  - Payroll clerk
  - Telephone operator
- Truck dispatcher —
  - Beauty operator
- Shipping clerk — 30
  - File clerk
- Assembly-line worker —
  - Textile mill worker
- Coal miner —
  - Sewing machine operator
- Taxi driver — 20
  - Waitress
- Janitor —
  - Cleaning woman
- Garbage collector —
- Shoe shiner — 10

NORC Occupational Prestige

SOURCE: Siegel, 1971.

vidualistic Americans rank occupational prestige in much the same way. But nobody noted the implication of these cross-national similarities for the question of American exceptionalism. In none of these countries do any gaps divide one class of occupations from another. Thus there seems to be no special affinity for continuous images among Americans that would explain their supposed lack of class consciousness.

The "robustness of the occupational prestige consensus" (Rossi, 1976) established the status-ranking model as the central fixture of American sociology. The occupational scales became the basis of the status attainment research industry that flourished in the 1960s and 1970s (e.g., Blau and Duncan, 1967; Duncan, Featherman, and Duncan, 1972; Sewell, Hauser, and Featherman, 1976; Hauser and Featherman, 1977; Featherman and Hauser, 1976; Jencks et al., 1972 and 1979). Here again the American cultural fixation on "making it" was paramount, translated now into the less romantic terms of raising oneself a couple of points on the Duncan socioeconomic index (SEI).

In the 1970s, dissent arose about the accuracy of the status hierarchy as a description of American society (e.g., Coser, 1975; Horan, 1978). Critics of the status quo attacked it as a distorted representation that ignored the real class divisions in the system (e.g., Wright and Perrone, 1977). But few challenged the popular *belief* in the ladder imagery among the American people. Conservatives who defend status rankings as an accurate model of the stratification system and radicals who attack it as an ideological myth both assume that the ladder imagery exhausts the content of Americans' perceptions of themselves; class divisions, however real, are not perceived to be real: "Class consciousness among manual workers is a transitional phenomenon . . . a clearly defined working class no longer exists, if it ever did" (Wilensky, 1966:12).

The evidence to justify this dismissal of class perceptions is embarrassingly thin. Class divisions have usually been ignored in research rather than proved irrelevant. The mistake made in interpreting the prestige studies is assuming that the perception of prestige ladders necessarily inhibits the consciousness of class divisions—as if Americans can have only one image of their society. The two models have been erroneously presented as mutually exclusive.

For example, as can be seen in Figure 3.1, there is an overlap in prestige scores between lower-status white-collar jobs and skilled blue-collar crafts. Machinists and electricians are ranked above reporters, building managers, and shipping clerks; beauty operators are ranked above file clerks. This overlap has led the prestige studies to dismiss the idea that the blue-collar–white-collar difference might be a class barrier: "The cleavage between white-collar, blue-collar, and farm occupations—if it exists at all—is based not so much upon matters of societal evaluations as perhaps upon the character of dress and work in the three groups" (Hodge, Siegel, and Rossi, 1966:327). In other words, since these particular "societal evaluations" can be shown to reflect a continuous status image of society rather than a bounded class model, it has been assumed that America uses a continuous status image in *all* "societal evaluations."[6]

The Left itself has assumed that status ladders and class divisions are mutually exclusive images of society. Early in this century the Hungarian Marxist George Lukács asserted explicitly that "status consciousness . . . masks class consciousness; in fact, it prevents it from emerging at all" ([1922] 1971:58). In the 1960s and 1970s, Lukács had a great influence on Left interpretations of the American working class. For example, Howard Wachtel, in his 1974 essay "Class Consciousness and Stratification," blames workers' concerns about status ladders for their abandonment of class consciousness:

> With the development of monopoly capitalism, labor has become stratified with workers acquiring sharp status differences, a fact which mitigates their identification with a class. The impact of this stratification process on consciousness is to divert workers' consciousness from a class orientation and replace it with an identification with one's strata in society. (1974:96,106)[7]

6. The existence of an overlap between blue-collar and white-collar occupations does not even imply that this class division is irrelevant for prestige judgments. The white-collar–blue-collar gap may be one among many considerations Americans use in judging the prestige of an occupation, and these other considerations (e.g., average income) may blur the class division without eliminating it. Otis Dudley Duncan (1961) warned against too quickly dismissing the class divisions on the basis of the prestige scores alone. He insisted on a direct quantitative comparison of the class dichotomy against the continuous status scales to measure their relative importance. When Duncan (1966) compared the effect of white-collar work, average education, and average income on the perceived prestige of the various occupations, he found that white-collar work conveys no special prestige in and of itself; it is only the greater average incomes and better schooling that cause higher prestige judgments (see also, Glenn, 1975).

7. Paul Sweezy (1967:38) has made a similar argument. See also Lopreato and Hazelrigg (1972:124) for the argument that status consciousness promotes individual action at the expense of collective movements.

The supposed conservative influence of these status differences became the central idea behind Richard Edwards's (1979) history of capitalism's co-optation of American workers.

None of this work ever asked whether status ladders actually do mask class consciousness, as Lukács presumed. The possibility was ignored that status and class models may *both* coexist in the popular imagination. Each way of looking at the world—as ranging along a continuous status ladder or as divided into opposed classes—may be useful in its own context and does not necessarily interfere with the use of the other model in other contexts. Why insist on a single vision?

Ralf Dahrendorf has argued that each model is useful for different purposes:

> In a sociological context, neither of these models can be conceived as exclusively valid or applicable. They constitute complementary, rather than alternative, aspects of the structure of total societies as well as of every element of this structure. We have to choose between them only for the explanation of specific problems; but in the conceptual arsenal of sociological analyses they exist side by side. Whatever criticism one may have of the advocates of one or the other of these models can therefore be directed only against claims for the exclusive validity of either. Strictly speaking, both models are "valid" or rather, useful and necessary for sociological analysis. (1959:183)

That is, class divisions are useful for understanding conflict in society: strikes, revolutions, absenteeism, and the like. Status ladders, or "social strata," are useful for understanding such phenomena as lifestyles, evaluations of worth, and mobility aspirations.[8]

The occupational prestige studies clearly fall into Dahrendorf's definition of studies of social strata, not social classes. They are popular rankings of general standing and thus naturally permit the "construction of a hierarchical continuum." The prestige research supplied response categories that were themselves steps along an obvious continuum ("poor," "be-

---

8. See also 1959:159. Dahrendorf's distinction between class and status avoids many of the conceptual fallacies of American sociology; e.g., Werner Landecker (1960) tried to discover class boundaries by observing where income, educational, and occupational prestige hierarchies coincide. Edward Laumann (1966) attempted to discover subjective class boundaries by testing for the statistical significance of the perceived social distance between pairs of occupations. Such studies are wrongly conceived because they seek to find class divisions not between conflict groups based on the organization of production but within status ladders that rank people and positions along a scale of desirability.

low average," "average," "good," and "excellent"), the sorts of graded criteria that Dahrendorf had in mind as "factors which define social strata but not social classes." It is not surprising, therefore, that people reacted by utilizing continuous criteria in their judgments and ignoring class divisions. The rankings are hierarchies of social strata, not perceptions of class position.

Thus, in arguing that Americans do perceive class divisions, we find no fault with the long tradition of prestige research. Prestige differences are recognized *also*—as are age, racial, ethnic, and gender differences. There is no need to quibble with the results of the prestige studies. Improvements may be possible, but no amount of tinkering with that research should ever be expected to test class perceptions. The investigators asked for status rankings, and within acceptable limits that is what they got.

But to grant that class divisions were irrelevant to this particular ranking task is not to say that class is *never* perceived. Different tasks and different situations may elicit different images of society. If we are to study class perceptions, we must ask for class perceptions. That research has a quite different tradition.

Subjective Class Identification

The alternative, class-oriented tradition of social psychological research began with Richard Centers's (1949) national surveys that asked Americans, "If you were asked to use one of these four names for your social class, which one would you say you belonged in: the middle class, lower class, working class, or upper class?" Centers found that a slight majority (51 percent) chose the working-class label. These working-class identifiers more often voted Democratic and endorsed more radical attitudes than did middle-class identifiers (1949:118–30). Centers somewhat grandly declared that his results would "convincingly dispel any doubt that Americans were class conscious" (1949:76).

Centers was reacting to studies published by *Fortune* magazine (1940), which announced that almost 80 percent of the American population considered itself "middle class."[9] For *Fortune*, this was reassuring news:

9. See also Hadley Cantril's (1943:78) conclusion that "the overwhelming majority of the American people identify themselves with some category of the great middle class," and a similar conclusion by George Gallup (Gallup and Rae, 1940). More recently, Ben Wattenberg

American capitalism had not created the class divisions that Marxists had expected. Instead, most Americans saw themselves as comfortably placed in the predominant middle. The middle class represented the "American way of life," was its main beneficiary and its guarantor of future stability.

Centers recognized the ideological bias in the research and revised the question to produce quite opposite results. *Fortune* had provided respondents with only three possible choices—lower, middle, and upper class. Faced with what they saw as the stigma of the lower class and the pretentiousness of the upper class, most Americans readily chose the safe and respectable middle-class option. Centers had only to add one more choice, "working class," and the percentage of middle-class identifiers dropped to 43 percent; in fact, the middle class was outnumbered by the 51 percent working-class identifiers (1949:77).[10]

Thus began a tradition of manipulating the wording of the question to produce whatever results the researcher desired. The later addition of an "upper-middle-class" option (Tucker, 1966 and 1968; Hodge and Treiman, 1968; Jackman and Jackman, 1983) restored a middle-class majority (62–66 percent). Open-ended questions that denied respondents any clues about the categories of interest likewise produced middle-class majorities. Debate raged about which was the "valid" measure of class identification, and as American sociology assumed a more conservative mold, Centers's research seemed largely discredited in mainstream sociology.[11]

Centers also lost his natural defenders on the Left. Once establishment social science adopted survey research as its own favored technique, radical critics responded by dismissing not just its conservative uses but survey research in general.[12] Centers's work was tainted by this association. It did not help that his principal monograph had an unorthodox—indeed,

---

(1974:51) has proclaimed a "massive majority middle class" in the United States, and Nathan Keyfitz (1976:30) has claimed that "in survey after survey most Americans place themselves in the middle class." This is yet another example of Richard Hamilton's (1975) point about how "restraining myths" live on despite ample disconfirming evidence.

10. Centers also rearranged the order of presentation (middle, lower, working, upper) to discourage a status-ranking orientation.

11. Gordon's verdict is perhaps representative: "a dubious methodology [that] has obfuscated the delineation of cleavages in politico-economic attitudes in American life" (1958: 201). However, the work of Jackman and Jackman (1973, 1983) has kept the question alive in American sociology. Kluegel et al. (1977) have now shown that the Centers class placement question has substantial reliability and validity.

12. For the reservations of a practitioner of survey research, see Portes (1971a:243).

naive—conceptual discussion of class. And since the Left, too, had its doubts about the class consciousness of American workers, Centers's claims undoubtedly appeared as extravagant to many on the Left as they did to established social science.

The fact that Americans would choose a class label in response to a forced-choice question could not, by itself, demonstrate that they were class conscious. Critics were quick to point out that class consciousness encompasses more than the mere choice of a class label—especially if that choice is limited by a fixed number of possible responses.[13]

Even Centers's name for the question, "class identification," stretches the meaning of the responses. Identification suggests something more central to a person's identity than is implied by a casual choice among four possible alternatives. Identification usually connotes an *affective* attachment to a class (see Landecker, 1963); there is nothing in the responses to Centers's question that suggests any affect. We will, therefore, refer to the Centers question as the class-*placement* question, not the class-identification question.

To this day, there are many sociologists who will reject out of hand any research using the class-placement question. Part of this hostility may be the result of Centers's own tendency to claim too much for his results, making his research especially vulnerable to the many critics eager to dismiss any mention of class divisions in the United States. Those critics, for a time, had their way, as not only class consciousness but class structure faded from attention in the research literature.

What is to be gained from rescuing Centers's work? We are convinced that there is much of value in the traditional class-placement approach—indeed, most of the interesting questions have still not been asked more than a third of a century after Centers's original analysis. We recognize the loneliness of our position, however. Both conservative and radical schools now have a well-developed resistance to research using the Centers ques-

---

13. Several sociologists have attempted to dissect the concept of class consciousness into various levels. Such armchair analyses have not been noticeably effective, and there is no agreement on what levels constitute a full class consciousness: e.g., both Mann (1973) and Lopreato and Hazelrigg (1972:126) identify five levels, but Mann's first level incorporates the first four of Lopreato and Hazelrigg's, while they subsume under their highest level what Mann requires four levels to describe. We believe also that these so-called higher levels of class consciousness have origins different from those of the direct experience that determines class perceptions (see Chapter 5).

tion; both will be skeptical and tend to evaluate new work in line with the failings of past interpretations.

There are some hopeful signs, nevertheless, that the time has arrived for a fresh consideration. Class divisions are now taken seriously in much of American sociology. In the 1970s new research borrowed the familiar tools of academic social science—including survey research—to demonstrate the continued importance of class divisions. These studies have understandably concentrated on the "hard" data of income, both personal and national, thus protecting themselves from most charges of biased measurement. There is no such safety for studies of "soft" phenomena like class perceptions. Measurement methods are crucial here, and inasmuch as methodological problems provoked the major accusations against Centers's research, we are working in more difficult territory. Still, now that class divisions have been demonstrated to have significant effects on Americans' income, it seems reasonable to ask whether they are also important to Americans' perceptions of their society.

If the responses to Centers's question did not indicate class consciousness, what *did* they signify? What did his respondents mean when they chose working-class or middle-class labels? One possibility was to reinterpret the question within the predominant status-ranking model of American stratification. The reinterpretation was promoted most skillfully by Hodge and Treiman's (1968) statistical analysis of a similar class-placement question. They found several joint determinants of class self-placements; income, education, and occupational prestige were the most important. Even so, only 20 percent of the variance in class placements could be explained by the stratification variables. The weakness of the relationships and the joint importance of quite different dimensions of stratification argued that there could not be a very clear class consciousness in the United States.

The final support for Hodge and Treiman's stratification model was their discovery of the importance of social contacts for people's self-placements: the status of friends, relatives, and neighbors helped determine class placements even among Americans with similar occupations, income, and education. Such social networks confused the picture even further for Americans trying to choose a class label. Besides, the importance of friends to the choice hardly suggested a conflict model of class divisions but emphasized instead the style-of-life concerns that were central to the status-ranking tradition.

Subsequent reanalysis by Jackman and Jackman (1973) suggested that social positions weren't nearly so obscure as Hodge and Treiman had inti-

mated. The several dimensions of social position that predict class placements are themselves closely related. Thus, education helps determine occupational status, and both of these determine income, and *all* of these
determine social contacts.[14] These linkages persuaded Jackman and Jackman to reject the "pluralist" model of Hodge and Treiman in favor of a
model that emphasizes the importance of social position in "constraining"
people's social lives.

But the Jackmans themselves never adopted a true class model. According to them, Americans derive their social positions from "general socioeconomic prestige and income" (1973:580); that is, from status rankings,
not from class divisions. The Jackmans attempted to evaluate a true Marxian model by testing whether capital ownership or self-employment made
people feel they were middle class. They found that neither of these Marxist divisions had any effect on how Americans placed themselves in the
class structure. The significant status effects and nonsignificant ownership
effects argue that self-placements are status judgments rather than class
perceptions.

The Jackmans' research strategy was a major advance over earlier analysis because it showed how to test what stratification models people use in
making their self-placements. If class divisions predict self-placements,
then we can accept the existence of class perceptions. If only status rankings predict self-placements, then there is no evidence for class perceptions, and Americans have indeed fully adopted status-oriented criteria of
social position. The logic is sound, and we accept their research strategy—although by extending it, we end up questioning their anticlass conclusions.

The problem the Jackmans faced was the inadequate means available
for testing the importance of Marxian class divisions. They relied only on
measures of capital ownership or self-employment—as was conventional
at the time. Unfortunately, a 1975 expansion of the Jackmans' original
analysis into a major survey came too soon to incorporate much of the re-
surgent interest in class. It is evident from their 1983 description of these
results that the Jackmans still don't take the idea of class divisions in
America seriously. Their rewording of the class-placement alternatives

---

14. Subsequent research questioned whether social contacts had much importance at all
(Jackman and Jackman, 1983:188–89). As the Jackmans put it, "It appears that frequent interaction with his superiors on the job does not make the chauffeur middle class."

into "poor," "working class," "middle class," "upper-middle class," and "upper class" reveals their status ladder orientation. Their analysis makes a halfhearted attempt to investigate the differences between blue-collar and white-collar workers, but the cryptic description of the results (no numbers are reported) and their dismissal of a statistically significant collar-color effect betray their lack of interest in a class perspective.

The Marxist analysis of contemporary class structure has now progressed beyond such simplistic notions of class division. Class structure cannot be reduced to the simple legal ownership or nonownership of productive property; nor is collar color an adequate measure of the social relations of production. The role of authority in an enterprise (Dahrendorf, 1959; Poulantzas, 1974; Wright, 1980, 1985) and the design of the work process (Poulantzas, 1974; Braverman, 1974) are better recognized now as central in the capital accumulation process and thus in the exploitation of the working class. This more complex but more accurate analysis of contemporary class structure requires that we raise again the question of whether self-placements reflect a true class division in American society.

CHAPTER 4
WHO IS WORKING CLASS?

In 1848, Marx and Engels predicted that capitalism would create a growing polarization between capitalists and workers:

> Our epoch, the epoch of the bourgeoisie, possesses . . . this distinctive feature: it has simplified the class antagonisms. Society as a whole is more and more splitting up into two great hostile camps, into two great classes directly facing each other: Bourgeoisie and Proletariat. (Marx and Engels [1848], 1976: 485)

In one sense, they were correct. The capitalists have become ever bigger: in 1950 the largest 200 corporations in the United States owned 48 percent of all manufacturing assets; in 1980 this had grown to 60 percent (U.S. Bureau of the Census, 1983:535; see also Baran and Sweezy, 1966). Meanwhile, the old middle class (the "petty bourgeoisie") declined. At the time of the Declaration of Independence, some two-thirds of Americans were economically independent: self-employed artisans, shopkeepers, and farmers. In 1985, roughly 8 percent of Americans were self-employed.

But Marx's prediction was wrong about the proletariat. True, the formerly self-employed became employees, but as the old middle class declined, a new middle class emerged as a buffer to absorb class conflict and stabilize capitalist society. As firms grew, an army of managers, professionals, and white-collar employees took over some of the managerial functions previously reserved for capitalists alone. These salaried officials work for owners of productive property, just as blue-collar workers do, but earn generous incomes and enjoy substantial prestige. And—what is crucial for a *class* analysis—the new middle class also shares in some of the *power* that capital has exercised over workers.

The Problem of the Middle Class

Conservative critics of Marx have interpreted the growth of the middle class as evidence disproving Marx's prediction about class polarization.[1] For example, Ben Wattenberg (1974:51) claims that America is now united in a "massive majority middle class": that is, no proletariat, no class conflict.[2] "Postindustrial" theorists have taken a somewhat more sophisticated view: classes still exist but have changed; Marx's nineteenth-century division between capital and labor is no longer the crucial one. According to John Kenneth Galbraith's (1967) *New Industrial State*, middle-class technocrats dominate society because their *knowledge* has supplanted industrialists' *capital* as the crucial resource. In a similar vein, Daniel Bell (1973) identifies the explosion of middle-class professions and services as the harbinger of a new class order. John Naisbitt's (1982) *Megatrends* helped popularize the idea that advanced technology creates a new class system—a system in which the struggle between capital and labor becomes irrelevant.

Marxist interpretations of the middle class

Twentieth-century Marxists responded more slowly to the growth of the middle class. Much of their thought was hobbled by a misplaced loyalty to Marx's emphasis on the division between owners of productive property and hired labor. Many Marxists seemed to regard the new middle class as only a bourgeois idea designed to obscure the division between capital and labor.[3] They reasoned that managers, engineers, and professionals—like factory workers—sell their labor to an employer; therefore, they are—like

1. Many Marxists also accepted the stabilizing impact of the new middle class; see, e.g., Bottomore (1966:48), who explains the continuation of American exceptionalism based on the growth of the new white-collar middle class.

2. For Wattenberg, the middle class is just a statistical range whose boundaries can be manipulated to suit any purpose. To justify the "massive majority" label, he stuffs assembly-line workers and corporate executives into the same class receptacle.

3. The importance given to the new middle class by revisionist Social Democrats such as Eduard Bernstein ([1899] 1961) may account for orthodox Marxism's rejection of the concept.

factory workers—part of the working class.[4] Such an analysis homogenizes 90 percent of America into an exploited working class opposed to a handful of capitalists who own the principal means of production.

This analysis will not do as a description of contemporary America. It provides no insight into the changing nature of class conflict in the twentieth century and cannot explain the durable grip of capitalism on the state and economy. An adequate analysis of contemporary class divisions cannot focus exclusively on the legal ownership of productive property. That does not explain much of the current class conflict, and it certainly does not describe the class divisions perceived by Americans.

What is needed is a class analysis that recognizes a position for the new middle class without abandoning the importance of conflict between capital and labor.[5] Such an analysis is now available and is essential for our understanding of how Americans perceive the working class. Earlier work on class perceptions was confused about the middle class and the role it plays in modern class conflicts. The middle class is not merely an arbitrary range along some status scale; it is a genuine class with interests *in opposition to the working class*. We believe that Americans recognize this opposition and use a true class model in identifying the division between the working and middle classes.

Our objective in this chapter is to demonstrate Americans' perception of this class division. The task requires two steps: first, we must identify the

4. Some Marxists (e.g., Mallet [1963], 1975) even anointed the new technicians and professionals as a "new working-class" vanguard who would, in the twentieth century, finally fulfill Marx's revolutionary prophecy (see Low-Beer, 1978).

5. We should first settle a point about terminology. Our use of the term "middle class" does not follow that of most other class analysts. "Middle" connotes an intermediate position on a ranking and thus suggests a range within a status model rather than a bounded category engaged in class conflict (cf. Lopreato and Hazelrigg, 1972:143). To avoid any status-ranking connotation, class theorists have replaced the term "middle class" with such inventions as the "new petty bourgeoisie" (Poulantzas, 1974 and 1977); the "PMC," for professional–managerial class (Ehrenreich and Ehrenreich, 1979); and "contradictory class locations" (Wright, 1980). We do not quarrel with these, but we think more is to be gained by staying with the familiar "middle class" designation; doing so builds a bridge between a rigorous class analysis and the popular perceptions of class. "Middle class" is the term in popular usage; it is, of course, imprecise because people often use it in ways that have nothing to do with twentieth-century class conflict. But our research shows that there *is* a genuine class content in the popular perception of the middle class. It seems to us most profitable to grasp the class content already signified by "middle class" and "working class" and to provide more rigorous definitions for terms already accessible to most people.

conflicts that divide the middle class from the working class; second, we must demonstrate that Americans define the middle class in a way that takes these conflicts into account. Our real interest is the second step, but to accomplish it, we must first understand the role of the middle class in contemporary conflicts between labor and capital. Once we recognize the distinctive class position of the middle class, we can ask how Americans perceive that role and therefore how they identify the working class in to-day's society.

The three dimensions of control

In the last decade, many conflict-oriented sociologists sought to rescue the concept of class without denying the reality of the growth of the new middle class. One of the first of these attempts, by the Greek Marxist, Nicos Poulantzas, remains the best. Poulantzas studied law at the University of Athens, went to Paris during the intellectual ferment of the 1960s, and first attracted notice as part of the circle around the Marxist philosopher Louis Althusser (see Jessop, 1985). Today, Poulantzas is better known for his work on politics, but his authoritative, *Classes in Contemporary Capitalism* (1974), provides the best starting point for an analysis of the middle class. Poulantzas places the middle class within the larger context of the struggles between capital and labor by identifying three divisions within the class structure that keep workers subordinate (1974:14).[6] He begins with the familiar *economic division* separating owners of productive property from productive labor. He gives the economic division primacy because the overriding conflict in capitalist society remains the economic exploitation of labor by capital.[7] But Poulantzas recognizes that capital's

---

6. Our emphasis on Poulantzas's three-dimensional analysis differs somewhat from Erik Wright's interpretation which places greater stress on Poulantzas's distinction between productive and unproductive labor (see Wright, 1976, and, especially, 1985). The three dimensions reflect the influence of Althusser and, thus, may seem unfashionably structuralist today. In fact, Poulantzas combines a structural appreciation of how the new middle class contributes to capitalist accumulation with a practical concern for its political role in the struggles between capital and labor. Although Poulantzas would have denied it, the three-dimensional approach also has a decidedly Weberian ring to it (cf. Weber [1921], 1978:926). As Frank Parkin (1979:23) has remarked, "Inside every neo-Marxist there seems to be a Weberian struggling to get out."

7. The importance attached to the capital–labor conflict separates Poulantzas's analysis from other revisionist approaches to the middle class, such as Dahrendorf's (1959) exclusive emphasis on authority and Wright's (1985) multidimensional scheme that weights each division equally as reflecting an independent mode of production. We do not take up Poulantzas's

ability to get work out of labor does not depend on its economic power alone. Capital also directly supervises at the work site to ensure maximum effort from labor. This authority defines a *political division* between workers and their bosses. Third, capital plans how work is to be organized and tries to shape the workplace and eventually even the whole society in support of its need to accumulate capital. Poulantzas interprets this planning power as an *ideological division* separating the manual labor of workers from the mental labor of professionals and managers. Together, these three aspects of power—ownership, authority, and mental labor—determine the class divisions in contemporary society. It is the joint influence of all three social relations that subordinates the working class to capital.

Middle-class Americans who are not themselves capitalists share in the exercise of these types of control. Supervisors direct workers; engineers design factories; social workers help regulate the poor. The power that people in these positions exercise separates them from working-class Americans who do not have such power. Neither working class nor capitalist, such positions can best be described as middle class.

The Poulantzas analysis of the middle class avoids the conventional emphasis on affluence and status; instead, the central focus is on power and exploitation. For Poulantzas, the middle class is a true *class*, not just an intermediate stratum straddling the center of a continuous status scale. Being middle class requires people to enter into specific social relations with capitalists on the one hand and workers on the other. In particular, the middle class dominates labor and is itself subordinate to capital. It is this simultaneous dominance and subordination that puts it in the "middle." Its relations with capital and labor—economic, political, and ideological relations—have developed gradually over the last century out of the conflicts between the two polar classes. It is this history that has shaped the roles played by the middle class in the functioning of modern capitalism.

The middle class as a class

Four principles distinguish Poulantzas's theory of the middle class from other class approaches: domination of the working class, subordination to capital, historical development, and a functional role within capitalism. Later works may incorporate some of these, but no other theory is faithful

---

other economic distinction between productive and unproductive labor. Although we find this distinction important for fitting the working class within the larger process of capital accumulation, we have been unable to find its reflection in class perceptions.

to the full set.[8] They are worth specifying in some detail, as they will recur in our analyses of each of the three dimensions of class domination.

1. The middle class stands in opposition to labor. Its members are part of the control apparatus over workers, either the direct supervisory control exerted by line officers or the more indirect control that plans the institutions and environments that help keep workers in their place. Supervisors are the direct agents of capital in obtaining work from the workers. Engineers, teachers, lawyers, doctors, nurses, advertisers, welfare workers, and state officials act to control the lives and opportunities of workers. They stand in opposition to workers not merely because they engage in creative work while manual workers do not but because they have taken over the design and planning activities that workers once had (Poulantzas, 1974:246). The Ehrenreichs have emphasized the opposition most clearly:

> Thus the relationship between the [middle class] and the working class is objectively antagonistic. The functions and interests of the two classes are not merely different; they are mutually contradictory. True, both groups are forced to sell their labor power to the capitalist class; both are necessary to the productive process under capitalism; and they share an antagonistic relation to the capitalist class. . . . But these commonalities should not distract us from the fact that the professional-managerial workers exist, as a mass grouping in monopoly capitalist society, only by virtue of the expropriation of the skills and culture once indigenous to the working class. (Ehrenreich and Ehrenreich, 1979:17)

2. Whatever the capability of the middle class to dominate workers, its power is constrained by the ultimate power of capital (Poulantzas, 1974: 270). The great mistake of the postindustrial theorists has been to discount the power of capital.[9] Middle-class subordination is often hidden: supervi-

---

8. These principles can be compared with Erik Wright's (1985:34) list of "conceptual constraints." Both sets emphasize the relational and antagonistic nature of middle-class positions. Wright includes in his constraints the consequences of class divisions for class formation, class struggle, class consciousness, and the history of social change. We prefer to consider such consequences as empirically testable propositions rather than as criteria of class definition. We find Wright's treatment especially deficient on the historical origins of the middle class: his reliance on John Roemer's (1982) abstract model of economic exploitation often leads Wright into a totally ahistorical analysis. As a result, his scheme neglects the subordination of the middle class to capital.

9. Daniel Bell (1973) ignores capital almost completely. Galbraith (1967) at least ad-

sors, mental labor, and the petty bourgeoisie appear to have a great deal of freedom in pursuing their goals. But the middle class exercises power only so long as it helps support the accumulation of capital. Only on the rare occasions when the middle class confronts the interests of capital directly, do we observe the ultimate power of capital. Managers who do not make profits get sacked. Professional organizations working for "the public interest" atrophy at the expense of those working within the corporate establishment.

Recognizing this power, the middle class usually aligns itself with capital.[10] The general foreman that Studs Terkel (1974:184) interviewed understood where his loyalties lay:

> Prior to going on supervision, you think hourly. But when you become management, you have to look out for the company's best interests. You always have to present a management attitude. I view a management attitude as, number one, a neat-appearing-type foreman. You don't want to come in as sloppy, dirty. You want to come in looking like a foreman.

The capitalist orientation carries over outside the factory as well. The Lynds' observations about the Muncie middle class (what they called "the business class") are typical:

> On the other hand, the business class, in the main, either embraces or huddles toward the [Ball family, the town's leading capitalists] because they know that the system through which they earn their salaries, receive dividends, buy new Buicks, and send their children to college depends upon the enterprise of men like these. The [Balls] symbolize security to the Middletown business class. (Lynd and Lynd, 1937:94)

3. The analysis of the middle class is necessarily historical; the middle class has developed within and because of the class struggle between capital and labor. No static analysis can hope to understand the position of the middle class. We must know the origins of middle-class positions and trace

---

dresses the conflict between capital and mental labor ("technocrats"); he was wrong, however, about who was stronger.

10. Poulantzas labeled the new middle class a "new petty bourgeoisie," in part because of the procapitalist positions it took on most issues. American data (Hamilton, 1972:202) confirm the political similarity of the old and new middle classes. But see Therborn (1982:33) for a dissent on conflating the new and old middle classes.

their growth and decline. Only this historical picture can detect the larger social forces that govern middle-class strength. Thus Braverman's (1974) case for the distinct class position of engineers rests on a historical analysis of corporate efforts to get more work out of their employees. Similarly, the analysis of social workers as a control mechanism (Piven and Cloward, 1971) rests on the historical correlation of the creation and expansion of welfare with riots and other threats to capitalist stability.

4. Positions are defined on the middle-class side of the divide not so much through a microanalysis of the content of their work (there is no need for a new wave of time-and-motion studies to determine how much work is spent in creative endeavor and how much in mere execution, or in supervision and in taking orders) as in the context of the entire class system and how it supports the demands of capitalist accumulation. This is especially important in considering mental labor. Many jobs that involve autonomous work—like those of skilled workers, for instance—are not middle class because their mental labor does not control other workers. Engineers and quality-control specialists control workers; machinists do not. Both require creative thought, but engineers are middle class; machinists, working class. Or, to take a different sort of example, the positions of advertising specialists depend on the peculiarly capitalist—in fact, monopoly capitalist—need to create and expand demand, giving them an orientation to the maintenance of monopoly capitalism which is fundamentally different from that of workers.

The perception of the middle-class– working-class division

Do Americans see the working class as divided from the middle class, or is the working class just a rough range along a status scale? Conflict occurs between identifiable groups (Dahrendorf, 1959:179–93): Blacks and whites, Republicans and Democrats, Americans and Russians. If Americans recognize a true class division, then we can expect class conflict to occur along this line.

We believe that most Americans do in fact recognize a division between the working and middle classes, if only implicitly. The division is defined by the three dimensions of control: economic, political, and ideological. In this sense, popular practice has anticipated social theory in the understanding of class relations. Moreover, we believe that Americans put more weight on these three dimensions of class division than they do on the conventional scales of occupational prestige. What matters is not how much prestige one's job has but how much power it confers.[11] To be middle class in America is to own productive property, or to have supervisory authority, or to perform mental labor at the expense of manual workers.

In what follows we consider each dimension separately, first analyzing how it subordinates workers and then demonstrating that Americans use it in assigning themselves working-class or middle-class labels.

Authority

The most obvious form of control over the working class is direct supervisory authority. The most tried and trusted of capital's methods for subordinating labor remains intensified supervision. Management's first instinct when labor trouble arises is to increase the scope and intensity of supervision.

For example, even after General Motors had precisely designed its new Lordstown, Ohio, Vega plant to minimize the possibility of worker disruption, the company had to resort to intensified direct supervision to reach its original goals (Rothschild, 1973). In October 1971, shortly before the great wildcat strike of March 1972, GM installed a completely new management at Lordstown. The new managers came from a separate branch of the company, the General Motors Assembly Division (GMAD). They quickly introduced stiffer, more militaristic discipline.

> GMAD is charged, at Lordstown and throughout the corporation, with a more general rearrangement of factory discipline. At Lordstown this rearrangement took the form of layoffs, increased severity by foremen, the assigning of extra tasks and extra penalties for failure to perform these tasks—the sort of changes that have earned the division a national reputation for ruthlessness. (Rothschild, 1973:113)

These details are classic examples of the exercise of supervisory authority. The methods differ little from those of nineteenth-century mill owners, ex-

---

11. Most sociologists have assumed just the opposite, without benefit of (or even interest in) any empirical evidence; e.g., Daniel Bell (1973:72) assumed that the new middle class was primarily concerned to maintain the status of its largely petty-bourgeois origins and its "clean cuff occupations."

cept perhaps that GM used a larger cadre of supervisory personnel to carry
them out. GM also had more sophisticated control mechanisms in its reper-
toire, but it chose intensified supervision to solve its problems.

> The GMAD intensification of discipline is a characteristic extreme expression
> of modern Fordist attempts to increase auto productivity. Just as factory plan-
> ning is cheaper than mechanical planning, so managerial discipline is cheaper
> than inspection or time study or other similar corporation techniques. Managers
> are trained to identify and eliminate waste moments. And beyond such training,
> the managers learn (for free) a lasting attitude of tough-mindedness, to be
> shared by executives and plant managers and middle managers and general su-
> pervisors and foremen on the line. (Rothschild, 1973:115)

The exercise of this sort of authority naturally produces class conflict of
the most ordinary and divisive kind. Both sides accept conflict as the natural state of industrial life. General Motors almost boasts of the strikes that
GMAD provokes; as its vice-president for industrial relations explains:
"Ten consolidations [by GMAD] have produced eight strikes. It should
be apparent, to employ an understatement, that these consolidations are
difficult to accomplish without conflict" (Rothschild, 1973:121). Old-
fashioned supervisory discipline caused these strikes. Although Lordstown
became notorious for the monotony and the impersonality built into its factory design, intensified authority was the immediate cause of the strike
there.

> Workers' grievances at Lordstown concerned not only the speeding up and in-
> tensification of jobs, but also the disciplinary character of plant management—
> where workers must ask, and wait, to leave their jobs for one or two minutes;
> must ask, and wait for, permission to get married on a Saturday; must show a
> doctor's note if they stay home when they get sick; or a note from the funeral di-
> rector when they go to their father's burial; or a garage bill if they arrive at work
> late because their car broke down. (Rothschild, 1973:115–16)

In the twentieth century, salaried supervisors issue the orders that workers must execute; it is these supervisors who come into direct conflict with
workers. Most supervisors are not owners; they are employees like their
subordinates. In the past, capitalist entrepreneurs both owned their enterprises and supervised the workers within these enterprises. As firms have
grown into giant corporations, the two functions of ownership and control
have become increasingly differentiated: shareholders own, supervisors
control.

Dahrendorf

The German sociologist and Social Democrat Ralf Dahrendorf saw these organizational changes as requiring a change in class theory. Dahrendorf (1959) wanted to update Marx without dropping Marx's emphasis on class conflict. He therefore substituted authority for ownership as the principal class division in contemporary society.[12]

In his new class theory, Dahrendorf separates from the working class all those managerial positions that exercise authority in the work place. Supervisors, middle and top management are in a class position antagonistic to working-class interests. This categorization excludes many white-collar workers, such as the army of clerical workers, who are often claimed for the middle class. Since clerks exercise no formal authority, they belong with manual workers in the contemporary working class.

Dahrendorf's theory is a breakthrough, but he overstates his case in claiming that authority has totally supplanted capital as the basic class division. Dahrendorf overlooks the subordination of managers to capital, the relation that makes them a true *middle* class.[13] Sporadic conflicts break out between capital and management; for example, capital threatens management with unfriendly takeovers, and management responds with its own array of defenses.

As in all class conflicts, the outcomes of these contests are not all predetermined, but the balance of power remains clear. Over the long run, managers are not free to run their enterprises against the interests of capital; if they try, they are eventually sacked. Even in the 1960s, when corporate chiefs had reasonably secure tenure, the most common cause for executives' dismissal was low profits for capital (James and Soref, 1981). Maurice Zeitlin (1974:1093–94) relates a revealing incident about Anaconda Copper. When it suffered heavy losses after Salvador Allende's na-

---

12. In fact, Dahrendorf argues, it has always been the exercise of authority that separated the dominant class from workers. The original overlap that gave early capitalists both authority and ownership of the means of production led to Marx's confusion in identifying ownership as the differentiating characteristic of class relations. Only now that ownership has been separated from authority can we see that it is the exercise of authority that determines capitalist class conflict.

13. It is their emphasis on managers' subordination to capital that distinguishes the neo-Marxian theories (Poulantzas, 1974; Wright, 1976 and 1980; Carchedi, 1977) from Dahrendorf's. Nonetheless, the neo-Marxian approaches owe an often unacknowledged debt to Dahrendorf for first emphasizing the importance of authority (Parkin, 1979:23).

tionalization of its Chilean mines, the company's board of directors immediately replaced the chief executive officer with the vice-chairman of the
Chase Manhattan Bank—a complete neophyte to the copper business but a
representative of big New York capital—and the new boss proceeded to
dismiss half of Anaconda's former management. Incidents like this one
aptly illustrate the relative power of capital and managerial expertise; capital's power is less visible, but in a crisis it overwhelms managerial authority.[14]

Capital retains control over management by an array of positive incen-
tives that usually obviate the need for dismissals. Bonuses, profit sharing,
and stock options closely tie managers' incomes to their firms' profitabil-
ity. These plans yield great rewards for managers, but they also ensure
managers' subordination to capital's interest in profits.

Empirical research

Research on the actual characteristics of positions of authority blossomed
in the late 1970s and early 1980s. We now know (Wright and Perrone,
1977; Robinson and Kelley, 1979; Kalleberg and Griffin, 1980) that supervisors earn higher incomes than other employees of the same educational
training and occupational status. It is not their ability or background that
earns them higher pay; it is the class position of boss. (Supervisors' incomes are below those of similarly qualified owners, however—a re-
minder that supervisors are a middle, not a dominant, class.) Being a boss
is also more personally fulfilling; supervisors' jobs are more challenging
and allow more personal growth (Kalleberg and Griffin, 1980). Bosses are
also more likely to be Republicans (Robinson and Kelley, 1979).

Perceptions of supervisors' class position

We are interested, however, in whether Americans recognize authority as
one of the criteria of middle-class position. Is the division between bosses
and subordinates perceived as a class division? Robinson and Kelley
(1979) report that male (but not female) supervisors are more likely than

14. Managerialism theories (Berle and Means, 1932; Dahrendorf, 1959; Galbraith, 1967)
flourished in the prosperity of the immediate postwar period when corporate affluence made
the profit constraints on managers largely invisible. As firms encountered losses in the stagnation of the 1970s, the subordination of managers to capital became more readily apparent.

subordinates to identify themselves as middle class in both the United States and Britain. Beyond that research, we have a lot of anecdotal evidence that authority has great subjective impact on workers. The interviews of Studs Terkel capture well the feelings of everyday Americans. One steelworker describes the division between workers and bosses this way:

> This one foreman I've got, he's a kid. He's a college graduate. He thinks he's better than everybody else. He was chewing me out and I was saying, "Yeah, yeah, yeah." He said, "What do you mean, yeah, yeah, yeah. Yes, Sir." I told him, "Who the hell are you, Hitler? What is this 'Yes sir' bullshit? I came here to work, I didn't come here to crawl. There's a fuckin' difference." One word led to another and I lost. (Terkel, 1974:xxxiii)

On the other side of the authority divide, bosses also recognize the importance of the gap that separates them from the working class. This general foreman is well aware of the difference, in spite of his lip service to American egalitarianism:

> There's a few on the line you can associate with. I haven't as yet. When you get familiarity it causes—the more you get to know somebody, it's hard to distinguish between boss and friend. This isn't good for my profession. But I don't think we ever change much. Like I like to say, "We put our pants on the same way." We work together, we live together. But they always gotta realize you're the boss. (Terkel, 1974:183)[15]

Workers return this ambivalent class distrust, as a spot-welder attests:

> Oh yeah, the foreman's got somebody knuckling down on him, putting the screws to him. But a foreman is still free to go to the bathroom, go get a cup of coffee. He doesn't face the penalties. When I first went in there, I kind of envied foremen. Now, I wouldn't have a foreman's job. I wouldn't give 'em the time of day. (Terkel, 1974:161)

The point for the welder is not that the foreman is free from hassles—a foreman still has a boss "knuckling down on him"—but that a class line

---

15. In fact, the class position of first-line supervisors is somewhat ambiguous. They often are not the "lowest level of management" but are on a rung that is unconnected to the rest of the management ladder. They come from working-class—not middle-class—backgrounds; they are not college educated; and they rarely get promoted to higher levels of management.

still separates him from workers: the foreman has control of his time and, more important, control of the welder.

General Social Surveys results

A statistical analysis of the class placement question (Chapter 3) provides a more systematic test of how Americans perceive authority in the class structure. For this analysis we use mainly the General Social Surveys (GSS), a series of national surveys from 1972 to 1984 (see the chapter appendix).

In the GSS, 47 percent of full-time employed men and 34 percent of full-time employed women report some supervisory responsibility.[16] These estimates are based on responses to the overly broad question, "In your job, do you supervise anyone who is directly responsible to you?" The general frame of reference ("anyone") does not specify whether the people being supervised are direct subordinates, clients, students, or even people totally outside the employing organization, and that ambiguity probably explains the high reported levels of supervisory responsibility. This crude measure, however, is the best available in these data.[17]

We are interested in whether supervisory authority confers middle-class position, in the view of our American sample. In a simple comparison it is easy to demonstrate that supervisors more often see themselves as middle class than do nonsupervisors: of the male supervisors, 63 percent accept middle-class labels; only 40 percent of men without supervisory authority so classify themselves—a difference of 23 percentage points. The difference is only 8 percentage points among women (50 percent versus 42 percent), but again, more supervisors than nonsupervisors claim middle-class position.

16. All means and standard deviations for variables used in this chapter are presented in the chapter appendix (Table 4.A).

17. A similar question has been used in other empirical studies of authority (Fox et al., 1977; Wright and Perrone, 1977; Robinson and Kelley, 1979; Wright et al., 1982). Besides not specifying who is being supervised, the GSS question does not specify what type of authority is being exercised: e.g., general oversight, task assignment, hiring and firing (see Wolf and Fligstein, 1979; Wright et al., 1982). The measure therefore subsumes many different types of authority, and it is likely that the respondents were not consistent in interpreting the meaning of the question. While we can lament the fact that so central a concept is so poorly measured in empirical research, we must nevertheless use what data are available to estimate the results that might be achieved with more valid measures.

This difference is not surprising; neither conservative nor Marxist interpreters of American society would expect the results to be otherwise. The important question is *why* supervisors see themselves as middle class. Supervisors differ from other workers in many ways: they earn more money, have usually had more education, enjoy higher prestige, and so on. But these factors—income, education, and occupational prestige—are primarily status advantages they enjoy, not a division between dominant and subordinate classes. What we want to test is whether supervisors more often see themselves as middle class because of their greater authority (that is, their class position) or because of the higher esteem and income their work is given (that is, their status ranking). If we can show that their authority determines (at least in part) their middle-class self-placement, then we can conclude that Americans perceive more than status ranks; they recognize class divisions as well.

We can answer this question because we can make separate estimates of how class position and status rank affect class perceptions. Since there are ranges of status among supervisors and among nonsupervisors, we can compare the class placements of supervisors and nonsupervisors with those of similar status levels; similarly, we can measure the association of higher status with class perceptions within each class.

Like most statistics, the analysis is best understood in graphic form. We will consider three possible outcomes of an analysis of the simultaneous class and prestige effects on class perceptions (see Figure 4.1). Their interpretations, however, are decisively different.

In Figure 4.1a there is no class effect on the self-placements; "class" perceptions are entirely a function of occupational prestige. Bosses would still see themselves as middle class more often than workers, but only because they have higher prestige, not because there is a sharp class division separating them from subordinates.

In Figure 4.1b, the reverse is true. The measure of continuous occupational prestige explains nothing beyond the supervisor-worker class dichotomy. In this case we would be justified in interpreting the class placements as reflecting the perception of a true class division, not merely of a crude status ranking.

Figure 4.1c illustrates both class and occupational prestige effects. High-prestige supervisors (corporate executives) more often consider themselves middle class than do lower-prestige supervisors (building superintendents); high-prestige workers (architects) more often than low-prestige workers (receptionists). But at equal levels of occupational pres-

FIGURE 4.1. Possible joint effects of class and status on class
perceptions

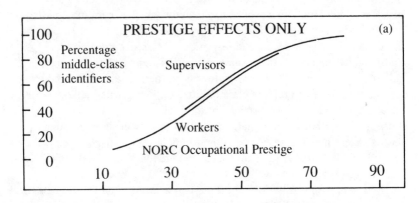

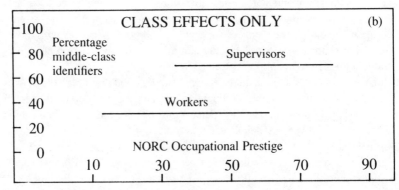

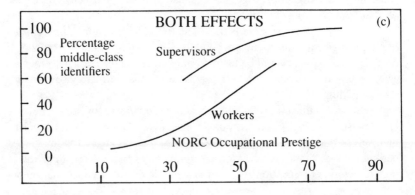

tige, those wielding authority (building superintendents) are substantially more likely to see themselves as middle class than those without authority (receptionists). In this case, we would infer that the class placements reflect the perception of both class divisions and status ranks.

Besides enjoying higher occupational prestige, supervisors also earn more money and are better educated than other workers. Earlier research and our own data tell us that income and schooling both increase middle-class placements (Hodge and Treiman, 1968; Jackman and Jackman, 1973 and 1983). The supervisors' more frequent middle-class placements may be due to their greater income and education rather than to the power they exert over subordinates. A fair test of class perceptions contrasts the class self-placements of supervisors and workers who are otherwise alike: that is, who earn the same salaries, have had the same schooling, and hold jobs of similar prestige. Thus, we must compare supervisors and workers only after matching them on all status factors.[18]

In Figure 4.2 we compare middle-class placements of equivalent supervisors and workers.[19] For men, supervisory power alone increases middle-class placements by an average of 10 percentage points.[20] This is not a great difference, but we must remember that we are comparing supervisors and workers who are exactly the same on all other class and status characteristics. As we will see below, other class divisions have a greater impact on class perceptions. Nevertheless, as Figure 4.2 makes clear, the author-

18. Controls are included for years of schooling, family income in the preceding year, and occupational prestige (see the appendix). We also control for the other two class dimensions as well, i.e., class placements are computed for both supervisors and nonsupervisors who have average probabilities of being self-employed and engaging in mental labor. For clarity of presentation, we discuss the relation between class divisions and class perceptions in separate sections. However, all multivariate analyses in this chapter have included all three dimensions of class position.

19. The plotted points represent the class placements for occupations at each prestige level averaged across nine prestige points and adjusted for the effects of the other class and status variables. We have also drawn the best-fitting curves, normal ogives, elongated S-shaped curves that are estimated by probit analysis. These curves are close to the results reported in the appendix in Table 4.B; the only difference is that in the plot we have calculated separate prestige curves for supervisors and workers (i.e., we have introduced an interaction term for prestige and authority). This interaction term is not statistically significant.

20. This and other percentages cited in the text are calculated from the probit equations in the appendix, Table 4.B. We substitute the mean values for all the control variables and calculate predicted scores for supervisors and nonsupervisors; these scores are then transformed into percentages according to the cumulative normal distribution.

FIGURE 4.2. Effects of supervisory authority and
occupational prestige on class perceptions

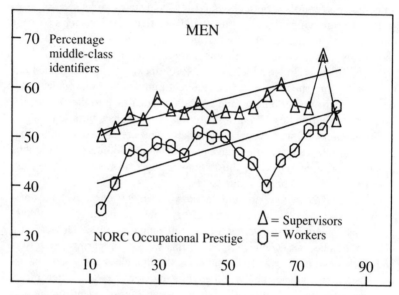

SOURCE: General Social Surveys.
NOTE: Fitted curve and plotted points are calculated after controls for mental labor, self-employment, family income, and years of education. Each plotted point is
a weighted average across ± 4 prestige scores.

ity division determines class perceptions as much as occupational prestige
does. For workers at average occupational prestige (42—about the prestige of mail carriers or tool-and-die makers), gaining an authority position
would increase the frequency of middle-class placement from 47 percent to
57 percent, somewhat more than moving to the highest prestige occupation
possible (a prestige score of 82 would, without any supervisory authority,
have a 54 percent predicted rate of middle-class placement). In fact, the effect of occupational prestige on class perception is less than we might expect by chance alone. What matters is whether one gives orders to other
workers or not.[21]

21. As with all the analyses in this chapter, we attempted to replicate these findings with
the Election Sample—a second, independent sample based on a different series of surveys.

For women (these results are not shown in the figure), authority is not important. This pattern—that men put more weight on their class position than do women—will hold true throughout the remaining analyses of class self-placements.[22] We address the reasons for this gender difference in more detail in Chapter 8; suffice it to say here that the difference results from differences in the nature of "women's work" and from the confounding effects of the husbands' class positions for the wives in the sample.

Mental Labor: The Managerial Class

The specialization of mental labor within the firm

The new middle class includes more than supervisory managers.[23] Many jobs that have no direct supervisory authority nevertheless permit substantial control over workers in particular and over society in general. The engineers who design factories determine the work lives of factory employees as much as do the plant managers who supervise those factories. The marketing manager has more say over what products the worker manufactures than does the production supervisor. The personnel officer and the labor relations specialist may not directly supervise any workers, but they

---

Using a quite different measure of authority, that analysis confirmed its effect on class perceptions (see the discussion in the chapter appendix). With the GSS data, we also attempted to explore the effects of different levels of authority (see Lopreato, 1968; Fox et al., 1977; and Jackman and Jackman, 1983:118). Respondents who supervised others were asked whether any of the people they supervised were themselves responsible for supervising others. Then a three-category scale was constructed: supervisors with one level of authority are 9 percent more middle class than workers without authority (all else being held constant). Supervisors with two levels of authority are only very slightly more middle class (3 percent) than the first-line supervisors; this slight difference is not greater than we might expect by chance. Thus, authority itself seems to have a truly dichotomous effect, as Dahrendorf suggested (1959: 171).

22. It may be also that we need a more stringent test of authority. Wolf and Fligstein (1979) show that women lack higher levels of authority (e.g., to determine pay: 37 percent of men, 14 percent of women; to hire and fire: 28 percent of men, 9 percent of women) even more than they lack supervisory authority (61 percent of men, 38 percent of women).

23. Several Marxist interpretations would disagree (e.g., Wright and Perrone, 1977; Reich, 1978:180).

have great influence over how workers are organized and treated. The oversight of the accountant and the quality-control inspector threatens workers as much as the authority of their supervisors. To include only direct supervisory management in the middle class and to exclude the engineer, personnel officer, marketing chief, and accountant is to create an artificial division between "line" and "staff" management. Both have control over workers and stand in much the same class position vis-à-vis both the working class and capitalists.

A class division between line and staff is especially absurd from a historical perspective. The specialized staff tasks of work planning, quality control, timekeeping, personnel, and the like, originally belonged to supervisory management. In early factories, line managers exercised all these powers. If we did not classify staff specialists in the middle class with supervisors, we would be compelled to conclude that these control activities passed out of the hands of management into those of the working class, a new stratum of white-collar workers. In fact, the opposite was the case, since the functional departments provided *more* control over labor than could be gained by simple line hierarchies.

The rationale for using staff specialists is often couched in terms that have little to do with class relations. Engineers introduce new technologies in order to increase technical efficiency, not to subordinate workers. But the new technology almost always has the consequence of reducing the latitude of the workers' independent action and extending the control of capital over workers' time. Workers realize this. A steelworker interviewed by Sandy Carter (1979:112) is quite explicit: "As far as I'm concerned I got no use for the intellectual—the so-called expert, who sits around all day dreaming up new ways to control my life."

Taylorism. Harry Braverman's (1974) classic study, *Labor and Monoply Capital*, traces the growth of these "so-called experts" in eliminating workers' control over production (see also Clawson, 1980). Some of his best evidence is the popularity of the time-and-motion studies and "scientific management" championed by Frederick Winslow Taylor in the early twentieth century. Taylor was quite explicit about his objective of controlling workers more thoroughly.[24] Taylor developed scientific man-

---

24. Taylor also sold the new methods as more technically efficient: he claimed that scientific management could figure out the one best way of producing something. In fact, it rarely did, and skilled craftworkers easily outperformed Taylor's cookbook methods.

agement in order to force workers to work harder. He advocated the routinization of every task and the detailed calculation of piece rates, not because they were inherently more efficient but because they were weapons in the struggle against the great evil of "soldiering," the deliberate limitation of output by workers.

But Taylor's schemes required management to understand better the details of the production processes. Workers could often resist employers' demands because they knew better how to manufacture the product (Gutman, 1973; Montgomery, 1979). Experienced workers could claim that it was impossible to produce at a faster rate, and their capitalist bosses had insufficient knowledge to overcome such objections. Taylor insisted, therefore, that to get control over workers, management had to eliminate workers' mental skills. Bosses must separate design and execution: "All possible brain work should be removed from the shop and centered in the planning or lay-out department" (1903:98–99). Formalized, written instructions, dictated by the employers, weakened the informal control of workers over work and, for a while, overcame some (but certainly not all) working-class resistance to management's demands. Employers were thus able to squeeze more profit out of their workers than would otherwise have been possible.

But—and this is crucial for understanding the modern middle class —the functions of work design were not taken over directly by capitalists themselves; they were entrusted to a new legion of managerial employees who also worked for capitalist wages. The result was the expansion of the corps of managerial, engineering, and professional positions during the twentieth century. The separation of design and execution created two classes of wage labor: the bulk of the workers who have little (and decreasing) say in the design of work, and the middle-class managers and professionals who have assumed those responsibilities. Thus the "new" middle class owes its very position to the destruction of workers' control, and this history makes the mental–manual division an antagonistic *class* division. It results from the employers' need to extract more labor from workers. Workers and middle-class managers have opposed interests in the organization of production. Two case studies make this historical conflict clear.

The steel industry. Katherine Stone's (1975) history of the steel industry also shows how the separation of mental and manual labor fit into a larger strategy of increasing control over the labor process. In the early days, skilled workers controlled the steel production process: they determined the pace of work, divided the labor among members of a crew, and sometimes even hired and paid their own unskilled labor. They lost these powers at the end of the nineteenth century. After management eliminated unions in the 1892 Homestead strike, the steel companies pursued a two-pronged effort to subordinate workers (Stone, 1975:55). First, supervisory authority was intensified; supervisors were forbidden to perform manual labor themselves; and training courses instilled a management orientation into first-line supervisors. In Poulantzas's terms, corporations reinforced the political relations of production.

But second, and equally important, the corporations took the *knowledge* of production processes away from the skilled workers and relocated it in management; that is, they reinforced the ideological relations of production. Training courses for narrow specialized skills replaced union-controlled apprenticeships. Labor-saving machinery eliminated skilled jobs. New dispatching systems and flow charts kept managers informed of the progress of production. These procedures, which are standard elements of managerial practice today, were innovations in the steel industry then. Because of them, the skilled workers lost control of the flow of production. The new organization required not only closer line supervision but a new cadre of staff officials. Just as the supervisory authority of the skilled workers was transferred to first-line supervisors, their overall knowledge about production was transferred to the staff managers. To fill the latter positions, employers began hiring a new class of white-collar employees, who became the bottom rung of the management hierarchy (Stone, 1975: 60). What is important here is the similar roles played by supervisory authority and mental labor in the class struggle within the steel industry.

GM's Lordstown plant. Mental labor played a similar supportive role at the Lordstown, Ohio, Chevrolet plant (Rothschild, 1973). General Motors designed the plant to incorporate the most advanced technology of the 1970s: computer controllers replaced human supervision and inspection; layout planning reduced workers' free time; automation replaced skilled work (machining and welding) with unskilled work (handing materials to robots). All these changes were the product of mental labor devising means to extract more labor out of the workers' time. As we emphasized in the section on authority, GM later applied more traditional supervisory pressures to increase production still further. The important point is the complementarity of supervision and mental labor in subordinating the workers. Both methods, the original plant design and the direct hierarchical pressure from bosses, were aimed at the same objective: securing maximum labor from the worker's hours on the line. In fact, the GM management hoped the control obtained through planning would be superior to strictly supervisory methods. GM's ideal system put workers "largely under the direction of machines," not of human supervisors.

GM prefers the control exerted by the staff specialists because it is more impersonal and more pervasive. It does not depend on having a supervisor constantly looking over someone's shoulder. Nor does it suffer from the human temptation to soften discipline in an attempt to secure a more friendly compliance. Its impersonality makes the control more difficult to resist. As Terkel's steelworker puts it, "Who you gonna sock? You can't sock General Motors, you can't sock anybody in Washington, you can't sock a system" (1974:xxxii). To include supervisory managers but not these staff specialists in the middle class is to ignore how the modern corporation seeks to control its labor.

What is important for a class analysis is that this specialization in mental labor involves a social relation between planners and executers: it distinguishes the mental labor of the engineer from the mental labor of the skilled craftsperson. Both the engineer and the skilled mechanic enjoy substantial autonomy deriving from the lack of routinization in their work. They differ, however, because the engineer plans work primarily for other workers; the mechanic plans primarily for his or her own work. In the engineer's case, therefore, the mental labor defines a class relation because it entails control over others; in the skilled craftsperson's case, the mental labor does not alter the worker's class position. The engineer is therefore middle class; the skilled craftsperson, working class.

Mental labor outside the factory

The issue becomes more complex outside the factory gates, where many professionals are in positions of substantial control over workers' lives but are not part of a productive enterprise. The class interpretation of these professionals is especially controversial because beyond controlling workers, they are engaged in providing many services; indeed, their control function is often unspoken if not vigorously denied. Thus social workers channel many benefits to those in need, but they are also responsible for ensuring that the unemployed and the poor do not sink so low that they disrupt the smooth working of the system. Indeed, the growth of welfare can be largely traced to this need to prevent disruptions (Piven and Cloward,

1971). Teachers instruct children (and adults) in countless skills, but schools are also the major screening device in modern society for allocating people to good and bad jobs, a function that gives them enormous power over workers and their children. Doctors make people healthy, or at least try to, but in doing so they exercise a control over people's lives that often extends far beyond what any boss could hope to achieve.

If the middle class is defined by the control it exerts over other people, then, it necessarily incorporates the social worker, teacher, and doctor as well as the first-line supervisor and plant manager. What the social worker, teacher, and doctor share with the engineer, accountant, and personnel officer is a specialization in mental labor: they all plan, design, and analyze, but their plans, designs, and analyses are largely executed by others.

Recognizing a class distinction between mental and manual labor helps to interpret the failure of the New Left that we described in Chapter 2 (Ehrenreich and Ehrenreich, 1979). One of the obstacles to the extension of radical protest outside campus walls was the students' reluctance to recognize a class division between themselves and the workers they were trying to reach. Students too readily accepted the naive assumption that because they were not capitalists, they too were working class, thus conveniently reinforcing their self-definition as the revolutionary vanguard —a vanguard that workers were bound to follow because of their common class position. This attitude only reproduced the mental–manual division in society: the student New Left, primarily from middle-class origins, would be responsible for designing the protest that workers would execute. The Ehrenreichs suggest in retrospect that the New Left's recognition of a class division separating students from workers would have cautioned a more deliberate and respectful effort to bridge that division.

Classifying jobs as mental labor

Unlike authority and self-employment, no one survey question will suffice to draw the line dividing mental from manual labor. Ideally, we would have a class analysis of each major occupation in the economy, a renewed sociology of occupations but one focusing on the conflict and macrosocietal implications of the division of labor.[25] Lacking this, we are some-

---

25. We have reservations about the practice of Wright et al. (1982) in defining a similar mental-labor division (what they call "semiautonomous labor") on the basis of survey responses to questions on the extent of work autonomy. This seems to concentrate too much on the microspecifics of an individual's working conditions and thus to ignore the social relations

what reassured to find that the major theorists of mental labor all sketch roughly the same division: mental labor is defined as all those occupations[26] in the census classifications of professionals and managers—the only exception being technicians, who, Braverman (1974) astutely argues, are really only a new kind of skilled worker.

This definition draws the line between mental and manual labor somewhat higher than the conventional white-collar–blue-collar line often used to denote a working-class–middle-class division (Weber, 1921; Lockwood, 1958; Parkin, 1971; Giddens, 1973; Gagliani, 1981). The problem with the white-collar–blue-collar line is that the routinized white-collar positions such as clerical and retail sales are as separated from the design and planning of office work as are blue-collar workers from the mental labor of factory work (Gorz, 1967; Braverman, 1974:293–374; Glenn and Feldberg, 1977).[27] It is for this reason that we categorized the lower white-collar workers in Figure 1.2 as working class. The issue is controversial since if these workers are included in the middle class, then the growth rate of the new middle class is so greatly exaggerated that it becomes the majority class in contemporary America. Even without them, the new middle class now constitutes over 20 percent of the labor force.

---

between mental labor and the working class. In particular, the concept of semiautonomous labor does not distinguish between the autonomy retained by skilled craftspersons and the autonomy enjoyed by mental labor, which capital has created *at the expense of the working class*. It is only this latter type of autonomy that merits a separate class location.

26. The use of census occupational classifications to create a class distinction has drawn sharp criticism from some class theorists. Wright (1979) insists that occupational data measure the *technical* relations of production and thus must be kept distinct from class divisions determined by the *social* relations of production. Carpenters, e.g., may be either employers, supervisors, or workers. This critique is a thoughtful corrective to the functionalist or even atheoretical use of occupational data in the past, but we think it overstates the case in at least two ways. Occupational classifications were not created solely to measure the technical relations of production; in fact, they do include social relations as well (e.g., between store managers and store clerks, or between construction foremen and construction workers). Moreover, the technical content of work for many occupations (social work, engineering, etc.) is very much the product of the historical development of class conflicts. To say that these positions are defined solely by the technical relations of production is to ignore their special role as agents of control over the working class.

27. Poulantzas is more inclusive in his definition, classifying clerical work, retail sales, and some service work as mental labor. But he acknowledges that these categories have an "objectively proletarian polarization" (1974:316–27) compared with the managerial-professional cadres isolated by Braverman and the Ehrenreichs. Although professionals are also subordinate to capital (see Derber, 1982), they retain control over others' lives in a way that clerical workers do not.

Empirical research

Several studies of American social structure have documented the *actual* separation of managers and professionals from the rest of the working class. Even before much of the theoretical and historical work had been done, Richard Hamilton (1972) found that the principal class division in American politics located the lower-paid white-collar workers within the working class. In national opinion polls, the decisive division in political attitudes separates both blue-collar and lower-white-collar workers from the "upper-middle" class (especially from the white Protestants who predominate in this class) that forms the core of conservative Republican politics in America (Hamilton, 1972:359–61).

Vanneman (1977) used cluster-analysis procedures to sort occupations into classes according to their patterns of residential isolation, father-son mobility, and friendship choices. For each analysis, the middle-class–working-class line was drawn at a place that separated professionals and managers from manual, clerical, and technical workers. For example, the residential distribution of technicians, bookkeepers, and other clerical workers more closely resembles the residential pattern of manual workers than that of professionals or managers. (However, retail sales workers cluster with other middle-class occupations, not with the working class, as in the Braverman and Ehrenreich analyses. A cluster analysis based on father-son mobility patterns shows that clerical workers have parental origins more similar to those of the working class than of the middle class.[28]

A persuasive rationale has accumulated, therefore, that in the contemporary United States a true class division separates the mass of workers from the professionals and managers who control work and help stabilize capitalist society. The division is not just status superiority but is based on class interests derived from antagonistic functions in the maintenance of capitalist society. The question remains whether this manager-worker class division is perceived by Americans themselves. Are working-class and middle-class labels used, at least in part, to distinguish between the two classes who engage in mental and manual labor?

---

28. Breiger (1981) reports more recent results that argue for the more conventional manual-nonmanual division. The most complete set of analyses (Pomer, 1981) explains the discrepancy. Clerical workers' origins are similar to those of blue-collar workers, but their children's occupations are more similar to those of white-collar children.

The perception of the mental-manual division

Workers' comments. There is substantial anecdotal evidence that workers do recognize the antagonism between mental labor and the working class: for instance, the steelworker (quoted above) who "has no use for the so-called expert who sits around all day dreaming up new ways to control my life." The middle class also recognizes the power inherent in mental labor. As one advertiser told Studs Terkel: "My career choice in advertising, which I've drifted into, is connected with the fantasy of power. I have a sense of slowly increasing power, but the limits are very frustrating" (1974:77).

Perhaps the best example of the popular perception of mental labor as an antagonistic class comes from E. Wight Bakke's (1940) study of the Depression unemployed. An American mechanic interviewed by Bakke anticipated Poulantzas, Braverman and the Ehrenreichs by more than a third of a century. The mechanic is worth quoting in detail because he notes most of the themes we have considered. He begins with *pro forma* protestations about the uncertainty of class structure in the United States, then zeroes in on the mental-manual division.

> You know it's hard to tell just what class divisions there are in America, and I don't know just how to say it. It seems to me it's something like this, that when you've a job where there's some call for planning, some call for figuring out things—I think that's the word, figuring out things—in your head, you feel that you're in a different class from the fellow who handles things.

For the mechanic, this mental-manual division is clearly a class division, not just a status differential. Indeed, he discriminates between the categorical class division separating manual and mental labor and the status differentials within each category:

> Now, I think that's the big class division in America, a division that comes right in the experience of men, something that's real, something that they see every day. And it usually works out that the "figuring-things-out" group is the same as the bosses and employers and the ones that tell you what to do. Now, of course, within the *figuring-out* group, and in the *handling-things* group, there's a lot of divisions too, but those aren't real class divisions.

His quick list of positions in the dominant class includes precisely those that Braverman and the Ehrenreichs have identified:

> [The fellow who figures out things] doesn't feel out of place when he's associating with men like professors, lawyers, and doctors—and oh say—bankers. He doesn't feel that he's out of place. He associates with them and he's sure of himself.

The mechanic is equally clear about what does *not* constitute a class division. First, he rejects the simple owner-employee distinction of the older Marxists:

> Now that fellow, I'll tell you right now, that fellow feels that he is just about next to the top notch, even though he is paid a salary just like others are paid wages, but just the same, he feels that he is important.

Even his "next to the top notch" description is apt, implicitly reserving the apex of the class structure for the genuine capitalist. He also rejects a simple money image (cf. Goldthorpe et al., 1969) of the class structure:

> Now, sometimes, you know, a man who's a real skilled artisan will be getting more money than that fellow, but it isn't always the money that makes the difference; it's the fact that you're figuring out things or you ain't.

The mechanic recognizes the association of a college education and mental labor, although the importance of formal schooling to class distinctions is clearly subordinated to the actual role of mental labor.

> If you've had a long experience of doing that sort of thing [figuring things out]. you get a confidence and an assurance that just naturally makes you feel a bit superior. Some men get that by going to college. Sometimes it ain't so; sometimes they don't do much figuring out in college, but at least they think that they've done it; but it isn't necessary to have gone to college if your training has been that of figuring out things. You feel pretty much the same way. (Bakke, 1940:89–90)

Bakke's mechanic is an unusually astute analyst, more perceptive than the best social scientists of his time, and quite as articulate. We do not claim that all American workers can provide such a clear analysis. We do suggest that this mechanic's image of the class structure is implicit in most

Americans' class perceptions. Not everybody can spontaneously describe that image in such detail, but most workers would recognize it as an accurate representation of the American society they know and work in.

The GSS results. In the GSS, 38 percent of the men and 30 percent of the women fall into the mental labor (that is, professional-managerial) class. The differences in class self-placement between these managers and other workers is striking—much greater than the differences between supervisors and nonsupervisors. For men, 68 percent of the mental laborers and only 23 percent of the workers identified themselves as middle class—a difference of 45 percent. Among women, the difference is 29 percent, since 62 percent of the mental laborers and only 33 percent of the workers identify with the middle class.

Of course, people in professional-managerial positions also earn higher incomes, have more prestigious occupational titles, and have usually acquired considerably more education. Is it their greater status rather than the power conferred by their mental labor that makes them middle class?[29] When we compare mental and manual labor for workers of equivalent education, income, occupational prestige, and other class positions, the results are striking—much more so than for direct supervisory authority. For both men and women, the mental-manual class division is the single most important determinant of class perception. The graphs in Figure 4.3 convincingly demonstrate the role of mental labor in determining class perceptions. The gap between mental and manual labor is substantial at every level of occupational prestige. For men, the average difference is 25 percentage points. The entire range of the occupational prestige scale has a smaller effect (11 percent) on class perceptions. *The crucial job characteristic for class perceptions is class position, not status rank.* For women, the difference between mental and manual labor is somewhat smaller—an

29. Mental labor is also often associated with supervisory authority: 60 percent of the mental-labor class also directly supervises subordinates; and only 30 percent of the manual-labor class has any supervisory power. But it is the close association between mental labor and occupational prestige that raises the most methodological questions. This multicolinearity makes it difficult to separate statistically the effects of mental labor and prestige on class perceptions. Fortunately, the overlap between mental labor and prestige is not so great that our results are endangered (see appendix, Figure 4.A). Our sample sizes provide sufficient numbers of low-prestige mental laborers and high-prestige manual laborers for separate estimates of the two effects on class perceptions.

FIGURE 4.3. Effects of mental labor and occupational
prestige on class perceptions

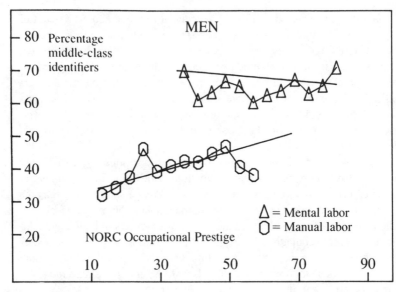

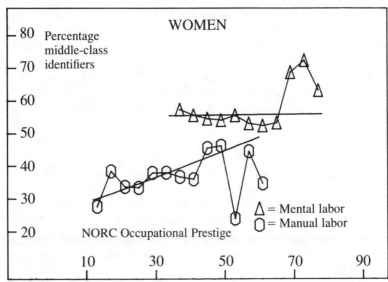

SOURCE: General Social Surveys.
NOTE: Fitted curve and plotted points are calculated/after controls for supervisory
authority, self-employment family income, and years of education. Each plotted
point is a weighted average of ± 4 prestige scores.

average of 12 percentage points—but still noticeable across the whole range of occupational prestige.[30]

The comparison of the mental-labor class effect with the occupational prestige effect demonstrates that the difference between managers and workers cannot be explained by the prestige differences between them. Without detailed analysis, we cannot tell whether it is the managers' dominant class position or their higher social status that places them more often in the middle class, but the results in Figure 4.3 eliminate the social status explanation. Occupational prestige is too unimportant in class perceptions to begin to explain the gap between the placements of mental and manual labor. If it is not the higher prestige, income, or education characteristic of mental labor that makes these managers see themselves more often as middle class, it must be their greater power—that is, their class position.

Ownership of Production: Self-Employment

The last class division to consider is the economic division between the self-employed and wage labor. The self-employed are the *old* middle class: the shopkeepers, artisans, independent professionals, and small farmers, whose numbers have dwindled (see Figure 1.2) but who are nevertheless still with us. This division has historic priority; even Marx acknowledged the intermediate position of the "petty bourgeoisie." Their class position must be distinguished from workers because their labor does not contribute to the profits of others. Capitalists make money from the labor of workers; the self-employed receive the full value of their own labor.

This economic difference generates different class interests: the petty bourgeoisie do not share the same interest in the transformation of capitalism as workers do. As a result, the self-employed generally act as a conservative force within capitalist societies (Lenin [1920], 1975 [vol. 3]:310); in fact, the old middle class has acquired a particularly nasty reputation for supporting reactionary regimes. In Chile it was the independent truck driv-

---

30. The Election Sample confirms the substantial effect of mental labor on men's class perceptions (see appendix, Table 4.B). However, for women the difference between mental and manual labor is small and not statistically significant.

ers who helped bring down the socialist Allende and install General Pinochet. And the self-employed in Germany, especially the rural Protestant self-employed, helped bring the Nazis to power (Hamilton, 1982).

The conservatism of the old middle class loomed large in many explanations of American exceptionalism. Their great numbers in early U.S. history provide a convenient explanation for the weakness of the American Left. Tom Bottomore's analysis is typical:

> In the USA, in contrast with the European countries, the ownership of property was quite widely diffused in the early part of the nineteenth century. . . . America was, predominantly, a society of small farmers, small traders, and small businessmen; the closest approach there has been to a "property-owning democracy." (1966:48)[31]

With the proportion of self-employed now down to 8 percent of the labor force, the old middle class can hardly be an explanation for American exceptionalism any longer.[32] Yet its decline has not brought an intensification of class conflict. This suggests that either the old middle class was not an important cause of American exceptionalism or that its role in muffling class conflicts has been assumed by someone else — in particular, by the new middle class of managers and professionals (see Bottomore, 1966: 50).

Today, the self-employed are important more for their theoretical significance than for their numbers. Unlike the self-employed, the working class must labor for some employer; all other forms of capitalist domination derive from this economic subordination (for Poulantzas, it is "determinant in the last instance"). The self-employed escape this subordination, and when they are themselves employers, they benefit from it. If workers do not recognize this division, they cannot understand the principal way in which they are kept subordinate.

---

31. Cf. labor historian Selig Perlman (1928:157): "The enormous strength of private property in America, at once obvious to any observer, goes back to the all-important fact that, by and large, this country was occupied and settled by laboring pioneers, creating property for themselves as they went along and holding it in small parcels." See also de Tocqueville [1835, 1840], 1954 (vol. 2): 267, and Karabel, 1979:211.

32. The old middle class may still have a conservative influence well beyond its meager numbers. The self-employed are disproportionately active in politics. Realtors, shopkeepers, morticians, and local attorneys still dominate the rhythms of local politics in hundreds of towns and small cities across America. These are people whose economic struggles have made them conservative individualists and the backbone of antilabor sentiment.

The genius of capitalism, as compared to such earlier methods of organizing workers as slavery and feudalism, is that employers trap labor into "voluntary" subordination. Capitalism transfers to workers the responsibility for better performance. Because employers can so easily dismiss their workers and hire new ones, they can pick and choose the best producers. To survive economically, much less to prosper, workers must exert themselves; slaves and serfs were under no such compulsion. This economic subordination can be seen most clearly in times when it is most threatening: absenteeism, turnover, and strikes all decline during periods of high unemployment. Workers afraid for their jobs are more submissive.

Capital's economic power underlies the other forms of power. Both the giving of orders and the reorganization of work depend ultimately on the fact that the job belongs to the company and not to the worker. Michael Burawoy, who generally discounts the importance of economic power, reports an incident from his own experience in a machine shop: "When I was resisting new inspection controls, a foreman came up to me, shook his fist angrily, and reminded me that a few days ago hundreds of auto workers had been laid off" (1979:130). The foreman was using the company's economic power to reinforce his supervisory authority and to impose new planning controls on workers.[33]

The economic division based on ownership is more than a means to an end; it is the end itself. Labor supports this compulsion by producing more value than it is paid in wages. Owners earn higher incomes than either supervisors or workers who have the same occupation and the same education and experience (Wright and Perrone, 1977; Robinson and Kelley, 1979; Kalleberg and Griffin, 1980). It is for the purpose of *economic exploitation* that the other forms of control are devised.

But Burawoy claims that workers do not understand their economic exploitation. For him (1979:28–29), the characteristic feature of capitalism is its ability to obscure economic exploitation in a way that slavery and feudalism never did. What must be studied, he says, is the way capitalists mystify economic relations and thus "manufacture consent" among workers so that they willingly participate in their own economic exploitation.

---

33. Burawoy was a Ph.D. candidate at the University of Chicago at the time he worked in the machine shop, so his employer's economic power over him was negligible. Moreover, the recessionary period he describes as rather ineffective in increasing the subordination of workers was, by a fluke, a time when the factory was expanding employment and demanding substantial overtime: i.e., a period of labor shortage for that firm. Those circumstances are not likely to provide a convincing demonstration of capital's economic power.

We believe that Burawoy assumes too much. There is, in fact, considerable evidence that workers are not "mystified." They do recognize their exploitation; they merely lack the power to do anything about it. The evidence comes in two forms: directly in comments about the value of their labor to their employers, and indirectly in their recognition of a distinct class position for the petty bourgeoisie who escape this exploitation. Most of this section concentrates on the second kind of evidence, the perception of the class position of the self-employed—this provides the broadest-based evidence that workers recognize the importance of the ownership division. But the occasional comments of workers also suggest that they understand how the economic relations benefit capital at their expense.

Petty bourgeois aspirations

The dream of self-employment still captivates workers' imaginations, however unrealistic the possibility may be.[34] The postwar automobile workers studied by Eli Chinoy (1955:86) entertained "widespread interest in small business." A former farmworker confirmed this fascination with self-employment among the working class:

> All farm workers I know, they're always talking: "If I had my own place, I'd know how to run it. I'd be there all the time. My kids would help me." This is one thing that all Chicano families talked about. We worked the land all our lives, so if we ever owned a piece of land, we knew that we could make it. (Terkel, 1980:168)

Such petty bourgeois illusions are said to explain American exceptionalism in that they divert workers' consciousness from the possibilities of collective action. The problem with such explanations (see Chapter 11) is the scarcity of evidence that workers' personal desires for getting ahead do in fact reduce their class consciousness. The opposite seems equally plausible: those workers who most fervently wish to escape the working class may be precisely those who most resent their capitalist bosses. One survey (Schlozman and Verba, 1979:160) showed aspirations for self-employment more closely related to personal unhappiness than to belief in the

---

34. Aspirations for self-employment have fallen considerably since the first half of the century: from 71 percent of employees in 1939 to 34 percent in 1976 (Schlozman and Verba, 1979:156).

American Dream. Self-employment may be attractive precisely because it is an escape from working-class subordination. Workers may both aspire to self-employment *and* be class conscious. To one machine operator, for example, the appeal of small business was precisely the possibility of escape from class domination:

> The main thing is to be independent and give your own orders and not have to take them from anybody else. That's the reason the fellows in the shop all want to start their own business. Then the profits are all for yourself. When you're in the shop there's nothing in it for yourself. When you put in a screw or a head on a motor, there's nothing for yourself in it. So you just do what you have to in order to get along. A fellow would rather do it for himself. If you expend the energy, it's for your own benefit then. (Chinoy, 1955:86)

Not only does self-employment mean "giving your own orders" (Poulantzas's political division); it also means "the profits are all for yourself" (Poulantzas's economic division). For the autoworker the dream of self-employment is one *expression* of his class consciousness, not a denial of it. The same resentment of capitalists' domination that prompts the petty bourgeois aspirations may also lead to militant class conflict. The direction that the resentment takes is probably a function of what seems most possible for the worker at the moment. To many American workers, self-employment—however remote a possibility—seems to offer a more realistic chance to escape from working-class subordination than does a socialist transformation. But our point is that petty bourgeois aspirations may be compatible with class conflict, given a good opportunity for class protest. Most of the American exceptionalism literature has not considered such a possibility.

Artisan origins of working-class movements

History teaches us that petty bourgeois *origins* have often contributed to successful working-class resistance to capital. The nineteenth-century Lynn, Massachusetts, shoemakers studied by Alan Dawley built one of the first radical unions in America on the basis of their previous artisan self-employment.

> Factory workers in the shoe industry were able to organize because most of them had been [self-employed] shoemakers in prefactory days. This gave shoe-

workers a common identity through a continuity of shared ideas and experiences. . . . Artisan protest inspired factory protest. Artisan organization engendered organization among factory workers. The Mutual Benefit Society of
Journeymen Cordwainers and the Mechanics Association left a legacy that became the Knights of St. Crispin [the first shoemakers' union]. The legacy contained not only the *experience* of organizing but also the stubborn conviction
that a worker had as much *right* to organize as anybody else. (1976:176–77)

In Lynn there was continuity between the artisans' resentment of their loss
of independence and the growth of working-class consciousness.[35] The
two sentiments were compatible and perhaps mutually reinforcing. Both
the working-class consciousness and the artisan independence rejected the
capitalist exploitation of their labor. Similarly, the autoworkers' dreams of
escape into small business should be interpreted not as an endorsement of
capitalism but as a rejection of it.

But does the dream of going into business for oneself really represent
an escape from the working class? Do Americans still equate being self-
employed with being middle-class? Or is self-employment no longer important—a meaningless vestige of an outdated Marxism? The next section
explores the issue by comparing the class self-placements of the self-
employed and the salaried.

The GSS results

The General Social Surveys include the customary measure of ownership
of the means of production: whether the person is self-employed or an employee. Hodge and Treiman (1968) and Jackman and Jackman (1973) used

---

35. Craig Calhoun (1982:123–26) identifies similar artisan origins of early nineteenth-
century English radicals, but he argues that an artisan background prevented the English
workers from developing into a class-conscious proletariat; instead, they were trapped in a
backward-looking "reactionary radicalism" that was anticapitalist but not prosocialist in even
a rudimentary form. It sought only to restore the privileges of the earlier artisan community
and was thus distinct from the later radicalism of the urban factory workers who were the real
"making of the English working class" (cf. Thompson, 1963). The distinction between the
two types of anticapitalist sentiment is an issue we will pick up again in Chapter 12. For now,
the important issue is whether the American worker was anticapitalist at all, or whether—as
Sombart maintained (1906:20)—"he loved it." The artisan origins of the Massachusetts and
English working-class protests suggest that petty bourgeois aspirations need not be procapitalist but may contribute to anticapitalist sentiments.

this measure (without success) in their studies of class placements. More recently, Wright and Perrone (1977) and Robinson and Kelley (1979) incorporated a self-employment variable in constructing class categories to study income inequalities.

In the GSS, only 12 percent of the men are self-employed and 8 percent of the women. These percentages are far too small to account for many of the middle-class placements in U.S. society. Nevertheless, the difference between the self-employed and wage laborers still addresses the important theoretical question about the role of ownership of productive property in the perception of class position. If the self-employed more often see themselves as middle class than do wage laborers (when we control for other influences), we can infer that the conventional Marxian emphasis on ownership of the means of production still plays some role in the popular perceptions of class position.

For men, self-employment does have an effect on class perceptions. In Table 4.1, men are 7 percentage points more likely to see themselves as middle class than are employees with the same income, education, and occupational prestige and in the same authority and mental-labor class positions. The difference is modest, but these are the first results that have found a middle-class ownership effect (cf. Hodge and Treiman, 1968). The difference for women is smaller and not greater than chance expectations.[36] Even for the men, the self-employment effect is smaller than the effects for authority and for mental labor. It might help if the surveys had more information about the nature of self-employment: for instance, how much property is owned and whether employees are hired. But with the available data we can conclude, somewhat tentatively, that American men do perceive self-employment as a class division that separates the middle class from the working class.

36. The Election Sample also included a measure of self-employment, with an intermediate category for people who are both self-employed and wage laborers: 14 percent of the men were fully self-employed; another 1.6 percent were partially self-employed. In this sample, self-employment has little effect on class placements once the other class and status variables are controlled (see appendix, Table 4.B). We suspect a measurement difference between the two surveys. A separate analysis of personal income in the 1976 and 1978 election surveys found no effect of self-employment; in the GSS, a similar analysis found the well-established relationship between self-employment and income. Thus the Election Sample measure of self-employment is unrelated to either middle-class placements or personal income; the GSS measure is related to both. Since the self-employment effect on earnings is well established, we put more trust in the GSS results showing a self-employment effect on class perceptions.

TABLE 4.1. Effects of self-employment on class perceptions

	Adjusted Percentage Middle-Class Placements	
	Men	*Women*
Self-employed	57	49
Employees	50	44
Difference	7	5

SOURCE: General Social Surveys.
NOTE: Adjusted percentages are calculated after controls for supervisory authority, mental labor, occupational prestige, family income, and years of education.

Conclusion

This chapter has reviewed evidence that mental labor, authority, and ownership each contribute separately to a middle-class placement.[37] American men use class labels, in part, to reflect actual position in the class structure: to exercise authority, to participate in the design of work, or to be in business for oneself is to be middle class; the working class enjoys none of these advantages.

American men perceive these divisions as *class* divisions; at work, it is their class position that determines middle-class placement, not just the

37. We have investigated these three dimensions as independent effects on class perceptions because we feel this best reflects Poulantzas's analysis of the middle class. Other Marxist analyses have instead combined the dimensions to create various class categories (see Wright and Perrone, 1977; Wright 1985). We feel this categorical approach is overly complex and theoretically unnecessary. Moreover, we did not find any statistically significant interactions among the three class effects (see McNamee and Vanneman, 1983, for an earlier report of this analysis).

higher status levels associated with managers, supervisors, and the self-employed. Even among men with exactly the same levels of occupational prestige, income, and education, mental labor is more middle class than manual labor; supervisors are more middle class than nonsupervisors; the self-employed are more middle class than wage laborers. Class divisions do determine class perceptions.

In fact, mental labor, authority, and self-employment have more noticeable impacts on class perception than does occupational prestige. For men, the estimate of prestige effects is less than what we might expect by chance (see chapter appendix, Table 4.B); thus, this analysis gives us no reason to believe that occupational status makes much difference at all to class perceptions. What counts is class position: managerial control, ownership of the means of production, and authority in the enterprise. For women, the results are less clear; mental labor determines their class perceptions but authority and self-employment do not. Even the mental-labor effect is weaker than for men. The explanation of this gender difference is complex, and we defer a more detailed analysis to Chapter 8.

Appendix

The statistical analyses of the class-placement question use data from two sources. The principal analyses are based on the 12 General Social Surveys (GSS) completed between 1972 and 1985. In the GSS the question was worded as follows:

> If you were asked to use one of four names for your social class, which would you say you belong in: the lower class, the working class, the middle class, or the upper class? (Davis and Smith, 1985:207)

We also analyzed data from the American National Election Studies between 1966 and 1978. For the longitudinal analysis (Chapter 6), we add the 1952 through 1964 election studies. In the Election Sample, the question was worded:

> There's been some talk these days about different social classes. Most people say they belong either to the middle class or to the working class. Do you ever think of yourself as belonging in one of these classes? [if yes] Which one? [if no] Well, if you had to make a choice, would you call yourself middle class or working class? (ICPSR, 1975:242)

Among the four choices offered in the GSS—lower, working, middle, and upper class—very few respondents chose the lower (1.6 percent) and upper (1.8 percent) extremes; thus, this question offers a basic dichotomy. We collapsed the two additional categories with the working and middle categories for our analyses. More drastic tinkering (e.g., adding an "upper-middle" category: Tucker, 1966; Hodge and Treiman, 1968; Jackman and Jackman, 1973 and 1983) changes the nature of the question and should be expected to yield quite different results (see Hamilton, 1966b).

Our rationale interprets the traditional "class identification" question as an exercise in cognitive judgment—respondents are asked to place a particular individual within a class structure. We infer the cognitive rules used in such placements from the pattern of results. Thus, we can use the statistical relationships between people's social position and their class self-placements as an index of the criteria used to assign people to classes. The important questions are which variables determine the self-placements (class or status) and how the social context (e.g., time, race, gender, or national culture) affects the relative strengths of those associations. Self-placements offer the advantage that respondents have full knowledge of the person they are classifying; no relevant characteristics are unknown to the respondents.

Our use of the self-placement question assumes that self-perceptions of class position follow the same rules as perceptions of the class positions of others. The equation of self-perceptions with other-perceptions is supported by a long tradition of psychological research (e.g., Bem, 1972). It is also an integral part of the symbolic interactionist approach and was one of the great insights of George Herbert Mead (1962).

Of course, since a respondent is classifying only a single person, we cannot develop a complete picture of each person's image of the class structure. But by aggregating responses across a great many interviews, we can develop a complete picture of how class labels are applied in the entire society. Do foremen typically place themselves in the middle class? Do clerical workers place themselves in the working class?

Samples

Together these surveys include data on the class perceptions of more than 20,000 Americans. There is no great virtue in these large numbers: for estimating national averages a sample of 2,000 is almost as good as a sample of 20,000. But we can use so many cases to get reliable estimates for subgroups that happen to be of special theoretical interest: line foremen and payroll clerks, Polish- and Scottish-Americans, women working in predominantly male occupations and men in predominantly female occupations.

All these national samples combine data from several surveys, and some of the surveys include much larger samples than the others (e.g., the 1972 Election data), though the larger samples represent populations that are virtually the same size as in other years. To correct for the fluctuating sample sizes, respondents were assigned weights so that each survey was weighted equally in the analysis (to the harmonic mean of sample sizes, see Winer, 1971). In addition, many of the samples included internal weights reflecting over- or under-sampling of certain parts of the population. These were included in the weighting of each respondent by multiplying the weight for that survey year by the internal weight (which usually had to be adjusted downward to reflect the true sample sizes).

All analyses have been computed for the white nonfarm labor force.

Only labor-force members are included because of the different interpretations given to occupation and even to income outside the labor force. Farmers are excluded because of their ambiguous position in a dichotomous, industrial class structure. Blacks require a separate analysis since there is substantial evidence (see Chapter 10; Jackman and Jackman, 1973 and 1983; Goyder and Pineo, 1974; Cannon, 1980; Cannon and Vanneman, 1986) that racial oppression shapes the perception of class. Separate analyses are computed for men and women because there are important differences (see Chapter 8) in the perceived class structure of men's and women's jobs.

Statistical analysis

The statistical technique used to test most of the empirical questions throughout this book is probit analysis (Hanushek and Jackson, 1977), a first cousin of the more familiar multiple regression using ordinary least squares. Probit analysis is more appropriate to the task of assessing dichotomous outcomes such as choices between "middle" and "working" class labels. Most of the estimated coefficients are presented in the tables appended to the appropriate chapters. The conclusions drawn from these statistical tests are presented in graphs; the coefficients are transformed into simple descriptive statistics such as percentages and included in the body of the text.

Variables

The three main class variables—authority, mental labor, and self-employment—are described in the text. The election surveys included no direct measure of authority, but we devised an alternative measure for a separate analysis described below.

Occupational prestige. Occupational prestige was recoded from the 1970 U.S. Census occupational codes as reported in the General Social Surveys codebook (Davis and Smith, 1985:448). In the Election Sample, occupational prestige was recoded from modified 1960 U.S. Census occupation and industry codes (ICPSR, 1968: 216–34). Both codes are derived from a direct measure of subjective occupational prestige (Siegel, 1971) and should therefore represent the best contrast to objectively defined class distinctions.

Education. Education is scored as years of school completed except that precise data are not available for the college-educated categories in the Election Sample. All Election Sample respondents with incomplete college were coded as having 14 years of school and respondents with graduate degrees were coded as having 18 years.

Income. The income measure is based on total family income from all sources. The surveys reported income according to different categorization schemes in different survey years. To achieve comparability, each income category in each year was recoded to the dollar value of the midpoint of that category. The top category was open-ended (e.g., $25,000 and over) so Pareto estimates were used (Shryock and Siegel, 1975:366). Because each set of surveys spans several yeras of high inflation, the income data are converted to real 1985 dollars (1978 dollars for the Election Sample) by adjusting for the relevant consumer price index. The logarithms of these values are used in all analyses rather than the actual dollar values, because we assume that income effects are likely to be proportional (i.e., the increase from $10,000 to $20,000 is equivalent to the doubling of $20,000 to $40,000, not to an increase from $20,000 to $30,000).

Authority in the Election Sample

There is no direct measure of authority in most of the election surveys. However we devised an alternative measure of authority from the *Dictionary of Occupational Titles* (DOT) codes (U.S. Department of Labor, 1965). One of the DOT codes rates the nature of a worker's interaction with other people, especially subordinates, on the job. In the past the DOT "People Code" has been interpreted as an index of "job complexity" (Kohn and Schooler, 1969; Miller, 1971), but closer inspection shows that the "people" referred to are almost all subordinates, not coworkers or superiors. For this reason, we feel the code is best interpreted as a measure of authority.

The code clearly implies authority in its higher categories: *mentoring*, the counseling functions performed by doctors, lawyers, and the clergy; *negotiating*, the executive management functions of "formulating policies and programs and/or arriving jointly at decisions, conclusions, or solutions"; and *instruction*, the exercise of authority over students. Two other categories also imply authority: *supervising*, "determining or interpreting work procedures for a group of workers, assigning specific duties to them";

and *speaking-signaling*, "giving assignments and/or directions to helpers or assistants."

Of the three remaining categories in the DOT People Code, *serving* (0.8 percent) clearly does not imply authority. *Persuading* (7.6 percent), however, occupies a special position. It is defined as "influencing others in favor of a product, service, or point of view." The attempt to influence, as well as the dominant interpersonal style typical of sales work, gives this classification something of the character of authority without genuinely fulfilling the condition of legitimized power. A separate measure was therefore created to isolate this type of relationship. The remaining small (0.2 percent) category, *diverting*, was combined with persuading because of a similar requirement to please and convince others.

The DOT code does not measure authority on the job as directly as does the supervision measure used in the GSS. But the DOT captures more of the richness of official occupational responsibilities; it reflects qualitative rather than quantitative distinctions. Further, the DOT measure does not depend on the worker's own subjective definition of authority (see Wright and Perrone, 1977:36). In sum, we feel that the DOT code has compensating advantages and disadvantages for measuring authority. Taken together with the GSS supervision code, the two different measures should provide a more rigorous test of the importance of authority in class perceptions.

For the men in the 1966 to 1972 election surveys, we recoded the occupations recorded in the original surveys according to the DOT codes. The five authority categories taken together represent 35 percent of the Election Sample, and when compared with the nonauthority categories, they do confer more middle-class position (see Table 4.C). On the average, the authority positions are 9 percent more middle class than the nonauthority positions. As in the GSS results, the authority effect is modest but more than we would expect by chance alone.

Each of the authority subcategories is more middle class than the nonauthority category. Mentoring (0.692), negotiating (0.472), and instructing (0.423) are all well above the nonauthority occupations (0.000). However, supervising (0.226) and speaking-signaling (0.128), although more middle class than the comparison, are less different than what we might expect by chance alone.

TABLE 4.A. Means and standard deviations

	General Social Surveys		American Election Surveys	
	Men	*Women*	*Men*	*Women*
Supervision (%)	43.3	34.5	—	—
Mental labor (%)	39.4	34.6	39.7	26.5
Self-employed (%)	12.7	7.2	14.9	8.6
Occupational prestige	42.4	42.3	42.9	39.9
	(14.3)	(13.2)	(14.1)	(13.7)
Years of education	13.1	12.9	12.3	12.4
	(3.1)	(2.6)	(3.2)	(2.6)
Family income (log)	10.09	9.91	9.72	9.47
	(0.77)	(1.00)	(0.66)	(0.77)
Sample size (unweighted)	2,808	1,781	3,425	2,451
Sample size (weighted)	2,798	1,784	3,295	2,292

NOTE: Standard deviations are in parentheses.

TABLE 4.B. Probit analyses of class perceptions: class and status
variables

	General Social Surveys		American Election Surveys	
	Men	*Women*	*Men*	*Women*
Supervisory authority	.2458	−.0088	—	—
	(.0542)	(.0667)		
Mental labor	.6436	.2856	.4965	.0848
	(.0759)	(.0900)	(.0634)	(.0867)
Self-employment	.1842	.1152	.0481	.1338
	(.0859)	(.1244)	(.0728)	(.1092)
Occupational prestige	.0041	.0094	.0079	.0097
	(.0023)	(.0030)	(.0020)	(.0025)
Years of education	.1108	.1152	.1319	.1652
	(.0093)	(.0130)	(.0082)	(.0121)
Family income (log)	.3264	.1906	.3435	.2973
	(.0374)	(.0325)	(.0364)	(.0386)
Constant	−3.0862	−4.0427	−.2767	.0074
Fit	.8086	.5628	.7852	.6505
Sample size (unweighted)	2,808	1,781	3,425	2,451
Sample size (weighted)	2,798	1,784	3,295	2,292

NOTE: Standard errors are in parentheses.

TABLE 4.C. Probit analyses of class perceptions:
           DOT-defined authority

	Probit Coefficients
DOT authority	.2161
	(.0752)
DOT persuading	.5081
	(.1320)
Mental labor	.3311
	(.0675)
Self-employment	−.0303
	(.0506)
Occupational prestige	.0109
	(.0034)
Years of education	.1304
	(.0127)
Family income (log)	.3861
	(.0612)
Constant	−.2628
Sample size (unweighted)	1,841
Sample size (weighted)	1,769

SOURCE: American Election Surveys, 1966–1972; men only.
NOTE: Standard errors are in parentheses.

FIGURE 4.A. Status distributions among mental-labor managers and workers

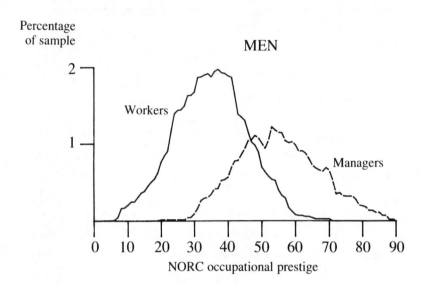

Percentage of sample

MEN

2

1

Workers

Managers

0 10 20 30 40 50 60 70 80 90

NORC occupational prestige

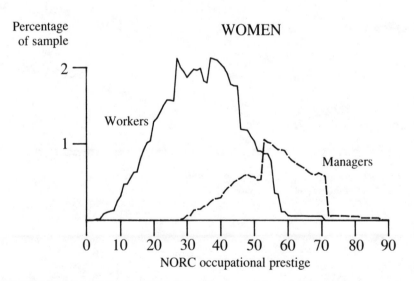

Percentage of sample

WOMEN

2

1

Workers

Managers

0 10 20 30 40 50 60 70 80 90

NORC occupational prestige

SOURCE: General Social Surveys.
NOTE: Percentages are moving averages across ± 5 percentage points.

CHAPTER 5
CLASS IMAGES

Critics of Richard Centers's class-perception question complain that it forces a particular class model on all interviewees. They have a point—that we need to explore other class images beyond those labeled working class and middle class—but they exaggerate its importance by claiming that the possibility of other class images necessarily invalidates the use of Centers's fixed choices.

Methods

The study of alternative class images usually begins with a simple, open-ended question asking people how they interpret class divisions. The best-known of these studies is the 1962 British survey of "affluent workers" (Goldthorpe et al., 1969),[1] which posed this question to a small sample of autoworkers: "People often talk about there being different classes—what do you think?"

The investigators eventually coded the varied responses into money models, 54 percent; prestige models, 8 percent; power models, 4 percent; a residual "other," 26 percent; and no images, 7 percent (Goldthorpe et al., 1969:150). Workers with power models, although uncommon, were the most class conscious; they saw society divided into two opposing classes: "bosses and men" or "the employing class and the rest of us." At the oppo-

---

1. For other examples, see Willener, 1957 and 1975; Popitz et al. [1957], 1969; Lopreato and Hazelrigg, 1972; Bulmer, 1975; Coleman and Rainwater, 1978:18.

101

site extreme, workers with prestige models were the least class conscious; they saw social differences stretched out along multiple gradations based on lifestyle or social background.

Between the class conscious and the status conscious were the majority of workers, who interpreted class primarily as a matter of the amount of money one has. All these models pictured a large central class to which most wage and salary earners belonged—disregarding the blue-collar–white-collar division that has been so central in British sociology. There were several variations on the money theme. A number of workers saw two income classes, the "very rich" and the "working class"; others added a third class below those two, "the very poor"; some distinguished two distinct classes at the top, "millionaires" and "the well-to-do."

Problems with open-ended questions

Goldthorpe et al.'s direct approach to studying class images, using open-ended questions, may seem at first to be the easiest and most natural approach: if we are interested in how Americans see class divisions, why not just ask them and record what they say. And, indeed, the method is well suited to in-depth interviews that permit relaxed and thorough probing (e.g., Bott, 1957; Lane, 1962; Sennett and Cobb, 1972; Garson, 1973; Rubin, 1976; Hochschild, 1981). But the luxury of extended interviews is not feasible for studying representative national samples. When open-ended questions are transferred to large-scale surveys, they raise four great problems.

First, open-ended questions are often more ambiguous; the more unstructured they are, the more baffling they tend to be for the people being interviewed (Schuman and Presser, 1979; Jackman and Jackman, 1983: 14–15). Usually the researcher has a very specific purpose for asking the question but leaves the respondent to guess at that purpose ("What does he mean, 'What do I think about social class?'"). The open-ended format is sometimes championed as the more democratic method—let the people decide for themselves what they mean by "class"—but in fact, this is a counterfeit democracy: the researchers know their intention in asking the questions, but since "class" may take several different meanings, the respondent is asked to guess which of the possible meanings the interviewer has in mind.

Second, open-ended questions give the sociologist extraordinary leeway in classifying the responses into categories that the people may never have intended.[2] From the bewildering assortment of replies that such questions provoke, what kinds of responses does the analyst encode as "class conscious?" The classifications are rarely clear-cut. American workers do not, standing on their doorsteps, expound a theory of class struggle based on the expropriation by capitalists of the surplus value workers produce. We cannot insist that workers be trained Marxist ideologues before we classify them as class conscious, nor is that necessary for radical protest (Moorhouse, 1976; Tilly and Tilly, 1981:17). Since Marxist theorists themselves disagree about the correct definition of the working class, we can hardly expect workers to have definitively resolved all these issues for themselves.

As a result of the ambiguity in the responses, then, researchers develop idiosyncratic coding schemes that are rarely replicated in subsequent studies. The prestige, power, and money models of the affluent-worker studies did not match the categories used in earlier analyses (e.g., Bott, 1957; Willener, 1957; cf. Goldthorpe et al., 1969:147), nor have later studies adopted the affluent-worker categories. Thus little cumulative knowledge—such as has developed, for instance, from the steady stream of research with the Centers class-perception question—has resulted from these attempts.

The coding problem suggests a third difficulty. The direct strategy depends on how well Americans can *articulate* their class images, not whether they *perceive* class divisions. Perception and articulation are distinct processes. Workers may experience class conflict and perceive the divisions around which that conflict is organized without being able to articulate precisely those perceptions. Yet unverbalized perceptions often exer-

2. This problem also confronts unstructured and in-depth interviews—resulting in such divergent interpretations as those of Lane (1962), Sennett and Cobb (1972), and Garson (1973). Sennett and Cobb interpret their working-class interviewees as suffering from a lack of respect—such as being addressed by their first names while their white-collar neighbors are always called "Mister." But their interviews also reveal how the workers resent the power that the middle class exercises over their lives. For example, an electrician's apprentice gripes, "It's a question of, like am I working for someone? I . . . I feel like I'm taking shit even when, actually, even when there's nothing wrong" (1972:34). The authors neglect the more class-conscious themes of dominance and subordination in such material and prefer a status-oriented interpretation. Both interpretations may be correct given the multiple consciousness of each American worker, but the neglect of the class themes creates the erroneous impression of weak class consciousness.

cise an important influence over thought and behavior.[3] One of the more important advances in psychological research has been the recognition that *implicit* cognitive models can determine behavior without ever becoming fully conscious. Our use of language provides a good example of this phenomenon: we learn to talk according to regular patterns long before we are taught explicit rules of grammar. These language patterns shape the way all people talk in everyday life, although we leave to professional linguists the task of articulating those rules.

In their research on patterns of language usage, linguists do not ask a sample of the population direct, open-ended questions about what rules they use in forming sentences. Those rules, however important and ingrained in patterns of speech, are not usually conscious. Indeed, if linguists did ask that question, the best answer they could hope for would be a recitation of the rules of "proper" grammar learned years before in school. Whether the school "rules" truly reflect actual patterns of speech or not would remain an open question. Nevertheless, sociologists have often studied the perception of class exactly this way—by asking respondents what rules they use to sort people into different classes and assuming that these answers accurately describe the pattern of usage.

The final flaw in open-ended questions is their assumption that people have only one image of the class structure. A person is classified as having *either* a money model or a power model; either a two-class or three-class or multiclass model. Nobody is classified as having *both* money and power models, or both two-class and multiclass models. For example, John Goldthorpe and his colleagues attached great significance to the predominance of the money models over the more conflict-oriented power models. The money models implied a less hostile image of society, appropriate for these more affluent workers. But H. F. Moorhouse (1976) later showed that money models and power models are not as mutually exclusive as were first supposed; in fact, he found that for much of the population, "statements about money are statements about power" (1976:474). And in John Leggett's (1968) study of working-class consciousness in Detroit, it is clear that for many workers, "money is power." When workers were asked who enjoyed special powers or privileges in Detroit, they replied:

---

3. The converse of this is often true, too. As Michael Burawoy (1979:139) observes in his observation of machine shop workers, "The idiom in which workers couch and rationalize their behavior is no necessary guide to the patterns of their actual behavior." (See Chapter 11.)

"The wealthy"; "The people that have the money. If you don't have money, you don't get much privileges"; "People who have more money could enjoy more power" (1968:161–62).

Similarly, several studies have thought it important to determine who has a two-class, three-class, or multiclass image of society; supposedly, the two-class models are more conflict oriented, perhaps even proto-Marxian. But this is a futile enterprise. Someone with a two-class image can distinguish subgroups within each of the major classes (see Lenski, 1952). Conversely, someone with a multiclass image can be persuaded to collapse the categories into fewer and larger classifications. Whether such a person responds to an interview question with a two-class or multiclass model depends chiefly on the momentary demands of the situational context.

Our objection to the assumption that each person has just one class image is the same as our comment on the occupational prestige studies—people have quite varied and flexible perceptions of their society. The fact that under one set of circumstances someone describes a particular image of the stratification system—be it a two-class, continuous status–ranking, or money model—does not mean that at other times and in other circumstances the same person will not use quite different images.

Few studies have been as sensitive to the multiple nature of class images as the early interviews of Elizabeth Bott (1957). In her intensive probing into the class images of Londoners, she was struck by the many seeming inconsistencies in the interviews.[4] The criterion of class position would shift from income to power and then to occupational prestige without arousing any sense of contradiction in the respondent. The level of focus would also adjust from one context to another, so that at one point the respondent would talk of what seemed like a quite homogeneous working class but would later break that class down into well-defined segments. From this she concluded that

> usages vary according to the immediate social situation and the specific purpose of the comparisons and evaluations. It follows that there is no one valid way of

---

4. Intensive interviewing often corroborates the complexity of workers' understanding of society. David Garson (1973) found that Massachusetts autoworkers would *both* endorse the standard American ideology of individual responsibility for success *and* advocate class solidarity to confront bosses. He interprets their ideas as typical of the multiple consciousness of American workers.

finding out what people *really* think about class, for each method will reveal
. slightly different reference groups, although there is a strain of consistency
and continuity running through each couple's usages at different times. (Bott,
1957:171)

The direct approach of asking people their class images often fails, then,
because people sometimes cannot articulate a class model they do perceive, and the class model they do verbalize may not be the only model
they perceive.

Structured questions

We would like to put to rest, therefore, the still-prevalent idea that unstructured direct questions ("What do you think?") are necessarily better than
more structured questions that allow respondents to choose from a series of
possible answers. Because answers to unstructured questions are more
"spontaneous," they have been thought to reflect better what respondents
really think about class; structured questions, by comparison, are said to be
guilty of gratuitously imposing on respondents a framework that may be
completely foreign to them (Gross, 1953; Case, 1955; Kahl and Davis,
1955; Haer, 1957; Gordon, 1958; Lopreato and Hazelrigg, 1972; Schlozman and Verba, 1979).

But this critique of structured questions loses its validity once we realize
that everybody has multiple images of society. A "spontaneous" response
would be preferred only if we could assume that the respondent has only
one class image. But if people have several complementary images, then
we have no way of knowing whether the "spontaneous" image first elicited
is a person's only image or what additional kinds of class perceptions he or
she may have developed.

By contrast, a series of more structured questions can be fairer to the respondent by providing a more explicit context, so that people seem better
able to understand what the researcher is asking. Of course, answers to
structured questions can be misleading if the context provided is meaningless to most respondents. The validity of structured questions depends on
the skill of the question author; our point is just that structured questions
cannot be judged a priori invalid. Nor are we suggesting that unstructured
questions are always invalid. Indeed, there can be no substitute for intensive interviewing where the interviewer has the time and skill to explore
the multiple perceptions of class structure. Studies such as Elizabeth Bott's

can elicit new and valuable insights. We doubt, however, that most survey research meets these conditions.[5]

The appropriate strategy for studying class images is to observe *many* concrete instances where such images must be used and to abstract the images from the specific behavior. The emphasis is on the "many," since no single rule will determine all concrete instances. In some circumstances, an authority-subordinacy distinction might be the decisive criterion; in others, income or education may be more important. That is, we must allow for the possibility that respondents, like sociologists, can work with different models, depending on the circumstances and the appropriateness of the model. But differences among individuals can also be observed by tendencies to utilize different models in the same situation.

Skillful intensive interviewing uses precisely this strategy to elicit multiple instances of respondents' use of class images. In the study reported in this chapter, we experiment with a structured format more suitable for survey research; we presented what is called a "triads" task to a small sample of Chicago respondents.[6] We listed three occupations and asked respondents to tell us which two of the three were in the same social class. Then we presented another set of three occupations and again asked them to choose the two in the same class. We proceeded in this way until we had asked all combinations from a list of eight occupations. Different parts of the sample were given different lists, but the main set that we analyze here comprised eight occupations taken essentially from the industrial sector: big corporation executive, plant manager, industrial engineer, factory foreman, skilled machinist, truck dispatcher, payroll clerk, assembly-line worker.[7] This list includes both high- and low-prestige positions, occupa-

5. How are we to interpret the answers people give to unstructured questions about class perception? It seems likely that the class images described often simply comprise categories and phrases picked up from popular culture—like the recitation of school grammar rules. In the United States, to be sure, the popular culture is largely bereft of class categories (Markwick, 1980). Neither the dominant American cultural institutions (the media and the schools) nor working-class–oriented organizations (unions and the Democratic Party) supply workers with the vocabulary they need to articulate the class divisions that surround them (Mann, 1973). It is expecting too much to presume that workers should develop this vocabulary *de novo*.

6. The details of the survey and its statistical analysis are presented in the methodological appendix to this chapter.

7. Some earlier research with occupational differences (e.g., Burton, 1972; Coxon and Jones, 1974) found that respondents often distinguished occupations by organizational set-

tions at various levels of prestige with direct supervisory authority and others without authority, and some blue-collar and some white-collar occupations. The mix enables us to test what criteria the respondents would fix on to make their judgments.

Tendencies in class images

The objective of research on class images must be to look for the "strain of consistency" that Bott (1957) found in her London interviews. People *do* differ in the way they perceive the social order, but we need not classify every person as having one and only one image of the class system. Some of the problems of earlier research in this area might be resolved if we looked for general *tendencies* in constructing class images rather than trying to identify complete models that precisely fit each observer's cognitive map of the social order. We believe that two such tendencies are basic to the broad range of class images that people most often report.

First, there is a tendency to see a strong division near the top of the social order that separates the bulk of the population into a large subordinate class. Most of the models that Goldthorpe et al. (1969:148) report for their English autoworkers reflect this tendency. So does the image suggested by the class-placement analysis in the previous chapter, which puts above the dividing line mental labor, the self-employed, and those in authority — all of whom are minorities in the work force. (The size of the elite in Goldthorpe's research would appear to be considerably smaller, however, since the English workers do not include all administrators and professionals in the top category; 1969:149). We call this tendency the *working-mass* tendency, since it groups most of the labor force in a subordinate, working-class position. The large mass at the bottom would include not only the less-skilled manual workers but also craftworkers and the white-collar proletariat.

A second common tendency draws the major division in society near the bottom: it sees the unskilled workers as a separate lower class but assimilates affluent blue-collar workers into the "middle mass" of society. This

---

ting: differentiating bureaucratic occupations from occupations where work was individualized (e.g., gardeners, police officers, real estate agents). Because we wanted to avoid this "situs" distinction in the main analysis, we chose the list mainly from the industrial setting. See also Blau and Duncan (1967) and Laumann (1973) for similar organizational setting dimensions in patterns of occupational mobility and friendship choices.

middle-mass tendency combines many manual occupations with truly middle-class positions so that this more successful majority greatly outnumbers the vestigial working class.[8]

These tendencies are not exclusive alternatives. Given an appropriate situation, many people recognize divisions at both ends of the social order. People who emphasize the separation of a small dominant middle class from the working masses are not necessarily ignorant of the internal divisions between foremen and assembly-line workers, for instance. Nor do observers who see a large middle mass necessarily deny a class division between corporate directors and factory foremen. Synthetic class images (Ossowski, 1963) that incorporate two or more tendencies are more understandable if we consider these two main cognitive tendencies to be *independent* of each other rather than psychologically opposed. In many situations, people will unite the tendencies in a composite image. The combination can be quite cognitively consistent and may even be the most widespread model within a given population.

Nevertheless, we are interested also in the differences among people in their readiness to adopt one or the other tendency. Americans may have multiple images of their class system, but they may lean toward one or another model as a preferred perspective. The two tendencies therefore represent the "strains of consistency" that Bott found to hold across the many variations that occur in situational contexts.

Class Image Patterns

Two statistical strategies have been developed to abstract the general tendencies from concrete similarity judgments such as those in our triads task. We rely first on a technique known as "individual differences multidimensional scaling" (INDSCAL); we then supplement this technique by grouping the occupations through cluster analysis methods.

INDSCAL attempts to summarize the differences among the occupations as distances in a one-, two-, or multidimensional space (Carroll and

---

8. The working-mass image reflects the results of a proletarianization process that lowers many white-collar workers into the working class. The middle-mass image reflects the results of an embourgeoisement process that raises affluent blue-collar workers into the middle class (cf. Blumberg, 1980).

Chang, 1970). If occupations are frequently chosen as being in the same social class, they will be close together in this space; if they are rarely chosen together, then they will be quite far apart. INDSCAL has a great additional benefit in that the scaling dimensions also describe differences among the people making the judgments. Thus we can uncover both the major tendencies of ways of grouping occupations in a social class, and the different preferences of people for each of these tendencies.

One-dimensional solutions

We begin by looking at the one-dimensional solution that INDSCAL generates from the triads data. Not surprisingly, this dimension closely resembles a status ranking. Figure 5.1 reports the values assigned to the occupations by the INDSCAL analyses as well as their scores on the NORC prestige scales (Siegel, 1971). The two are highly correlated (0.96). There is a tendency in the INDSCAL results to cluster the occupations into three separate groups, but the rankings are remarkably similar. (Both the high correlations and the clustering tendency are observed also in the two other variants we used in these interviews: see the chapter appendix, Table 5.A.)

While the one-dimensional results reproduce the conventional prestige scale quite well, less than half of all responses to the triads task conform to the implications of the prestige scales. The distances along the NORC scale can be used to predict which two occupations should be chosen in the same social class, but only 47 percent of the actual responses agree with the NORC prestige predictions. Some 14 percent of the triad responses reject even the ordinal properties of the NORC prestige scale: That is, respondents chose the highest and lowest prestige positions as being in the same class. For instance, for the triad factory foreman (NORC prestige = 45.1), payroll clerk (41.3), truck dispatcher (33.5), the modal response (40.5 percent) placed the highest status position (foreman) and the lowest (dispatcher) in the same class. These two can be chosen only if prestige ranking is rejected as a model of social class judgments. The modal response to this particular triad suggests a predominance of an authority model over a prestige model: both the foreman and the dispatcher exercise authority over other workers; the payroll clerk does not. While the predominance of authority over prestige does not hold for all the triads, the extent of the poor fit to the prestige models suggests the existence of multiple criteria in the population.

FIGURE 5.1. One-dimensional representation of class image
                    ratings

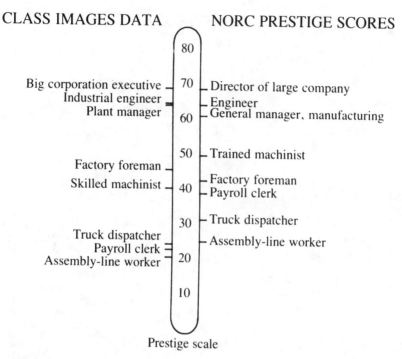

CLASS IMAGES DATA   NORC PRESTIGE SCORES

Prestige scale

SOURCE: Images Survey, Siegel (1971).

Multidimensional solutions

Our real interest with INDSCAL lies in the multidimensional solutions that
identify the alternative criteria people use in constructing class images. the
INDSCAL results represent the "meaningful psychological dimensions" in
the data (Carroll and Chang, 1970); that is, the "strains of consistency" that
run through people's many concrete judgments.

Figure 5.2 displays the two-dimensional results and identifies the
"working-mass" and "middle-mass" tendencies described above. The vertical dimension separates the three managerial positions from the remain-

FIGURE 5.2. Two-dimensional representation of class
image ratings

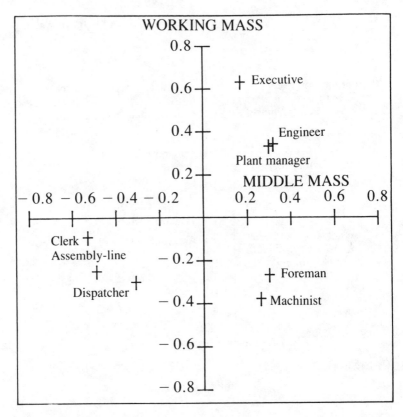

SOURCE: Images Survey.

ing five working-class positions. The big corporation executive is especially distinct in this perspective. On the other hand, there is little difference among the five working-class occupations; they represent an undif-
ferentiated mass of workers subordinate to their managerial "bosses."
Direct supervisory authority is not the issue here. The factory foreman
scores only slightly higher than the machinist, while the industrial engineer
is in the dominant group together with the more clearly supervisory plant

manager. The division is similar to a "mental labor" differentiation, as in Poulantzas's emphasis on the middle-class positions that help to reproduce the existing capitalist system. The criterion appears to be a worker's function in the larger system rather than the specific work situation.

The horizontal dimension describes the middle-mass perspective, grouping the intermediate positions of machinist and foreman with the managers. It is only the unskilled assembly-line worker and the low-prestige white-collar workers who are separated into a distinct (lower?) class —a vestigial working class that has not yet made it into the comfortable majority.

Two-dimensional results based on a somewhat different set of occupations are quite similar (see Figure 5.3). The horizontal or middle-mass dimension collapses the intermediate occupations (represented in this set by the carpenter and payroll clerk) with the three managerial and professional positions. The vertical or working-mass dimension collapses the intermediate positions with the assembly-line worker, janitor, and unemployed laborer. These are precisely the same tendencies we identified with the industrial occupations analyzed in Figure 5.2.

None of the respondents could be classified as "pure" types in weighting one dimension to the complete exclusion of the other. These dimensions should be thought of, therefore, as cognitive tendencies. The actual images are some weighted combination of the two tendencies. The image of the many respondents who weight the two dimensions almost equally approximates the one-dimensional results reported in Figure 5.1. When the results of respondents with both types of models are aggregated, we again obtain the familiar status gradations. Thus, the typical strategy of aggregating responses across individuals obscures the systematic "distortions" that some respondents are making at either end of the scale.

As interesting as what does appear in these results is what does not. Neither a supervisory authority distinction nor a manual-nonmanual division appears to be meaningful in sorting these occupations into social classes. A manual-nonmanual division can be obtained only if a four-dimensional solution is computed. (These results are reported in the chapter appendix, Table 5.A.) The skilled machinist and assembly-line worker score low on the fourth dimension (-0.44 and -0.72), while the remaining positions score from $+0.06$ to $+0.40$. The major division here is a manual labor distinction. Status is of less concern: similar status positions are separated while quite disparate positions are grouped together.

The four-dimensional results with the alternative occupational titles also

FIGURE 5.3. Two-dimensional representation of class
image ratings: alternative titles

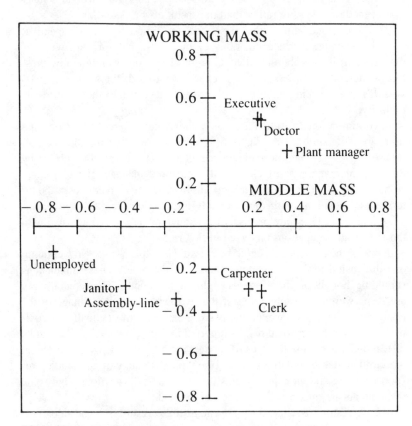

SOURCE: Images Survey.

yield one dimension that describes a manual-nonmanual division. In this model the eight occupations are sorted into two groups with the payroll clerk ($+0.41$) joining the other three nonmanual positions ($+0.30$, $+0.31$, and $+0.33$), while the carpenter (-0.14) is seen as closer to the manual positions (-0.45, -0.25, and -0.51).

The manual-nonmanual division is apparently a weak criterion, since there is no suggestion of it in the two-dimensional results. Nevertheless, earlier work that dismissed it as irrelevant in stratification judgments (Duncan, 1966; Glenn, 1975) is not supported by these techniques, which are more sensitive to individual differences. On the other hand, the weakness of this dimension suggests that for this American sample, at least, the manual-nonmanual gap is not so crucial a division as some researchers have maintained (Lockwood, 1958).

The authority-subordinacy distinction does not appear in any of these solutions. From results with our third subsample, however, we know that people are cognizant of an authority distinction among these occupations; they just don't apply it to social class judgments. In the third version of the questionnaire, we kept the same industrial occupations as shown in Figures 5.1 and 5.2. But instead of asking people to choose the two in the same social class, we asked them only to choose the two "most similar to each other." This reveals criteria of similarity that are quite removed from social class. In fact, the one-dimensional results do replicate a prestige hierarchy quite well. But the second dimension represents a work-setting criterion, distinguishing the strictly factory jobs (machinist, assembly-line worker, and factory foreman) from the office jobs (corporation executive and payroll clerk), with the plant manager and industrial engineer appropriately in between.

The third dimension is of special interest in this version of the interview: here, all authority positions score positively and all nonauthority positions score negatively. The plant manager is separated from the almost equally prestigious industrial engineer; the factory foreman from the skilled machinist; and the truck dispatcher from the payroll clerk. These distinctions show that the respondents recognize authority as an important criterion for differentiating between jobs. But the emergence of an authority dimension here rather than in questions of class implies that while authority may be a salient aspect of work, it is not especially relevant in determining class position.

This would suggest that the weak effect of supervisory authority on class placements (Chapter 4) may not be just a consequence of the poor measurement of authority. Supervisory authority may be less important to American class perceptions than was first supposed. On the other hand, both the class-images data in this chapter and the class-placement data in the last chapter demonstrate the primary importance of the division between managerial professional positions and the remaining workers not engaged in mental labor. For Americans, the mental-labor division appears more important than an authority distinction or a blue-collar–white-collar division.

Class Differences in Class Images

INDSCAL scores

If the working-mass and middle-mass tendencies are the principal influences on class images, do the working and middle class differ in their preferences for these tendencies? Our small sample sizes (only 103 respondents for the main interview version) prevent a detailed multivariate analysis of the INDSCAL tendencies, but the simple zero-order relationships suggest that the middle-mass perspective may be class-linked. The INDSCAL analysis generates two scores for each respondent describing how closely his triad judgments match the two scales reported in Figure 5.2. Managers and professionals score significantly higher than workers on the middle-mass dimension.[9] Thus, workers are less likely to put much weight on a perspective that lifts foremen and skilled workers out of the working class and locates them closer to the more dominant middle-class positions of plant managers and engineers.

The tendency to see such a division within the working class is, in fact, more characteristic of the middle class; workers themselves place less importance on the division. For example, on the triad industrial engineer, factory foreman, assembly-line worker, managers preferred (63 percent) to group the foreman with the engineer, whereas only 41 percent of the workers did so. Their preferred response (47 percent) put the foreman in the same class with the assembly-line worker.

There is no parallel preference of workers for the working-mass dimension. Working-class respondents do score somewhat higher than managers and professionals on this dimension, but the difference is not greater than what we would expect by chance.[10]

---

9. The difference between the managers' average (0.48) and the workers' (0.36) is 3.1 times the standard error of the difference.

10. The workers' average (0.48) is only slightly greater than the managers' (0.45). The difference amounts to only 0.62 times the standard error of the difference. Similarly, the manager-worker differences on form B of the questionnaire (listing the alternative occupation titles shown in Figure 5.3) were not statistically significant. The problem with this form was that dropping the two intermediate occupations, foreman and machinist, made the gap between the top and bottom groups so large that it forced most respondents to use the working-mass perspective for most of the triads. Thus, this form became less sensitive to individual differences within the sample.

Perceived division

The triad data also permit a direct calculation of the best-perceived division among the eight occupations. Any division of the eight into two groups implies a unique pattern of responses to the triads. For example, a working-mass division that sorts out the executive, engineer, and plant manager at the top implies that in a triad of plant manager, foreman, assembly-line worker, the respondent will class the foreman and the assembly-line worker together; a middle-mass division implies that the respondent will class the plant manager and foreman together. The perceived fit of these two divisions can be calculated from the proportion of triad responses that match what is implied.

There are 127 logically possible divisions of eight occupations into two groups, but only three are widely endorsed. There are significant differences between managers and workers on two of these three divisions.

As would be expected from the foregoing discussion, the division best perceived by the managers and professionals is the middle-mass division that separates the clerk, dispatcher, and assembly-line worker at the bottom and merges the foreman and machinist with the three managerial positions. This division matches 51.8 percent of the managers' responses to the relevant triads. For workers, the match is only 44.1 percent, a statistically significant difference.[11]

The working-mass division also matches the triad responses quite well, but there is little difference between managers (50.7 percent matching) and workers (50.2 percent). This confirms the nonsignificant differences in INDSCAL scores reported above.

The workers' preferred division is an even more elitist model than the working-mass division. A division that isolates the occupation of big corporation executive into a class by itself matches 56.7 percent of the workers' triad responses. Managers, however, are less likely to isolate the exec-

11. Chi-square = 25.2 with 1 degree of freedom. The rather low proportion of matching responses for even this best division reflects the range of perspectives among managers but also the variety of models that any one respondent may apply to the series of triads. We interpret the indeterminacy of this analysis—the fact that no one model is made to fit any respondent perfectly—as part of the merit of the triads method. The appropriate research question reveals the relative strengths of the different perspectives that each person combines in his or her own way.

utive; 48.2 percent of their responses match this division.[12] Thus the best match for workers is the opposite of the best match for managers: workers prefer to isolate a small elite at the top; managers prefer to separate a small lower/working class at the bottom.

The managers' tendency to a middle-mass division has a clear conservative connotation. It lumps most Americans together in a large middle mass, recalling Ben Wattenberg's (1974) complacent image of a "massive majority middle class." Some problems of inequality may be recognized at the bottom, but the larger part of American society is subsumed in a comfortable category that ranges from corporate executive to machinist.

In contrast, the workers' tendency toward an elitist model is potentially more radical. The capitalist is isolated at the top. Differences are recognized below that level, of course, but the fundamental division in the class structure is at the very top.

This is, in fact, not unlike the images that Goldthorpe et al. (1969) discovered with their English autoworkers. Both their power models and their various money models isolated small elites at the top, merging the middle class and working class in a large subordinate group. That study emphasized distinctions among these various elitist models, but our data suggest that such variants may be less important (cf. Moorhouse, 1976) than the difference between the elitist model and the middle-mass perspective. Goldthorpe and his colleagues did not find evidence for such middle-mass models, but their samples excluded managers and professionals—precisely the people who favor such models. Indeed, the popularity of middle-mass models in establishment social science may be mainly a reflection of a distinctively but understandably middle-class perspective within the U.S. social science establishment. The mistake has been to generalize this perspective to all Americans rather than recognizing its limitations as a middle-class tendency.

It would be another mistake to overextend our interpretation by calling these two images the working-class and middle-class images of American society. Both classes can and do recognize the relevance of both images. But the "strain of consistency" that Bott urges us to identify is different for workers than it is for their bosses. American workers tend toward what is, for them, a more class-conscious image: a society dominated by a small elite.

Our general argument on American exceptionalism is thus supported by

12. Chi-square $= 14.3$ with 1 degree of freedom.

these data. When we gather evidence on what American workers actually think, even a small exploratory study such as this one finds them to be more class conscious than they are generally believed to be. The weight of our evidence is properly cumulative, but the pieces are beginning to fit together. The American exceptionalism thesis suggests a lack of difference between American workers and the American middle class, but the results in Chapter 4 and the widespread acceptance of the proletarianization perspective demonstrate that this class division is in fact well perceived in American society.

Methodological Appendix

Sample

Respondents were 317 male residents of the Chicago metropolitan area, 25 years or older, interviewed by telephone during October and November 1974. Unfortunately, women were excluded, but this was done in order to simplify analysis of the effects of occupation on class images. Since other research (see Chapter 8) shows that women use both their own and their husbands' occupations in determining subjective class placement, the small sample of this study would have made it impossible to separate these effects reliably. Men younger than 25 were also eliminated in order to facilitate the analysis of the relationship of occupation to class image.

The response rate for this survey was disappointingly low: 53 percent. Some of this might be attributed to the post-Watergate, post-Vietnam alienation of the times; much is probably due to the difficulty of the triads task. In any event, the resulting sample was heavily skewed toward better-educated, more middle-class respondents. The sample included roughly twice the proportion of college-educated respondents as was reported in the 1970 census of the Chicago metropolitan area. To counteract the worst effects of this sample bias, we weighted the respondents to match the census distribution across six educational categories.

Triads

The question used for two-thirds of the sample was as follows: "Now I'm going to read the names of some occupations, three at a time. For each set of occupations, please tell me which *two* of the three you think are in the *same social class*." The remaining one-third of the sample was asked to choose "which two of the three you think are most similar to each other."

The disadvantage of the triads method is the large number of judgments required even with a small number of occupations: eight occupations form 56 triads. The method has the advantage of asking respondents for concrete judgments. In retrospect, it seems to us perhaps to carry this virtue to an extreme. After many repetitions, the task becomes quite trying. Moreover, many of the judgments are not easy, especially in a telephone interview. These problems may account for the low response rate. Reducing the occupations to five (by dropping the supervisory authority dimension, for instance) would present a more reasonable series of 10 triads.

A somewhat similar and very promising technique is the "vignette" method developed by Peter Rossi and his coworkers (see, for example, Alves and Rossi, 1978; Rossi and Nock, 1982). The vignettes offer the advantage of presenting respondents with a social composite including many characteristics beyond occupations. Laumann and Senter (1976) have resurrected a social distance methodology to study perceived differences between occupations. The analysis closest to our own is Coxon and Jones's (1978) multidimensional scaling of perceived occupational similarities. All three of these techniques could provide valuable new data if suitably adapted to incorporate class factors.

Statistical techniques

The 56 triads were first analyzed with the INDSCAL program, an extension of multidimensional scaling methods to incorporate individual differences (Carroll and Chang, 1970). The triads data were converted into perceived distances for each respondent by counting how often a pair of occupations was selected as most similar. With eight occupational stimuli, the maximum possible score was six, indicating that a pair was perceived as most similar each time it was included in a triad with any of the other occupations. The minimum score was zero, indicating that the pair was never chosen as most similar. "Don't know" responses were scored as one-third for each of the three pairs. In this way, a similarity score was computed for every pair of occupational stimuli (eight stimuli produce 28 possible pairs) for each respondent. These scores were the basis of the INDSCAL analysis.

The second analysis is a variant on a divisive clustering algorithm (Bailey, 1974). It computes directly the match between the actual pattern of triad responses and the patterns implied by each possible division of the eight occupations. Each possible division leaves some of the triad responses indeterminate: these triads are excluded from the calculation of the proportion of matching responses.

TABLE 5.A. Scaling perceived occupational differences

	One-dimensional Results	Two-dimensional Results		Three-dimensional Results			Four-dimensional Results			
	I	I	II	I	II	III	I	II	III	IV
Same class: industrial occupations										
Big corporation executive	.48	.63	.17				.52	.14	.66	.14
Industrial engineer	.39	.34	.32				.18	.33	.50	.06
Plant manager	.37	.33	.29				.56	.25	−.22	.13
Factory foreman	.01	−.27	.30				−.10	.28	−.44	.22
Skilled machinist	−.07	−.38	.26				−.42	.32	−.07	−.44
Truck dispatcher	−.36	−.30	−.31				−.38	−.30	−.23	.40
Payroll clerk	−.39	−.09	−.54				−.17	−.55	−.06	.21
Assembly-line worker	−.44	−.25	−.49				−.19	−.49	−.14	−.72

Same class: alternative occupations

Big corporation executive	.48	.50	.23	.51	.29	−.13	.30
Doctor	.48	.49	.24	.48	.37	−.21	.31
Plant manager	.39	.35	.36	.36	.33	.07	.33
Payroll clerk	−.18	−.30	.24	−.30	−.39	.24	.41
Carpenter	−.19	−.30	.18	−.38	.43	.25	−.14
Unemployed laborer	−.31	−.12	−.71	−.21	−.35	−.80	−.45
Assembly-line worker	−.32	−.34	−.15	−.26	−.36	.32	−.25
Janitor	−.34	−.28	−.38	−.20	−.31	.26	−.51

Similarity: industrial occupations

Big corporation executive	.51	.41	.48	.19
Industrial engineer	.32	.42	.00	−.34
Plant manager	.40	.36	.09	.37
Factory foreman	.09	.11	−.33	.45
Skilled machinist	−.25	−.07	−.44	−.48
Truck dispatcher	−.36	−.45	.00	.32
Payroll clerk	−.25	−.41	.57	−.11
Assembly-line worker	−.46	−.37	−.36	−.40

SOURCE: Images Survey.

CHAPTER 6
THE DECLINE OF SOCIAL CLASS?

The second half of the twentieth century brought enormous changes to the United States. Prosperity and labor peace characterized an "affluent society" (Galbraith, 1958) that most observers quickly interpreted as deadening the class consciousness of American workers.

It had not always seemed that workers were destined for such a fate. The first part of the century had been dominated by events that raised workers' consciousness: the concentration of capital in giant corporations, the rise of the Socialist Party, and the ravages of the Depression with its sudden explosion of union organization.

But the prosperity of the post–World War II period ushered in a new era of more comfortable working-class existence and a softening of class conflicts. The American Socialist Party had long since faltered, split up into warring factions, and self-destructed. The bitter labor disputes that had marked the growth of unionization in the 1930s had subsided into well-orchestrated collective bargaining. Unprecedented prosperity from World War II through the Vietnam War endowed workers with a standard of living that would have been inconceivable to their parents and grandparents. Not even the stagnation of recent times has done much to resurrect a moribund labor movement.

The "End-of-Ideology" Thesis

The stereotypes of American workers that arose from these two eras are starkly contrasting. If we conjure up a labor scene from the Depression, we may observe Walter Reuther's autoworkers battling company goons on the picket line in Detroit. But in the 1950s, the picture is one of workers mov-

125

ing to the suburbs, owning their own homes and cars, sending their kids to college, and generally winning their share of American abundance. The 1980s image shows workers quiescent or even defeatist, their politics inclining toward Ronald Reagan rather than militant protest.

Such stereotypes are mischievous at best. The supporting evidence is, and always has been, too thin to justify the pictures. In this chapter we describe some new evidence that portrays a more class-conscious transition during the twentieth century.

But it is also important to realize how the stereotype found its way into social science; indeed, academe shares much of the blame for foisting the distorted image on the American public. Grand theories about "the end of ideology" proclaimed a new society based on class accommodation. As Seymour Martin Lipset (1960:442) put it, "The fundamental political problems of the industrial revolution have been solved."

The end-of-ideology thesis interpreted the midcentury affluence as the final refutation of Marx. Marx had written in the midst of nineteenth-century industrialization when an ever-increasing division between workers and capitalists seemed likely, when society was "splitting up into two great hostile camps . . . Bourgeoisie and Proletariat" (Marx and Engels [1848], 1976:485). But the end-of-ideology school claimed Marx had been mistaken about the future. Working-class consciousness had waned, not waxed. The changes in modern society, which Marx could not have foreseen, had controlled and minimized the conflict between workers and capital. A widely held view of industrial relations (e.g., Kerr et al., 1960; Ross and Hartman, 1960) forecast that strikes would decline as the acceptance of collective bargaining and grievance procedures tamed the once-bitter labor strife. The successful containment of class conflict destined class consciousness to become a historic relic of the early industrial period.[1]

The end-of-Ideology school did not have the facts straight, however, even on the observable levels of class conflict. The record of strikes during the twentieth century (Figure 6.1) hardly reveals a long-term secular decline. Identifiable peaks define the wavelike nature of class conflicts (an international, not merely American, phenomenon; see Korpi and Shalev, 1980). The gradual decline of strikes in the 1950s and 1960s—the trend

---

1. See Blumberg, 1980, for a good review and refutation of these theories. Many scholars have noted that class conflict is most intense in early industrialization (see note 5, Chapter 1). In the concluding chapter we suggest an explanation for this phenomenon that does not rely on changes in working-class consciousness.

FIGURE 6.1. Strike involvement, 1880–1980

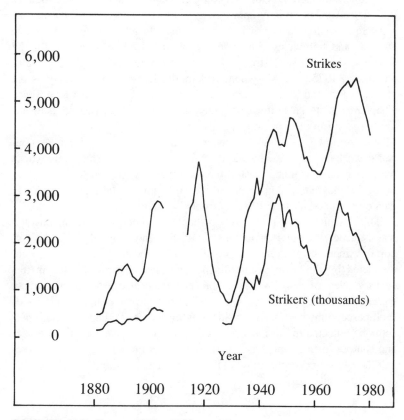

SOURCE: U.S. Census, 1973a, 1983.
NOTE: Strike rates are moving averages across ± 2 years.

that prompted many of the theories about the institutionalization of class conflict—was merely a trough in the cyclical pattern, not a final resolution of class divisions presaging the waning of class consciousness.

But the main problem with the end-of-ideology thesis is that its proponents rarely studied workers' class attitudes and perceptions. We know very little about *how* class consciousness changed or even when or in what direction; most of the theories only inferred changes from the observed outcomes of class conflict. The rise and decline of unions or radical political parties have been taken as the main indicators of class consciousness. This now familiar fallacy of psychological reductionism obscured the fact that there were rarely any appropriate data on workers' consciousness itself. Some of this lack was inevitable, since "dead men cannot be interviewed, and humble workmen left no written testimony behind for the historian's use" (Thernstrom, 1964:58–59; see also Laslett, 1970:6; Dubofsky, 1975:6). Even when workers did leave such testimony as the "fierce words and bitter feelings" uncovered by Stephan Thernstrom (see Chapter 2), historians often discounted its significance or twisted its meaning to reconfirm their preconceptions.

We are now in a somewhat better position than earlier researchers because we have survey data on several generations of Americans whose work lives have spanned most of the century. These data have their limitations, but they are an improvement over the almost total lack of historical data on workers' attitudes that confronted earlier theorists.

The evidence of the previous two chapters should caution us against too readily accepting any conclusions about the "end of ideology." Contemporary American workers do recognize class divisions, and they are not distracted by the many status distinctions that have proliferated in this century. Nevertheless, we have not yet looked at direct evidence about *changes* in class perception, and it is entirely possible that the clarity of such perceptions has faded considerably over time. Perhaps the class perceptions reflected in our most recent data are only a pale shadow of earlier and sharper distinctions that American workers drew between themselves and their bosses. We turn now to these historical questions.

Changes in Class Perceptions

The growth of the middle class

Figure 6.2 reports the changes in middle-class placements in the ten election surveys from 1952 to 1978.[2] The fitted trend line demonstrates the growth of the middle class during this period of postwar prosperity. The rate of change, about half a percentage point a year, is not dramatic. Even

2. The sample in this analysis and throughout the rest of this chapter comprises respondents between the ages of 21 and 64 who have recorded values on occupation, education, and income. See Schrieber and Nygreen (1970) for an earlier analysis of similar data.

FIGURE 6.2. Trends in class self-placements, 1952–78

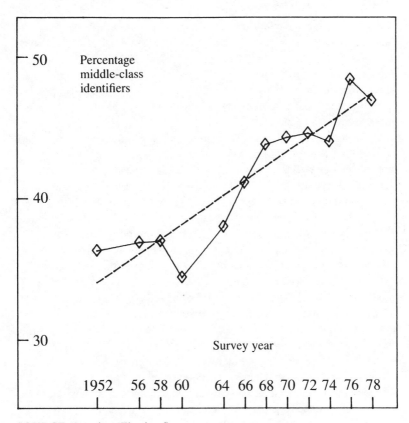

SOURCE: American Election Surveys.

by the end of the period there is little support for the "massive majority middle class" claims (Wattenberg, 1974:51) that supposedly heralded the "end of ideology." When we understand better the causes of this change, there is even less reason to believe that class divisions are fading from popular perceptions: the size of the classes may have changed, but the division between them remains as real as ever.

Generational effects

The first question we will ask is whether the increase in middle-class self-placements was the result of middle-class generations replacing working-class generations, or whether the prosperity of the period affected all generations equally to raise levels of middle-class placements within each generation. In the language of statistical analysis, is the change a cohort effect (generational replacement) or a period effect (a time trend that is uniform across all generations)?

Generational effects suggest a more enduring modification of American society. Two birth cohorts have had especially dramatic impact. The more recent, the "Baby Boom" generation born between 1946 and 1964, changed the face of America. This demographic bulge was responsible for such diverse results as the explosion of school construction in the 1950s and 1960s and the increased crime rate of the 1970s. The political impact of the Baby Boom generation has been less thoroughly analyzed. Only a few of its members get into the later surveys analyzed here; even so, we will see that they perceive a distinct class position for themselves.

Political analysts (e.g., Campbell et al., 1960; Oppenheim, 1970; Knoke and Hout, 1974; Converse, 1976) have more often singled out the "Depression cohort" of voters who entered the electorate during the 1930s and were captured by Roosevelt, the New Deal, and the Democratic Party.[3] These voters created the major party realignment of 1932 (Burnham, 1970). Even studies that include data through 1972—a full 40 years later—show a clear persistence of Democratic party identification among the Depression cohort; their party loyalty is greater than that of cohorts either before or since (e.g., Knoke and Hout, 1974; Converse, 1976).

It seems reasonable that the class consciousness of the Depression cohort, which entered the labor market during the greatest economic catastrophe in American history (Elder, 1974:3), would be equally distinctive. The

---

3. Unfortunately, research has not been consistent in its definition of the Depression cohorts. Some research has defined this generation very broadly as all birth cohorts from 1900 to 1930 (e.g., Knoke and Hout, 1974), or quite narrowly as only those from 1905 to 1912 (e.g., Converse, 1976). For our purposes, entering the labor force—not entering the voting population—during the Depression should be the important influence on class perceptions; therefore, we look especially at the birth cohorts from 1904 to 1923. These people were either in their mid-twenties in 1930 or had reached at least age 16 by the end of the decade—the ages when most Americans first enter the labor force.

Depression was difficult for almost everybody but most difficult for the groups least integrated into secure positions in the economy: the working class, minorities, and youth (Campbell et al., 1960:153). Their subordination to the larger economic forces may have indelibly imprinted a working-class identity on their class perception.

We can easily rearrange the survey data to compute class perceptions according to the year of the respondent's birth rather than the year of the interview. Figure 6.3 compares birth cohorts between 1887 and 1958.[4] The results suggest that the Depression cohort is indeed distinctive in its class placements. Its earliest members, those born soon after the turn of the century who were in their late twenties as the Depression hit, do indeed constitute the most working-class cohort in U.S. history. Those born earlier are more middle class, and there is a consistent though slow increase in middle-class placements over most of the cohorts from 1902 to 1945. But those born immediately after World War II, the beginning of the Baby Boom generation, are again more working class.

Figure 6.3 may be a misleading description of cohort changes because the averages are contaminated by the increases in middle-class placements between the 1952 and 1978 interviews (as seen above in Figure 6.2). The more recent (middle-class) cohorts appear more often in the later (more middle-class) surveys, while the Depression cohort appears more often in the surveys of the (more working-class) 1950s.

Age differences may also contaminate the cohort averages reported in Figure 6.3; for example, the nineteenth-century cohorts, who appear quite

4. We have coded birth cohorts into a series of dummy variables for this and following analyses. The sample was divided into 16 four-year intervals representing the birth cohorts from 1887–91 to 1947–51 and a seventeenth cohort including all respondents born between 1952 and 1958. In the analyses where age and time period were included, they too were categorized: age was divided into 11 dummy variables, one for each four-year interval between ages 21 and 64; time period into 12 dummy variables for the 12 survey years from 1952 to 1978.

It may seem that a cohort analysis requiring 40 dummy variables offers an unnecessarily complex alternative to the more obvious and parsimonious model including only the three interval variables: actual age, year of interview, and year of birth. However, this case dictates the more cumbersome approach: first, it seems unreasonable to assume that all age, period, and cohort effects are linear; second, to include all three dimensions in a single analysis results in a linear dependency among the measures—Cohort = Period − Age—which precludes a unique solution to the normal equations of the regression analysis. Dividing each dimension into a series of dummy variables and constraining some to equal effects helps eliminate that dependency; see also note 6, below.

FIGURE 6.3. Class self-perceptions of birth cohorts,
             1890–1954

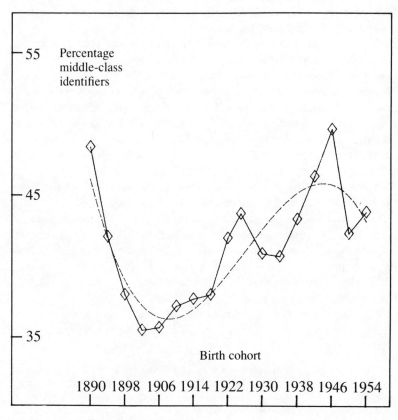

SOURCE: American Election Surveys.
NOTE: Smooth curve: class placements = 817.45 − 19.265 cohort + .156 cohort^2 − .00041 cohort^3. R^2 = .766

middle class, are also quite old by the time they get into our election surveys. Perhaps they are more middle class because older people tend to see themselves as middle class, not because that generation is distinctive. We would like to compare the nineteenth-century cohorts with the later cohorts when they were *all the same age*. Only then can we decide whether their middle-class placements are a fundamental generational difference or just a normal consequence of advancing age.[5]

Investigating the true cohort effect, uncontaminated by age and period changes, requires a sophisticated statistical analysis that allows us to look at birth-cohort differences among people of about the same age, interviewed in the same year (or period).[6]

We have plotted these "true" generational changes in Figure 6.4 together with the best-fitting curve to the points. The smooth curve provides a somewhat clearer picture of the historic trends.[7] Figure 6.4 confirms the extraordinary working-class orientation of the Depression generation. Middle-class placements are highest at 57 percent in the earliest birth cohort (1887–91). After that, middle-class placements decline sharply,

5. Because earlier studies were based on a single survey, they could not separate the effects of age and birth cohort. Schlozman and Verba (1979), with their more ambiguous open-ended question, found that older workers were more likely to place themselves in the working class, a result consistent with a more working-class Depression generation. They also found higher levels of working-class placements in a comparable 1939 survey. Centers (1949:167) found slightly more working-class placements among manual workers 30 to 49 years old, roughly the Depression cohorts in our analyses.

6. The technique follows each cohort throughout its life cycle and measures class placements at all ages. If birth cohort is the critical factor, we would expect the Depression generation to identify as more working class at all ages; if age is the critical factor, we would expect the older ages to identify as more working class in all surveys, regardless of even wide differences in birth cohort. But to trace such patterns—and thus separate age, period, and cohort effects—requires several surveys at widely separated points in time.

Constraining some of the time intervals to have the same level of class placements enables parameter estimation (Mason et al., 1973), but the results can be affected by which age groups, birth cohorts, or time periods are pooled. We have tested 15 different models constraining different combinations of cohorts, ages, and survey periods to be equal. All analyses produced similar results. We have reported the one with the fewest constraints. Largely for reasons of data management, ordinary least-squares regression is used in all cohort analyses rather than probit analysis. The number of cases and variables in these several analyses made the use of probit analysis computer routines impractical.

7. To plot the smooth curve, we regressed the middle-class percentage of each cohort interval on four polynomials (first on a linear cohort variable, then quadratic, cubic, and fourth-power cohort variables). Even the plot makes it clear that a straight line (the first-order polynomial) will not adequately describe the trend. Neither does the addition of a quadratic term (representing a U-shaped curve) fit the data well: $R^2 = 0.62$. A better fit is the cubic equation with an R^2 of 0.89. A fourth-order polynomial is unnecessary, since the additional term is not statistically significant and the increment to R-squared is negligible. The two inflexion points (bends) for the cubic curve estimate the times when the curve reaches a local minimum and maximum; a local minimum is observed at 1914 and a maximum at 1945.

FIGURE 6.4. Effects of birth cohort on class
self-perceptions, 1890–1954

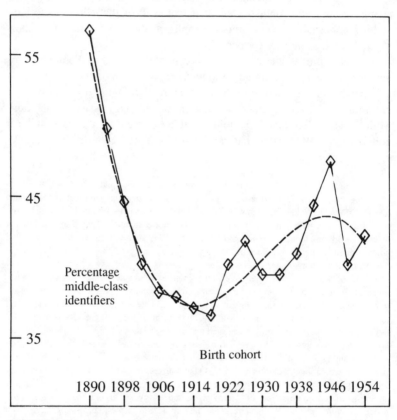

SOURCE: American Election Surveys.
NOTE: Effects are calculated with controls for age and survey year.

Smooth curve: middle-class placements $= 977.46 - 22.354$ cohort $+ .175$ cohort$^2 - .00045$ cohort^3. $R^2 = .886$

reaching their nadir at 37–38 percent in the 1904–19 birth cohorts. These
cohorts are the Depression generation: their early working experience
occurred during the decade of the 1930s. Our more careful analysis, eliminating the possible contamination of age and survey timing, confirms the
conclusion that the Depression cohort is the most working-class generation
in American history.

The cohorts immediately following the Depression adopt slightly more middle-class orientations, peaking at 48 percent in the 1945 cohort. An upswing after the Depression is not surprising, as these cohorts entered the labor force during the expanded economy produced by World War II. But the upswing is rather modest, not as dramatic as indicated in the previous figure suggesting that some of the apparent post-Depression increases are a general time-period effect, reflecting the good times during which these cohorts were interviewed. In fact, the post-Depression cohort appears more similar to the Depression generation (that is, more working class) than to the pre-Depression cohorts. Moreover, the second inflexion point at 1945 indicates that the post-Depression increases have not been maintained. After 1945, the curve dips again: the Baby Boom generation is more working class than the World War II generation. The most recent cohort in the sample, the post-1952 birth cohort, is 42 percent middle class, only 4 percentage points above the Depression cohorts.

The overall picture that emerges from this analysis is a Depression generation dramatically more working class than the cohorts that came before but only slightly more working class than the cohorts that came after. The Depression's effect in changing class perceptions appears to have been permanent.[8]

Cohort succession or time-period trend?

The cohort curve indicates that the trend in recent interviews to more middle-class placements (Figure 6.2) did not result from cohort succession processes: that is, middle-class cohorts replacing working-class cohorts. The recent birth cohorts entering the labor force are no more middle class

---

8. To understand why the cohort-class relationship took on this shape after controls, one needs to examine the parallel age and period curves. Although not presented here, the age-class relationship is an inverted-U pattern that counterbalances the U-shaped pattern of the birth cohort relationship. The age-class relationship therefore suppresses the early-cohort–middle-class relationship. Specifically, the early birth cohorts are observed mainly in their older ages when the tendency is to working-class identification. When the competing effects of age are eliminated through statistical controls, their relatively high levels of middle-class identification become apparent. Likewise, the recent cohort trends are confounded with period changes so that recent cohorts appear more middle class than they actually are. Recent cohorts entered the sample in more prosperous, middle-class periods. When the period trend toward middle-class identification is controlled, the recent cohorts are more similar to the Depression cohorts. In sum, separating the life-cycle and period trends in class perceptions from those across generations does not alter the strength of the cohort-class relationship but changes its form.

than those who are exiting through retirement or death. If we assume that the full cycle of cohort replacement takes about 45 years, then in the 1952 surveys the 1887 cohort (65-year-olds) were being replaced by the 1932 cohort (20-year-olds). Examining the curve at these two points reveals that the net effect of such replacements is toward *greater* working-class identification: the 1887 cohort is very middle class and the 1932 cohort is much more working class. This trend—working-class cohorts replacing middle-class cohorts—continues until about the year 1965. In 1965, the newer 1945 middle-class cohorts are replacing the equally middle-class 1900 cohorts. The net effect of this cohort replacement on the levels of middle-class placement is negligible.

Nor does the most recent period reveal any generational trends toward embourgeoisement. The Baby Boom generation is quite working class (unlike the World War II generation that immediately preceded it) and replaces an equally working-class generation from the early post-Depression era (the 1925–35 birth cohorts). The more working-class orientation of the Baby Boom generation prevented a sudden rise in middle-class placements. If the high middle-class orientations of the World War II cohorts had continued, middle-class cohorts would have replaced more working-class cohorts, thus accelerating the embourgeoisement of America. Instead, levels of middle-class placements fell among the Baby Boom cohorts. Even during the most recent surveys (1965–78) the entering cohorts were no more middle class than the departing ones.

Our conclusion, therefore, is that the recent increase in middle-class orientation remains independent of cohort succession trends. When we look at cohort replacements in the entire period 1952–78, at no point are recent middle-class cohorts replacing earlier, more working-class cohorts. The postwar trend to middle-class identification, therefore, must represent a true time-period change: a uniform move to more middle-class placements among all birth cohorts and all age groups. We will confirm this shortly, but first we must ask what causes the cohort differences.

Why is the Depression generation different?

Probably the most striking aspect of the cohort comparisons is the uniquely working-class sentiment of the Depression generation (the 1904–23 birth cohorts). The 1914 cohort is 10 percentage points more likely to identify as working class than their 1887 predecessors. The Depression cohorts are also more working class, by a few percentage points, than the cohorts that came after. Explaining the later trend toward more middle-class placements is relatively easy, so we take up that task first. Explaining the differences between Depression and pre-Depression cohorts is more difficult but, we feel, more interesting for understanding the long-term changes in American class consciousness.

The post-Depression cohorts. Americans born in the post-Depression cohorts see themselves as more middle class because they *are* more middle class: they more often hold managerial positions, and they have more college degrees than those of the Depression generation (see Table 6.1).

When we compare *equivalent* workers from different cohorts—that is, workers with the same class position, education, and income—the post-Depression generation appears very similar to the Depression generation. In Figure 6.5, the most working-class Depression cohort (in 1918) is 41 percent middle class; middle-class placements rise slowly to 46 percent in 1946—a small 5 percent increase, compared with the 11 percent increase for the same years in Figure 6.4. Thus the increased middle-class identifications of the recent cohorts are explained by the somewhat improved social structural conditions they entered.

TABLE 6.1. Cohort averages on class position, family income, and education

	Education (years)	Percentage Managerial	Family Income (1978 $)
Pre-Depression (1888–1903)	9.4	25.8	$ 7,990
Depression (1904–23)	10.8	28.2	$11,429
Post-Depression (1924–47)	12.2	30.8	$13,988
Baby Boom (1948–57)	13.1	25.0	$11,635

SOURCE: American Election Surveys.
NOTE: Managerial positions include the census classifications of managers and professionals but exclude technicians.

FIGURE 6.5. Birth-cohort effects for equivalent workers,
1890–1954

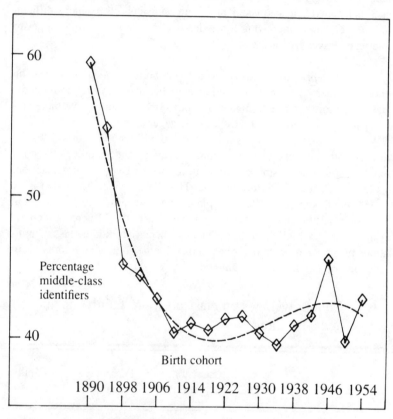

SOURCE: American Election Surveys.
NOTE: Effects are calculated with controls for age, survey year, managerial position, occupational prestige, education, and family income.

Smooth curve: middle-class placements $= 738.88 - 16.145$ cohort $+ .123$ co-
hort$^2 - .00031$ cohort^3. $R^2 = .903$

The pre-Depression cohorts. The same explanation is not available for
the pre-Depression cohorts. The early cohorts saw themselves as more
middle class (Figure 6.5) despite being less often managerial or college educated. When we compare workers in pre-Depression cohorts with equiva-

lent workers in later cohorts, the pre-Depression generation appears even more remarkably middle class. In fact, the most outstanding features of Figure 6.5 are the high rates of middle-class placements among the pre-Depression cohorts. There is a drop of 18 percentage points in middle-class placements from the 1890 cohort (59 percent) to the Depression cohort of 1918 (41 percent).

It is the pre-Depression Americans, not the Depression cohorts usually discussed, who are most unusual. No simple social structural differences can account for their high rates of middle-class placements; we think that a more psychological explanation is required. A further analysis suggests not only that the overall rates of middle-class placements are extraordinarily high, but that the class division between managers and workers is less clearly perceived before the Depression. Table 6.2 divides the birth cohorts into four main groups: the pre-Depression, Depression, World War II, and Baby Boom generations. When managers and equivalent workers are compared within each group, there are large differences in class perceptions for the last three cohorts but very small differences within the pre-

TABLE 6.2. Manager-nonmanager differences in class perceptions among four birth cohorts

	Adjusted Percentage Middle-Class Placement			
	Pre-Depression (1888–1903)	*Depression (1904–23)*	*Post Depression (1924–47)*	*Baby Boom (1948–57)*
Managers	53	47	49	46
Workers	48	47	49	46
Difference	5	13	18	12
N	695	5,469	10,054	3,231

SOURCE: American Election Surveys.
NOTE: Adjusted percentages are calculated after controls for occupational prestige, respondent's education, and family income.

Depression cohorts. Pre-Depression workers often place themselves in the middle class. It is the trauma of the Depression that solidifies working-class perceptions and changes the way Americans think about class. Pre-Depression workers appear more "confused" about class divisions in America. After the Depression, the division between managers and workers emerges as a main determinant of class perception and remains important through present generations.

In short, our results contradict the implications of the end-of-ideology thesis. Recent generations see class divisions as clearly as their parents did. A few more see themselves as middle class, but that is what we would expect from the increases in college education and managerial positions. Baby Boom generation workers are just as likely as those from the Depression generation to consider themselves working class; neither group has any special middle-class illusions. Instead, what emerges most strikingly from our analysis is the indication that the pre-Depression cohorts are the workers most confused about class divisions in America. The Depression transformed class perceptions in the United States, and, as far as we can see, the transformation was lasting.

Time-Period Changes in Class Perceptions

Causes behind the growth in middle-class placements

We began the analysis of birth cohorts by asking whether generational replacements could explain the middle-class increases between the first survey in 1952 and the last in 1978. By now it should be clear that it does not, although we think we have learned along the way much about how Americans have changed the way they think about class. The time trend pictured in Figure 6.2 is a true period effect: all ages and all generations increased their rates of middle-class placements during those decades. When comparisons are made within birth cohorts and age groups, the time-period effect remains virtually unchanged: the average yearly increase in middle-class placements changes from 0.515 percent per year to 0.502 percent per year.

An increase in middle-class placements should not be surprising. The period in which the surveys were conducted spans one of the most prosper-

TABLE 6.3. Structural changes in the United States, 1952–78

Year	Occupational Prestige	Family Income (1965 $)	Education (Years)	Percentage Managerial
1952	39.3	$5,499	10.2	25.1
1956	39.3	$6,837	10.8	26.8
1958	40.2	$6,970	11.0	30.4
1960	39.6	$7,593	11.1	25.6
1964	38.5	$7,807	11.1	26.3
1966	40.2	$8,224	11.5	27.9
1968	41.3	$8,794	11.7	31.2
1970	40.4	$9,019	11.5	28.6
1972	41.6	$9,263	12.0	31.4
1974	41.0	$9,350	12.2	30.4
1976	41.8	$9,062	12.4	33.6
1978	42.3	$9,638	12.6	33.6

SOURCE: American Election Surveys.

ous eras in American history. Managerial positions opened up, schooling lengthened, and incomes grew (see Table 6.3). It seems reasonable to expect that increased prosperity would increase middle-class placements, and the structural changes do in fact account for all the increases in middle-class placements. A comparison of workers in the same occupational position, with the same educational background, and earning the same salaries shows no measurable change in the rate of middle-class placements between 1952 and 1978. The overall increase, about 0.51 percentage point per year in Figure 6.2, drops to a decrease of 0.03 percentage point when comparing equivalent workers, as in Figure 6.6. This is no more than we

FIGURE 6.6. The effects of survey year for equivalent
workers, 1952–78

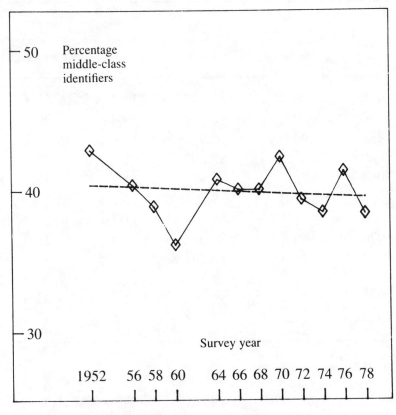

SOURCE: American Election Surveys.
NOTE: Effects are calculated with controls for age, birth cohort, managerial position, occupational prestige, education, and family income.

Middle-class placements = $43.366 - .034$ (year-1900). $R^2 = .023$.

might expect from chance fluctuations. Middle-class placements increased
because there were more college-educated managers earning high incomes
in 1978 than there were in 1952. But any given worker who stayed in the
same position throughout this period was not likely to change his or her
self-perception.

A universal embourgeoisement?

This finding would merit little attention except that at least two schools of thought would lead us to expect other results. The first, the "embourgeoisement" school, argued that growing prosperity infused *all* workers with a sense of middle-class attainment so that they all changed the way they thought about themselves. Mark Evers (1976:13), for instance, interprets growth in middle-class placements among a Detroit sample as reflecting "part of a general trend toward a universal 'middle class' existence and lifestyle, as so often heralded by commentators in the popular media."

In fact, however, there was nothing "universal" in the changes brought about by the postwar prosperity. *Workers* did not change, even though their relative proportions in the labor force did; that is, the decline in working-class self-placement was not a decline in working-class *consciousness*. Instead, it was a decline in the relative number of working-class positions. The point is similar to the one we made in Chapter 2: there are *structural* explanations for changes that are often attributed to psychological causes.

Absolute or relative standards of class perceptions

Studies of perceived well-being. A second school of thought is more subtle, but its failings are more revealing for understanding the psychology of class perceptions. In the early 1970s, as appropriate data became available, several social scientists began to ask whether the unparalleled prosperity of the postwar decades had translated into greater personal satisfaction. To their surprise, they found that most measures of well-being were unrelated to changes in national prosperity. Our class-placement results are less surprising in that regard, since they do reflect the increased prosperity. The different results for class perceptions and personal satisfaction suggest that different psychological processes link the national prosperity and individual perceptions. The personal satisfaction studies therefore will bear some closer scrutiny.

Richard Easterlin (1973) compared measures of personal happiness in 19 countries. Despite the fact that the countries ranged in overall prosperity (based on their gross national product) from the United States with $2,790 GNP per capita to Nigeria with $134 GNP per capita, there was no noticeable pattern of national averages in the happiness ratings. Easterlin found, to nobody's surprise, that within each country people with higher income reported greater happiness. Money, it seemed, could buy happiness for people but not for nations. Easterlin interpreted the paradoxical findings by concluding that people judge their own well-being relative to some social norm of what goods they ought to have. This norm varies among societies: the wealthier the society, the higher the norm against which one measures one's own well-being. Thus there are no national differences in perceived well-being because the people living in the more prosperous countries have a stiffer standard for what constitutes happiness. Every increment in prosperity for the whole country is matched by an increment in the standard to which personal well-being is compared.

Otis Dudley Duncan (1975) found the same paradoxical result when comparing changes in satisfaction in the United States between 1955 and 1971. Despite the increase in average income over the 16 years, Duncan found no increase in satisfaction with the standard of living. Within each year, however, Duncan also found that the wealthier Americans were, in general, happier Americans. Again, more money bought more satisfaction for individual Americans but not for the country as a whole.

Duncan also interpreted his results in relative terms: "The relevant source of satisfaction with one's standard of living is having more income than someone else, not just having more income. And satisfaction measures as such cannot tell us whether a population with a higher average income is really 'better off' than a population with a lower one" (1975:23). Even adjusting for inflation, people did not find the $10,000 they earned in 1971 to be as satisfying as the $10,000 they earned in 1955. A family earning $10,000 in 1971 was better off than 48 percent of 1971 families, but a family earning $10,000 (in 1971 dollars) in 1955 had been better off than 85 percent of 1955 families (U.S. Bureau of the Census, 1972) and therefore felt more satisfied than the 1971 family.

Lee Rainwater (1974) found evidence supporting this change in income standards. Results from 18 Gallup Polls between 1946 and 1969 showed that Americans had raised their standards for "the smallest amount of money a family of four needs to get along in this community." In 1946, Americans on the average thought an income of $4,614 (in constant 1971 dollars) was necessary; after 23 years of steady prosperity, the amount had increased by about half, to $6,878.

Class perceptions as absolute judgments. Class perceptions do *not* obey this logic of relative comparisons. Unlike satisfaction with living standards, middle-class placements increased between 1952 and 1978—there were more managers, more college degrees, and higher incomes in 1978 —but they had the same *meaning* in 1978 as in 1952. Comparing equivalent people in the two years yields a statistically nonsignificant change over the time period.[9]

We interpret these findings to mean that the class perception process obeys a more absolute logic. The meaning of "working class" and "middle class," unlike that of happiness and satisfaction, remains the same over time. The labels have specific referents (a managerial position or a college degree, for example) rather than a relative ranking in a status hierarchy (such as more education than average, or a higher prestige occupation than most people). This is exactly the point we made in Chapter 3 in comparing class perception and prestige studies, and in Chapter 4 in examining the determinants of class perceptions. Americans do interpret class in categorical terms with some absolute standard of reference; that is, they perceive *class*, not just *status*. When appropriate (in judgments of personal well-being or occupational prestige, for example), Americans can use a relative-comparisons model that ranks people along a continuum of social standing. But class divisions are also meaningful, and the evidence is that the terms "working class" and "middle class" are used in this categorical way.

9. A *relative*-comparisons model would predict a significant negative time coefficient, once individual social structural variables were held constant, as Duncan (1975) found. It is, of course, not possible to prove the null hypothesis, but the analysis reveals no support for the relative-comparisons model.

CHAPTER 7
U.S. AND BRITISH WORKERS

Same Consciousness, Different Opportunities

Much of the accepted wisdom about America's weak class consciousness is based, sometimes implicitly, often explicitly, on comparisons with the older European societies. Foreign observers, beginning at least with Alexis de Tocqueville in 1835, have filled their commentaries on the United States with glowing accounts of America's "inherited ideology of class-lessness" (Bottomore, 1966:51). The American Creed promised the opportunity to get ahead and thus constructed an image of American society as a "scheme of gradation" (Ossowski, 1963). The inequality that existed was continuous; American workers, unlike European workers, could not see themselves divided into a class separate from their bosses.

Research neither confirmed nor challenged the accepted wisdom; mostly, it ignored the issue. Other facets of the American Creed came under research scrutiny. But even as sociologists gathered the data to question America's more rapid mobility rates, they continued to endorse without examination the idea that American workers were protected from class consciousness by an "ideological egalitarianism" (Lipset and Bendix, 1967).

Occasionally, someone would remark on the lack of adequate comparative research on class consciousness. Treiman and Terrell (1975), in a study of mobility paths, cite the common belief that class is less salient in the United States than in Europe, but in a foresighted footnote they acknowledge that this belief rests on virtually no rigorous empirical research. Kahl (1957:174) had earlier noted the lack of systematic evidence for this widely held belief. Everybody seems to have overlooked the implications of a 1948 UNESCO study comparing class placements in nine countries (Buchanan and Cantril, 1953).[1] In this study, the United States had the

---

1. Kahl (1957:182) took note of the UNESCO study but dismissed its results for unspecified reasons. The most recent edition of that textbook (Gilbert and Kahl, 1987) omits any reference to either the study or the problem.

third highest level of working-class identification, exceeding such presumably class-conscious countries as France, Germany, Italy, and Norway. Only in Britain and the Netherlands did more people see themselves as working class. This surprising result led Buchanan and Cantril to question the "glib generalities" that America was a middle-class society. They called instead for a revision or, at least, a careful re-examination of the prevailing wisdom.

The research reported in this chapter attempts this re-examination. We will compare the class perceptions studied in Chapter 4 with similar data from Great Britain. The weight of the evidence suggests that there is, in fact, little difference in the way American and British workers perceive class divisions. At least in the separation of a working class from a middle class, the popular U.S. and British definitions are remarkably similar.

What makes the similarity in class perceptions especially interesting is that the psychological similarities coexist with continued political differences between the two societies.[2] The research reported in the second half of the chapter demonstrates that British politics are indeed more polarized by class divisions than are U.S. politics; the British Labour Party mobilizes working-class voters far more effectively than does the U.S. Democratic Party. We suspect it is the greater class structuring of British politics that sustains the belief in greater British class consciousness. But our results suggest that political differences may arise without any underlying difference in class consciousness.

Class Perceptions

Our strategy to detect cross-national differences in class perceptions relies on a comparative analysis of the class self-placement question. In effect, we recompute the analysis of class placements separately for each country and compare the results. If class is more clearly perceived in Britain, Brit-

---

2. Thus, our results should not be interpreted as yet another instance of the substantial "homogenization" of industrial societies. A popular school of sociology has developed the idea that all industrial societies converge toward a more or less common social structure dictated by the necessities of industrial production (Kerr et al., 1960). This industrial convergence theory seemed to be supported by the high cross-national correlations of prestige rankings (e.g., Hodge, Treiman, and Rossi, 1966). In contrast, what we find important is the juxtaposition of social psychological similarities and structural—especially political— differences.

ish workers ought to see themselves more uniformly as working class than do American workers; and British managers ought to see themselves more uniformly as middle class. Statistically, this ought to reveal itself in stronger relationships of the objective class divisions to the subjective class placements. But if the statistical relationships are similar in the two countries, then class labels are being assigned according to the same rules, and there is no noticeable superiority of British workers to identify their class membership.

The surveys

The most critical requirement for cross-national survey analysis is to select equivalent samples responding to equivalent questions that are coded into equivalent categories.[3] Fortunately, we begin with research studies that employed quite comparable designs. The U.S. data are from three of the American election surveys (1968, 1970, and 1972) in our Election Sample (see Chapter 4). The British data are from two surveys (1963 and 1964; supplemented in the voting analysis by a 1966 survey and 1970 reinterviews) from the study *Political Change in Britain* (Butler and Stokes, 1969, 1974). The resulting samples comprise 1,900 American and 1,163 British men, and 1,932 American and 1,485 British women.

Working class placements in Britain and the United States

The two sets of surveys asked virtually identical class self-placement questions: in each, respondents placed themselves in either the working or middle class. Britons selected the working-class label more often than Americans (74 percent versus 53 percent).[4] By themselves, the less common working-class placements in the United States imply nothing about less class consciousness. Americans are more often managerial, college educated, and affluent than the British; given more of the attributes of middle-class position, Americans should more often label themselves accordingly.

---

3. Details of the problems encountered in this analysis are reported in a methodological appendix to this chapter.

4. These differences are more pronounced but essentially similar to those in the 1948 data reported by Buchanan and Cantril (1953). Among the nine nations they studied, Britain had the highest rate of working-class identification (60 percent), while the U.S. rate was third highest (51 percent).

The more interesting question is whether a U.S. and a British worker *in equivalent positions in the social structure* are equally likely to label themselves working class. The trick here is to create statistical equivalency of social position in the two samples. Data in the two surveys allow us to come close.

The stratification measures

Both surveys have adequate occupational codes from which we can construct a managerial class dichotomy and a prestige ranking according to the NORC scores (Siegel, 1971). Both also identify the self-employed. (The remaining class dimension, authority, was identified only in the British surveys and so was dropped from this analysis.)

It is difficult to make education equivalent across the two countries. In Britain, the type of secondary schooling people receive (secondary-modern schools versus the more selective grammar and public schools) and the source of their postsecondary education (whether universities, teachers' and technical colleges, night schools, or apprenticeships) help determine their occupations and earnings (Treiman and Terrell, 1975; Burawoy, 1977; Kerckhoff, Campbell, and Trott, 1982). These qualitative distinctions ought to be important for middle-class placements as well and thus should be included in the analysis, together with the usual scale for years of education. The problem is to construct comparable qualitative measures from the U.S. data. Our solution has been to seek rough equivalents in the U.S. educational data wherever possible; where this is not possible, we add the remaining British distinctions separately.

The sample means for these variables are reported for each country in Table 7.1. As we expected, the U.S. averages are substantially higher on all variables except technical schooling. By using these dimensions as statistical controls, we can compare the class placements of U.S. and British workers in roughly equivalent positions. That analysis will tell us more about the levels of class consciousness in the two countries: if British workers are more likely than similarly placed U.S. workers to identify as working class, that would constitute some confirmation of the prevailing wisdom about weak American class consciousness.

American-British similarities

To present the results, we abstract four hypothetical composites with widely different positions on these dimensions. We then calculate the estimated class placements of these four composite cases in each country. For the men, the four composites are as follows:

TABLE 7.1. Class and status in Great Britain and the United States

	U.S.A.	G.B.
Men's jobs		
% managerial	38.8%	19.2%
% self-employed	14.8%	7.8%
NORC prestige	42.7	36.9
	(14.5)[a]	(14.3)
% defined[b]	85.1%	93.8%
Women's jobs		
% managerial	24.6%	13.7%
% self-employed	6.9%	4.5%
NORC prestige	39.6	31.5
	(13.4)	(13.2)
% defined[b]	34.4%	26.0%
Income (1967 $, U.S.)	8345.5	2646.4
	(5210.7)	(1447.4)
Education		
Years of schooling	12.2	10.7
	(2.2)	(1.2)
Postsecondary technical schools	14.1%	26.0%
College	31.4%	12.7%
Elite secondary	nd[c]	16.9%
Elite university	nd	2.0%
N	3,496	2,648

SOURCES: American Election Surveys, 1968, 1970, 1972; Butler and Stokes (1969), 1963 and 1964 surveys.

NOTES:

[a]Standard deviations are in parentheses.

[b]Men's jobs are defined for all men in the samples and for all women who are not themselves listed as heads of household (the jobs coded are for the reported head). Women's jobs are defined only for women who are employed.

[c]nd = not defined.

1. A plant manager (managerial class with an occupational prestige of about 61) with 15 years of education, including some college, earning $16,000 (in 1967 U.S. dollars).

2. A machinist (working class with an occupational prestige of about 47) with 12 years of education, including some technical school, earning $8,000.

3. A steelworker (working class with an occupational prestige of about 33) with 10 years of education, including some technical school, earning $4,000.

4. A janitor (working class with an occupational prestige of about 19) with 8 years of education, earning $2,000.

None of these is self-employed, nor does any in Britain have an elite secondary or university education. For women, we substitute a teacher, a bookkeeper, a hairdresser, and a waitress, occupations with the same class positions and prestige as the male occupations. Because for women's class perceptions we must also consider the jobs of the "heads of household" (see Chapter 8; Jackman and Jackman, 1983), we will assume that the women are married to men with the same class position and occupational prestige—to the four male composites, for example.

Figure 7.1 reports the estimated likelihood of a middle-class self-placement for each of these composite cases in each country. There are two important conclusions to draw from this figure. First, the levels of British and U.S. class placements are remarkably similar. The biggest difference is between the steelworkers, who are 14 percentage points apart; most others are within a few points of each other. Once we compare equivalent British and U.S. workers, the Americans are just as likely to think of themselves as working class—and the main exceptions run counter to the assumption that there is a stronger British working-class consciousness: it is the Americans who more readily choose a working-class label.[5]

Second, and perhaps more important, the gap between U.S. managers

---

5. We do not attribute much importance to this reversal. We are especially suspicious that the income controls overcorrect for American affluence. To test for this, we eliminated the national income differentials by recoding income into percentile ranks within each country. When we control for relative income rank rather than for actual dollars of income, the U.S. workers appear on average slightly more middle class than the British workers. Since the dollar estimates probably overcorrect for income differences and the percentile ranks undoubtedly undercorrect, it seems safest to conclude that neither country is more (subjectively) working class than the other.

FIGURE 7.1. Estimated class self-placements of four
            composites

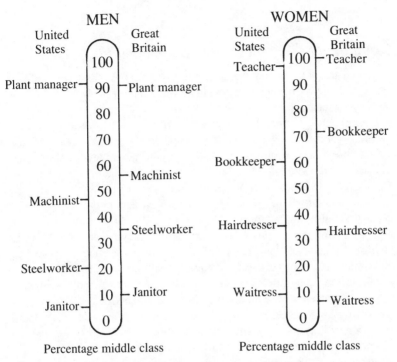

SOURCES: American Election Surveys: 1968, 1970, and 1972. Political Change
in Britain Surveys: 1963 and 1964.

and workers is as great as the gap between British managers and workers.
If class divisions were less clear in the United States, we would expect the
class placements to be less polarized: all the estimated class placements
would collapse toward the middle of the scale. In an "ideology of classlessness," more U.S. workers would assume middle-class placements, and
more U.S. managers would revert to working-class placements. In contrast, in the class-conscious British society, virtually all managers and professionals would be clear about their middle-class positions, and British
workers would be similarly clear about their working-class positions. Such

differences do not emerge in Figure 7.1. U.S. class perceptions are just as clear (or just as uncertain) as British class perceptions. The accepted wisdom about a unique American classlessness is not supported by this empirical test.

Comparing the impact of specific variables

We need to look beyond these overall comparisons, however, because specific class divisions may still be more important to British class perception. For instance, it might be that in Britain the difference between our hypothetical schoolteacher and waitress is primarily a consequence of their different managerial class positions, while in the United States the difference might be a result of their different educational levels. If the class divisions were more important in Britain, we would still be justified in concluding that Britain is the more class-conscious society.

The more detailed analysis shows that each determinant of class perceptions is also similar in the two societies. We illustrate the results by comparing how much class placements would change in each country with changes in each class and status variable. Table 7.2 considers hypothetical British and U.S. workers with an equal probability of placing themselves in the working and middle classes. In the United States a man's managerial position by itself increases middle-class placements by 18.3 percent, in Britain by 24.5 percent.[6] Although this difference suggests that British class perceptions are somewhat more sensitive to actual class position, the 6.2 point difference is smaller than we might expect by chance. Similarly, although the results suggest other small differences between the two countries, only one of these is greater than chance expectations. The exception is self-employment, which has a stronger impact on British class placements. This difference might be interesting except that we have already noted (in Chapter 4) that in the American Election Sample the measure of self-employment seems strangely irrelevant to a variety of relationships found in other U.S. surveys. On the other hand, the American GSS found a significant self-employment effect on class placements that more closely

6. The results seem to indicate that a woman's job has little effect on her class placement but that the job of the "household head" does. These data are not appropriate for addressing this issue, however, since we cannot distinguish in the British samples (and therefore do not do so in the U.S. samples) between full-time and part-time workers. The question of women's class self-placements is quite complicated; see Chapter 8.

TABLE 7.2. Effects of class and status on British and U.S. class perceptions

	U.S.A.	G.B.	Difference	T-Test[a]
Men's jobs[b]				
Managerial position	+18.3%	+24.5%	+6.2%	1.51
Self-employment	−2.4%	+14.8%	+17.2%*[c]	2.64
NORC prestige				
(14 points)	+4.0%	+1.6%	−3.4%	1.00
Women's jobs				
Managerial position	+0.6%	−1.3%	−1.9%	0.20
Self-employment	+1.7%	−1.4%	−3.1%	0.20
NORC prestige				
(14 points)	+5.6%	+7.3%	+1.7%	0.32
Income (100% increase)	+11.3%	+14.1%	+2.8%	1.20
Education				
Two years of school	+9.9%	+11.1%	+1.2%	0.47
Postsecondary				
technical school	+6.8%	+10.4%	+3.6%	0.76
College	+12.1%	+6.1%	−6.0%	0.97
Elite secondary	nd[d]	+7.7%		1.82
Elite university	nd	−2.0%		0.18
N (unweighted)		5,762		
N (weighted)		4,047		

SOURCES: American Election Surveys, 1968, 1970, 1972; Butler and Stokes (1969), 1963 and 1964 surveys.

NOTES:

[a]A t-test of greater than 2.0 indicates a difference between effects that is greater than chance ($p > .05$). The statistics are calculated from the interaction terms of the probit analysis.

[b]Men's jobs defined for all men in the samples and for all women who are not themselves listed as heads of household (the jobs coded are for the reported head). Women's jobs are defined only for women who are employed.

[c]* = $p < .05$.

[d]Not defined. Elite secondary and university schooling are defined only for the British sample. The reported t-test compares the British coefficient against zero.

parallels the British results. For this reason, we are reluctant to draw any conclusions about cross-national differences based on this single significant result.

The overall similarity of the results implies that the distinction between the middle class and the working class is made as easily in the United States as in Britain. Indeed, the cognitive rules used in relating objective position to subjective placement are almost identical. An additional year of education or a proportional rise in income will increase the likelihood of middle-class placement as much in the United States as in Britain. And in both countries, managerial class is an equally crucial determinant of class placement.

Other aspects of class consciousness

Thus far we have compared only class perceptions in the two countries. We should also consider more fully committed aspects of class consciousness that might yet explain differences between British and American class conflict. Even if Americans and Britons see class divisions in much the same way, they may feel quite differently about these perceived divisions. Perhaps these deeper feelings create the politically important differences between the two countries.[7] Our data are not perfect for investigating these differences, but what data we do have provide little support for British–U.S. differences at any level of class consciousness.

Class closeness. One wave of the British survey (1963) and three waves of the U.S. survey (1968, 1970, 1972) asked respondents whether they felt close to their chosen class or no closer to people in that class than to people in other classes. If members of the British working class are more class conscious, we would expect them to claim this closeness as an expression of their class solidarity. But there are negligible cross-national differences

---

7. Landecker (1963), e.g., stresses the difference between cognitive and affective components of class consciousness. The class-placement question addresses the issue of cognitive differences only. It may be that while class position is equally clear to Americans and Britons, Americans invest less affect in this identification. Giddens (1973) and Mann (1973) also propose several levels of class consciousness of which class perception is only the most basic. While we are skeptical of such "armchair introspection" into class consciousness, we would like to investigate each of these possibilities before we draw firm conclusions about cross-national similarities.

in response to this question. Among self-identified working-class people, 60.0 percent in Great Britain and 58.8 percent in the United States report feeling closer to their chosen class than to people in other classes; this difference is smaller than chance expectations; therefore, it appears that U.S. workers claim class solidarity just as often as British workers do. At this level of class consciousness, too, there is little evidence for American exceptionalism.

Class salience. Another dimension of class perception sometimes studied in surveys is class awareness or salience: the degree to which survey respondents report themselves as thinking in class categories. In both surveys, respondents were first asked whether they thought of themselves as belonging to any class before being asked for their specific class placements.[8] Of the U.S. working class, 63.5 percent agreed to thinking in class terms; of the British working class, 64.1 percent. Again, the difference is negligible and not statistically significant.[9] Thus, research results for class awareness, like those for class closeness and for class perception, provide no support for the supposed weak class consciousness of U.S. workers. The consistency of this result, together with the lack of any prior research finding U.S. differences, must call into question the conventional wisdom.

Perceptions of a dominant class. The foregoing analyses almost exhaust the capabilities of our data, but other comparisons are worth speculating about. First, British-U.S. differences that do not seem to occur along a middle-class–working-class division might still be observed if respondents were asked about a dominant or ruling class. A greater British consciousness of a ruling class would fit with the British history of feudal privilege (important to Louis Hartz, 1955, among others).

This intriguing question must go unanswered for now, as we can only

8. Previous research using this question (Guest, 1974) has linked such awareness to support for more "liberal" or collective-governmental strategies of social change as opposed to dependence on individual efforts.

9. A more complete loglinear analysis, not reported in detail here, shows that the American middle class reports itself as class aware more often than the British middle class (73.9 percent to 58.8 percent). We are reluctant to read too much into this result; however, a more class-conscious U.S. middle class would be consistent with our theory that the most exceptional characteristic of U.S. class structure is the greater strength of its dominant class (see Chapter 12).

look where the data currently exist. But where we do have data, the result
is not a trivial matter. The popular definition of the working class has been
thought basic for progressive forces in industrial societies. It is confusion
over the boundaries or even the existence of a working class that has been
blamed for the lack of a genuinely socialist alternative in the United States.
But the research reported here suggests, on the contrary, that U.S. workers
are as clear about the working class as British workers.

Perceptions of inequality. Second, though our data do not permit us to
compare more general attitudes toward economic inequality, a study by
Wendell Bell and Robert Robinson (1980) found no support for any greater
class consciousness among the British. They compared small samples from
London and New Haven, Connecticut, and found that the New Haven residents perceived *more* inequality than the London residents: for example,
stronger agreement—53 percent to 32 percent—with the belief that "people of higher social classes in this country get easier treatment by the police
and the courts than people of lower classes do." Moreover, the Londoners
expressed equally egalitarian values condemning the class differences that
do exist (Robinson and Bell, 1978): for example, similar levels of dis-
agreement with the proposition that "it's fair that rich people who can pay
fines can stay out of jail while poor people may have to go to jail for the
same crime." These results reverse the conventional wisdom (and the researchers' own expectations) that Americans hold more egalitarian values
but are less conscious of existing inequalities.

Attitudes on class. Cross-national research on other class attitudes—
what are sometimes called higher levels of class consciousness (Mann,
1973) —faces a crippling dilemma. On the one hand, surveys can ask
about broad ideologies. Past research indicates that workers often appear
quite conservative in such surveys (Free and Cantril, 1967; Mann, 1970;
Chamberlain, 1983). The problem with these results is that such general attitudes do not determine any behaviors of consequence (Schuman and
Johnson, 1976).[10] Only attitudes about specific policies or groups have

---

10. Nor are general beliefs a consequence of the class situation or personal economic experiences of survey respondents (Schlozman and Verba, 1979). Ideological beliefs are more often the result of direct socialization by parents, peers, and mentors (see Portes, 1971b, on the
sources of radical beliefs among the Chilean workers). Burawoy (1979:201) observes that the

been shown to affect subsequent actions. A prerequisite for research on class consciousness, therefore, ought to be that the ideas and attitudes being studied actually predict some class-relevant behaviors (but see Kluegel and Smith, 1981:49 for how rarely this is done)[11]. The class self-placement question, whatever its limitations, does determine political preferences; most other supposedly class-conscious attitudes fail even this test.

On the other hand, attitudes towards specific objects pose a different problem for cross-national research. If questions are asked about unions, political parties, or the government, American workers will inevitably interpret these questions in the context of American unions, political parties, and government. If they then appear more skeptical than European workers of these institutions, their reluctance may not be a failure of class consciousness but merely a reflection of the real differences in these American institutions. Most radicals distrust the AFL-CIO, the Democratic Party, and the U.S. government; they should not then expect American workers to endorse reforms that would depend on these institutions.

Given these problems, it is understandable that there has been so little cross-national research on class consciousness.[12] But neither the analysis in this chapter nor Bell and Robinson's results support the contention that American workers are less class conscious or that Americans have an "inherited ideology of classlessness." We can speculate that *other* psychological differences may exist between the United States and Britain, but where we have reasonably accurate data, we cannot find evidence for this particular one.

---

broad values socialized during childhood play little role in the class struggles on the shop floor.

11. The problem of behavioral relevance also disqualifies most survey questions that ask respondents how they feel about their own position in the social order. Collective action is motivated by perceptions about collectivities: about one's class, ethnic group, gender, or neighborhood. In Runciman's (1966) terms, it is fraternal not egoistic deprivation that is relevant (see also Vanneman and Pettigrew, 1972). Hamilton and Wright (1986:366) also find a sharp disparity between continuing high levels of personal satisfaction as reported in opinion polls and the dramatic drop in public confidence in the government and other national institutions. The perception of social structural problems appears to be largely independent of the perception of one's own well-being.

12. Wright (1985), using a six-item attitude scale, finds U.S. workers less class conscious than Swedish workers. But much of the difference in his class-consciousness scale derives from different attitudes toward strikes, and once union membership and other background variables are controlled, there is no more class polarization in Sweden than in the United States (1985:276).

U.S. – British Differences in Politics

How then do we explain the widespread assumption that class consciousness is much greater in Europe than in the United States? Such a belief did
not arise out of nothing. We suspect that the conclusions about class consciousness derived from observations about real differences in the political
systems. Class position determines party affiliation and voting more often
in Britain than in the United States (Alford, 1967); from this difference, it
was inferred that British voters must be more class conscious than U.S.
voters. This is again the familiar reductionist fallacy: all differences in behavior are attributed to differences in consciousness. The alternative explanation is not considered: that U.S. voters do not have class-oriented parties
to vote for, while the British voters do.

Kay Schlozman and Sidney Verba tell a revealing anecdote about the
Englishman trying to explain American politics to an English audience: "In
America, there are two political parties. There is the Republican party,
which is roughly equivalent to our Conservative party. And there is the
Democratic party, which is roughly equivalent to our Conservative party"
(1979:292). This "tweedledum-tweedledee" interpretation of U.S. politics
describes the choice offered to U.S. voters, not characteristics of the voters
themselves. We argue in this section that it is this structural choice that
makes U.S. politics exceptional, but that the choice does not result from
any weaker class consciousness of the voters.

Methods

Studying politics requires us to alter our research statistics, since we no
longer have a simple two-category outcome to predict. In the British surveys, while most of the electorate expressed a Conservative or Labour
preference, approximately 10 percent identified with the Liberal Party.
And both nations include many citizens who identify with no party or who
do not vote. Politics thus present us with many categories that do not fall
easily along a linear scale, and these nonlinearities cause problems for our
usual statistical techniques. Prior research has sometimes tried to escape
these complexities by dropping nonvoters, independents, and third-party
voters from the analysis, thus simplifying the statistics to a simple Republican versus Democrat (or Conservative versus Labour) choice. Alterna-

tively, the other groups might be coded as a midpoint between the two major parties. But both of those strategies, in forcing the multiple categories of political choice into a linear scale, obscure one of the most important facts to be discovered about U.S. politics. Therefore, we use statistics (discriminant function analyses) designed to analyze categorical dependent variables; we find, happily, that the methodological innovation uncovers a critical substantive insight.

Party affiliations

Both surveys asked respondents about their usual party affiliations. These affiliations, especially in the United States, provide a stable measure of political orientation and a convenient baseline for our later analyses of actual voting choices.

The discriminant function analyses find the "best" ordering of the party affiliations that maximizes the fit between the political categories and the array of class and status variables. For party affiliations (but not, as we shall see, for voting) the socioeconomic ranking of the parties yields no surprises (see Figure 7.2). Republicans and Conservatives top the scales; Democrats and Labourites hold down the bottom; independents (in Britain, respondents who refused to choose a party) are in between—in fact, almost equidistant from the two major parties. The Liberals in Britain rank quite high on these socioeconomic scales, resembling Conservatives more closely than they do Labour partisans.

A more revealing outcome of this analysis is the positions of our hypothetical composites along these socio-economic-political scales. As the discriminant function analysis creates the best ordering of the political parties, it also computes what combination of class position, income, education, and so on, determines people's positions along these political scales. When we compute the positions of the four composites along these scales (Figure 7.3), the contrast with the class-placement results (Figure 7.1) is immediately apparent. The distance separating plant managers from janitors, and teachers from waitresses, is narrower in politics than in class perceptions. This is no surprise, for we expect people's class positions to determine their class placements more closely than they determine political affiliations. More important are the striking U.S.–British differences in politics that were not found for class perceptions. The political distances are much larger in Great Britain than in the United States. British janitors and waitresses are more Labourite than U.S. janitors and waitresses are

FIGURE 7.2. Discriminant function analyses of
              party affiliations

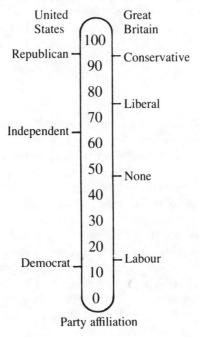

Party affiliation

SOURCES: American Election Surveys: 1968, 1970, and 1972. Political Change
in Britain Surveys: 1963 and 1964.

Democratic; British plant managers and teachers are more Conservative
than U.S. plant managers and teachers are Republican. The British system
is thus more polarized along class lines.

The comparison of the two figures tells us that while U.S. workers consider themselves just as much members of the working class as British
workers do, the U.S. workers do not so readily translate that class identity
into a political affiliation (and while U.S. managers are just as middle
class, they do not translate that identity as readily into a Republican affiliation). For U.S. workers, the class feelings are there, but the political loyalties do not follow.[13]

13. This can be seen also in path analyses constructed from the discriminant functions
(chapter appendix, Table 7.B). The path analyses add class placements as an intervening vari-

FIGURE 7.3. Estimated political partisanship of four composites

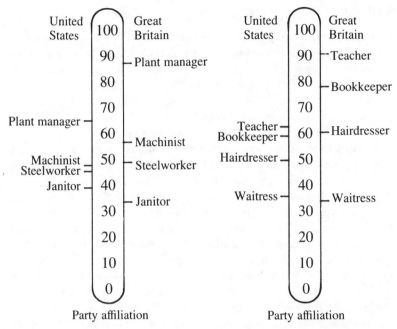

Party affiliation   Party affiliation

SOURCES: American Election Surveys: 1968, 1970, and 1972. Political Change in Britain Surveys: 1963 and 1964.

The simplest explanation for these results is that the U.S.–British difference lies not in different levels of class consciousness but in a different party system. British politics offer British voters a choice between a middle-class and a working-class party; U.S. politics offer no such choice.

---

able between the socioeconomic scales and the political party scales. The British results show that class placements are an important mediator between objective socioeconomic position and party affiliation: objective position determines class self-placements, which determine party affiliation. In the United States, this causal chain is broken at the second step: as in Britain, objective position determines class placements, but these self-placements are almost irrelevant to party politics. In a separate British regression of the political party scale on all the individual class and status variables, class placement had the largest zero-order correlation and the largest standardized partial regression coefficient with the political party scale. In the United States, class placement was not even statistically significant.

Thus, once Americans recognize their class position, there is still little they can do about it.

Voting

What happens to U.S. working-class voters when they see no class differences between the major parties? The answer is found when we analyze actual voting choices rather than party affiliations. The surveys encompass several national elections in the two countries. The British surveys include voting for elections in 1964 and 1966; each election is analyzed and reported separately. The American data include the 1968 (Humphrey-Nixon-Wallace) and 1972 (McGovern-Nixon) elections.

What is most interesting in the voting analyses[14] is the ranking of the voting choices along the socioeconomic scales (see Figure 7.4). Unlike the results for party affiliation, these results show an important difference between the U.S. and the British rankings of the political outcomes. British voting appears much like British party affiliations: Conservatives at the top, Labour at the bottom, and nonvoters somewhere between. The Liberal Party voters are again more similar to the Conservatives than to Labour, even outranking them in the 1966 elections. The U.S. ranking is completely different. While Republican voters are at the top, it is nonvoters who are lowest in socioeconomic status; Democratic voters are in the middle. This pattern reaches its extreme in the 1972 election, when McGovern voters are virtually indistinguishable from Nixon voters along this principal socioeconomic dimension.

In every election, the main social division in the U.S. electorate is between voters and nonvoters, not between voters for the different parties. The typical working-class response in the United States is to abstain. This is the argument of Walter Dean Burnham: "The 'real' class struggle, the point at which class polarization is most salient, is not found in the contests between Democrats and Republicans in the active electorate, but *between* the active electorate as a whole *and* the non-voting half of the adult population as a whole" (1980:37).

14. These results are reported in detail in the appendix, Table 7.D. The British composite scores are again more polarized than the U.S. scores, although the contrast is somewhat smaller for the voting analysis than for the party affiliations. Again, class position (managerial occupation and self-employment) determines political outcomes in Britain more than in the United States.

FIGURE 7.4. Discriminant function analyses of voting
choices

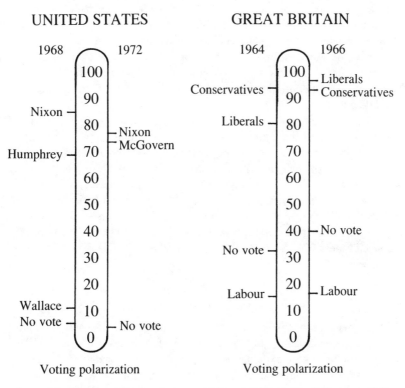

UNITED STATES   GREAT BRITAIN

SOURCES: American Election Surveys: 1968 and 1972. Political Change in Britain Surveys: 1964 and 1966.

    The contrast with Great Britain tells us what has happened to U.S. politics. The Democrats occupy a position that is occupied in Britain by the Liberal Party. It is U.S. nonvoters who hold the same position as the British Labour Party; the United States does not offer a party to capture the bottom of the socioeconomic ladder. Throughout the industrialized West, these workers vote for the Left: for a Labour Party in Britain or Australia; for a Social Democratic Party in Sweden, Austria, or Germany; for the Communist Party in Italy and France. The United States has no leftist party, so these workers sit out. It is this working-class nonvoting that is exceptional in U.S. politics: "The large decline in participation after 1900 and the exceptional working-class abstention rate today very much resemble a gap in the active American electorate that was filled elsewhere by socialist parties" (Burnham, 1974:679). The United States has one of the lowest rates of voting in the democratic world. In a typical presidential election, only half of the voting-age population casts a ballot; in off-year Congressional elections this proportion falls to one-third. Even India, facing obstacles of enormous poverty and massive illiteracy, has a better record than this.

The pieces of this cross-national puzzle fit well together: the United States has one of the highest rates of nonvoting among democratic countries. U.S. nonvoters are far more working class than voters for either of the major parties. In British elections, nonvoters are not distinctively working class. There, as in most other democratic systems, workers vote for the Left. The United States does not offer workers a leftist political alternative. Without a party to express their class interests, U.S. workers lose interest in the electoral process. What is exceptional here is not the consciousness of U.S. workers but the structure of the U.S. political party system.

Structural determinants of politics

All of this is more easily understood if we drop any assumption that politics, even democratic politics, simply reflect the ideas of the voters. That is, we ought to seek explanations of political behavior directly in the dynamics of political institutions; inferences about the motivations of the actors are likely to be mistaken in attributing psychological differences.

This has been the problem with many explanations of cross-national differences in political behavior. The difficulties arise when we try to attribute the lack of class voting in the United States to the lack of motivation among the individual voters. U.S. voters *seem* not to be class conscious because they rarely vote or organize politically along class lines. But it may not be the case that the psychological predisposition is lacking; it may be only that there is no opportunity provided to express that predisposition.

How does a political system develop to frustrate working-class consciousness? We must remember that politics involve a contest between opposing forces—not just a tallying up of people's wishes, like an opinion poll. Success in this conflict depends on many factors besides numerical strength. If one of the forces in politics is exceptionally strong—if it has great wealth, virtually uncontested social status, and a firm grip on existing political institutions—it can shape the political choices offered to the voters so that its dominance will not be seriously threatened.[15] This is the argument we sketch in the final chapter: what is exceptional about U.S. politics and about U.S. class conflict in general is the extraordinary power of U.S. capital. There are good reasons to conclude that U.S. capital has had more power than the capitalist classes of other Western democracies. In the face of this overwhelming power, the U.S. working class has had a more difficult time constructing political and class organizations to defend its interests. The typical mistake that scholars have made is to infer weaker class consciousness from these greater difficulties. The evidence in this chapter suggests that class consciousness is not the explanation.

15. Again, Burnham (1980:66): "The structure of political choices offered the electorate in the United States, and the major decisions made by political elites, have together produced more and more baffled ineffective citizens who believe that chance rules their world. This implies the long-term paralysis of democracy."

Methodological Appendix

Samples

Several restrictions were placed on our two samples to achieve equivalence and analytic clarity. Since much of the research focuses on the role of class divisions and occupational structure, the samples were restricted to men in the labor force and to women who were themselves in the labor force *or* whose "household heads" were in the labor force. We also restricted the samples to the 21–65 age range. As in the earlier analyses, minorities present special problems for research on class perceptions (see Chapter 10; also Jackman and Jackman, 1973 and 1983; Goyder and Pineo, 1974; in Canada, Pineo and Goyder, 1973). We have therefore restricted the cross-national comparison to whites in each country, there being insufficient numbers of nonwhites in the British sample for an adequate comparison.

The final counts are not the effective degrees of freedom for the analysis, since respondents are weighted by several criteria. First, the sampling design of the British survey imposed weights (ICPSR, 1972:iii–viii). Second, the British survey was a panel study, so the 1,263 interviews of British men represent only 721 distinct individuals. To be conservative, we weighted the British samples to reflect the number of distinct individuals, not the number of interviews. Third, we adjusted for the different sample sizes in the different surveys so that each year had an equal weight (the harmonic mean of the sample sizes) in the final analysis. Finally, in the analyses where we combined the U.S. and British data, we weighted the two nations equally (to the harmonic mean of the number of individuals). The result was a weighted sample of 1,045.3 men and 1,260.1 women in each country.

Variables

Prestige scores. For the cross-national comparison, we use the NORC scores on the assumption that the U.S.-derived scores are not substantially different from British rankings (Hodge, Treiman, and Rossi, 1966; Treiman, 1977).

Income. Income data are available for the total family in the United States and for the head of household in Britain. The U.S. family income data are multiplied by 0.8 to approximate head of household income (see

Lebergott, 1964). For both countries, income is translated into 1967 U.S. dollar equivalents by adjusting for the prevailing exchange rate and for changes in the U.S. consumer price index. The logarithm of this adjusted income is again used because it seems reasonable that class placements reflect proportional rather than absolute increases in income. After these adjustments, the British reported an average income only one-third that of the United States. This is undoubtedly an underestimate of the relative British incomes and probably an even greater underestimate of the relative standards of living.

Education. Four dummy variables have been created to estimate the effects of the qualitative differences in education. First, trade-oriented postsecondary schools are identified as night schools and apprenticeships in Britain, and as "vocational and technical training programs" in the United States (ICPSR, 1975:184–85). Second, a college-versus-noncollege dichotomy is created for both countries. The distinctions identify the more elite tracks of the British system: one for university education (as distinct from teachers' or technical colleges), and another for the kind of secondary school: the basic secondary modern track versus the elite tracks (grammar school, public school). No equivalent U.S. variable could be constructed, although if the data were available, it would be interesting to test whether the American "prep" school— admittedly a more limited phenomenon— might not have the same class-defining characteristics as the British grammar and public schools (cf., Mills, 1956; Domhoff, 1967) and whether a college curriculum within U.S. high schools had an effect equivalent to the British grammar school education.

Party affiliation. In the United States, the surveys asked:

Generally speaking, do you usually think of yourself as a Republican, Democrat, independent, or what? (ICPSR, 1975:63).

In Britain, the surveys asked:

Generally speaking, do you usually think of yourself as Conservative, Labour, Liberal, or what? (ICPSR, 1972: 180).

Note that the U.S., but not the British, surveys included an explicit choice of independent. The first wave (1963) of the British survey did not even include the final "or what?"

In addition, both surveys probed further for strength of party affiliations. We have ignored these further distinctions, since a separate discriminant function analysis revealed that strong and weak party identifiers did not fall along a linear scale of socioeconomic position.

Analysis

The figures in the text are computed from the detailed equations reported in Tables 7.A–7.D, below. We have endeavored to make the text presentation as straightforward as possible without ignoring the complexities of the results. In this regard, we have made two decisions that require further comment.

Pooling men and women. Throughout most of this chapter, we pool the men's and women's data to present a single set of results. Both the pooled and separate equations are reported in the following tables. The pooled results simplify the presentation; in general, the results for men and women are similar. We make an exception in reporting both genders when we focus explicitly on the occupational composites, since occupation is so closely linked to gender.

The analysis of class placements does reveal some differences between men and women. In the separate equations, some British–U.S. differences emerge that are not found in the pooled equation. We have not commented on these differences because there seems to be little pattern to the results. None of the male differences meet the usual criterion for statistical significance ($p < 0.05$). For women, two of the effects (income and head of household's self-employment) are more important in Britain; also, elite secondary schooling, a distinction defined only in Britain, has a significant impact on women's class placements. If we relax the criterion somewhat ($p < 0.10$), three of the male differences and one more of the female differences are statistically significant. But the patterns are not consistent across gender. Only self-employment shows a statistically significant cross-national difference for both genders.

Discriminant function analyses. We rescale the discriminant function results reported in the tables in order to make them more equivalent to the probit analyses of class placements. We approximate equivalent scaling factors by standardizing the constructed party and voting scales, much like the standardized cumulative normal that underlies the probit analysis. That is, we scale the discriminant function results so that the political party and voting scales (the dependent variables) have zero means and unit standard deviations. They are then transformed to 0–100 scales through the cumulative normal function, thus approximating the same scale used in the probit analyses of class placements.

TABLE 7.A. Probit analyses of class perceptions in the United
States and Great Britain

	Women & Men	Women	Men
Men's jobs[a]			
Managerial position	.4754*[b]	.4755*	.4655*
	(.0562)	(.0824)	(.0808)
Self-employment	−.0594	−.0777	−.0569
	(.0787)	(.1151)	(.1106)
NORC prestige	.0071*	.0065	.0064
	(.0025)	(.0036)	(.0035)
Defined	.1046	−.2108*	nd[c]
	(.0596)	(.0970)	
Women's jobs			
Managerial position	.0158	.0238	nd
	(.1118)	(.1106)	
Self-employment	.0420	.0373	nd
	(.1805)	(.1794)	
NORC prestige	.0100*	.0103*	nd
	(.0045)	(.0041)	
Defined	−.2864*	−.0868	nd
	(.0803)	(.0751)	
Income (logged)	.3842*	.3047*	.4700*
	(.0409)	(.0543)	(.0651)
Education			
Years of school	.1255*	.0845*	.1629*
	(.0132)	(.0190)	(.0186)
Postsecondary technical	.1752*	.3329*	.0308
	(.0567)	(.0806)	(.0820)
College	.3074*	.5753*	.1446
	(.0771)	(.1193)	(.1056)

Elite secondary[d]	.1954	.3708*	.0658
	(.1076)	(.1513)	(.1568)
Elite university[d]	−.0504	−.4815	.1836
	(.2759)	(.5264)	(.3260)
Nation (0 = U.S.; 1 = G.B.)[e]	.4135*	.5750*	.0047
	(.0448)	(.0618)	(.0657)

Interaction Variables (Nation × All Variables)

Men's jobs

Managerial position	.1820	.0374	.2919
	(.1205)	(.1762)	(.1722)
Self-employment	.4404*	.5561*	.3964
	(.1671)	(.2475)	(.2331)
NORC prestige	−.0050	−.0036	−.0034
	(.0050)	(.0073)	(.0072)
Defined	−.0076	−.3767	nd
	(.1227)	(.2035)	

Women's jobs

Managerial position	−.0491	−.1281	nd
	(.2444)	(.2451)	
Self-employment	−.0776	.0137	nd
	(.3965)	(.3978)	
NORC prestige	.0031	.0006	nd
	(.0096)	(.0084)	
Defined	−.2854	.0894	nd
	(.1751)	(.1634)	
Income (logged)	.1068	.2843*	nd
	(.0888)	(.1214)	

Education

Years of school	.0158	.0911	−.0740
	(.0334)	(.0477)	(.0490)

TABLE 7.A. *continued*

	Women & Men	Women	Men
Postsecondary technical	.0896	−.1953	.3349
	(.1183)	(.1644)	(.1776)
College	−.1551	−.2621	−.0021
	(.1600)	(.2518)	(.2236)
Unweighted *N*	5,762	2,943	2,819
Weighted *N*	4,047	2,146	1,901
Chi-square	1217.1	665.2	582.0
Fit	.784	.810	.790

SOURCES: American Election Surveys, 1968, 1970, 1972; Butler and Stokes (1969) 1963 and 1964 surveys.

NOTES:

[a]Men's jobs are defined for all men in the samples and for all women who are not themselves listed as heads of household (the jobs coded are for the reported head). Women's jobs are defined only for women who are employed. If a variable is undefined for any variable, the respondent is given a score of 0. A dummy variable ("defined") identifies those respondents for whom these variables are defined (coded 1). Thus, the coefficient for the men's managerial position represents the difference between men (or husbands) who are managers and men (or husbands) who are workers; the coefficient for "defined" represents the difference between respondents for whom these variable are defined and those for whom they are not defined. Managerial position includes the census classification of managers and professionals but excludes technicians.

[b]* = $p < .05$. Standard errors are in parentheses.

[c]nd = not defined.

[d]Elite secondary and elite university are defined only for the British sample.

[e]So that this variable yields meaningful results, the income, education, and occupational prestige variables have been centered at $5,000, 12.0 years of school, and 40.0 prestige. The coefficient therefore represents the difference between U.S. and British workers who are neither managerial nor self-employed, with an occupational prestige of 40, an income $5,000, 12 years of school, no technical school, no college, and no elite secondary or university.

TABLE 7.B. Discriminant function analyses of party affiliations

	Women & Men		Women		Men	
	G.B.	*U.S.A.*	*G.B.*	*U.S.A.*	*G.B.*	*U.S.A.*
Centroids[a]						
Conservatives/Republicans	1.333	1.370	1.259	1.422	1.455	1.349
Liberals	0.606		0.431		0.712	
No affiliation/Independents	−0.107	0.307	−0.373	0.277	0.104	0.305
Labour/Democrats	−1.073	−1.184	−1.082	−1.119	−1.047	−1.213
Discriminant Function Coefficients						
Men's jobs[b]						
Managerial position	.4901	.1113	.3147	−.0309	.6729	.1965
Self-employment	.5084	.0802	.4968	.1151	.2725	.0463
NORC prestige	.0008	.0044	.0019	.0095	.0001	.0008
Defined	−.4390	−.0069	−.4561	.0058	nd[c]	nd

TABLE 7.B. *continued*

	Women & Men		Women		Men	
	G.B.	U.S.A.	G.B.	U.S.A.	G.B.	U.S.A.
Women's jobs						
Managerial position	−.3958	−.0743	−.3659	−.0554	nd	nd
Self-employment	−.1148	.1015	−.1048	.1210	nd	nd
NORC prestige	.0153	.0017	.0148	.0010	nd	nd
Defined	.3196	−.0153	.2326	−.0078	nd	nd
Income (logged)	.1110	.0109	.2127	−.0343	−.0160	.0540
Education						
Years of school	.0842	.0304	.0477	.0513	.1003	.0052
Post secdry technical	.1709	.1155	.1840	.1253	.1984	.1053
College	.1932	.1423	.2342	.0746	.2274	.2801
Elite secondary	.2020	nd	.1604	nd	.3099	nd
Elite university	−.7255	nd	−.5892	nd	−.8033	nd
Constant	−1.424	−0.838	−1.906	−0.625	−2.096	−1.414

Computed Composites

Teacher/plant manager	1.260	0.268	1.167	0.270	1.017	0.332
Bookkeeper/machinist	0.673	0.050	0.693	0.181	0.126	-0.090
Hairdresser/steelworker	0.202	-0.104	0.217	-0.045	0.063	-0.148
Waitress/janitor	-0.439	-0.373	-0.443	-0.396	-0.451	-0.309
Unweighted *N*	2,327	3,320	1,247	1,815	1,085	1,818
Weighted N	1,237	1,715	670	940	570	1,018
Canonical correlation	.3871	.2035	.3634	.1989	.4206	.2230

SOURCES: American Election Surveys, 1968, 1970, 1972; Butler and Stokes (1969), 1963 and 1964 surveys.

NOTES:

[a]These coefficients are scaled somewhat differently from the coefficients reported in conventional analyses. Usually, the coefficients of the independent variables are scaled so that the discriminant function constructed from them has zero mean and unit standard deviation. The centroids of the groups are then computed along this function. We reverse this so that the groups are scaled to have a zero mean and unit standard deviation, and the discriminant function coefficients are scaled to predict these group scores. Our results are analogous to an ordinary least-squares regression of the political groups (coded to the computed centroids) on the independent variables.

[b]Men's jobs are defined for all men in the samples and for all women who are not themselves listed as heads of household (the jobs coded are for the reported head). Women's jobs are defined only for women who are employed. If a men's job or women's job variable is undefined for any respondent, the variable is given a score of zero. A dummy variable ("defined") identifies those respondents for whom these variables are defined (coded 1). Thus, the coefficient for the men's managerial position represents the difference between men (or husbands) who are managers and men (or husbands) who are workers; the coefficient for "defined" represents the difference between respondents for whom these variables are defined and those for whom they are not defined.

[c]nd = not defined.

TABLE 7.C. Regressions of party scales on class placements and socioeconomic variables

	Women & Men		Women		Men	
	G.B.	*U.S.A.*	*G.B.*	*U.S.A.*	*G.B.*	*U.S.A.*
Regressions[a] of Party Scales on						
Class self-placements	.2674	.0132	.2958	.0066	.2289	.0510
Discriminant function	.2716	.1965	.2267	.1960	.3323	.1952
Multiple R	.4583	.2029	.4485	.1988	.4771	.2253
Regressions of Class Self-Placement on						
Discriminant function	.4463	.4594	.4647	.4116	.4258	.5058
Indirect Path from Discriminant Function to Party Scale						
Discriminant function	.1193	.0060	.1375	.0027	.0975	.0258

SOURCES: American Election Surveys, 1968, 1970, 1972; Butler and Stokes (1969), 1963 and 1964 surveys.
NOTE: [a]Coefficients are standardized partial regression coefficients. Discriminant functions are computed from the socioeconomic variables from Table 7.B.

TABLE 7.D. Discriminant function analyses of voting choices

	Great Britain		United States	
	1964	*1966*	*1968*	*1972*
Centroids[a]				
Conservatives/Republicans	1.342	1.301	0.910	0.653
Liberals/Wallace	0.772	1.538	−1.251	−0.841
Nonvoters	−0.483	−0.282	−1.634	−1.773
Labour/Democrats	−1.036	−0.988	0.419	0.554
Discriminant Function Coefficients				
Men's jobs[b]				
Managerial position	.4845	.4708	.0738	−.0323
Self-employment	.4997	.5570	.1892	−.0841
NORC prestige	−.0004	.0036	.0031	.0104
Defined	−.2481	−.8256	−.0470	.2166
Women's job				
Managerial position	−.0001	−.3577	−.4589	.1771
Self-employment	−.2015	.5526	.0879	−.2546
NORC prestige	.0033	.0104	.0158	.0005
Defined	.2182	.0891	.3225	.1405

	Great Britain		United States	
	1964	1966	1968	1972
Income (logged)	.2122	.1759	.2265	.2240
Education				
Years of school	.0426	.0514	.1535	.0673
Postsecondary technical	.2140	nd[c]	−.1324	.0392
College	.3144	nd	−.5042	−.0119
Elite secondary	.2428	.1800	nd	nd
Elite university	−.6144	nd	nd	nd
Constant	−2.322	−1.465	−3.160	−3.113
Computed Composites				
Teacher/Plant manager	1.356	0.861	0.483	0.811
Bookkeeper/Machinist	0.499	0.506	0.510	0.275
Hairdresser/Steelworker	0.226	0.085	−0.220	−0.167
Waitress/Janitor	−0.260	−0.517	−0.817	−0.649
Unweighted *N*	1,056	1,198	792	1,312
Weighted *N*	604	639	511	485
Canonical correlation	.3894	.3797	.3188	.3189

SOURCES: American Election Surveys, 1968 and 1972; Butler and Stokes (1969), 1964 and 1966 surveys.
NOTES: See notes to Table 7.B.

CHAPTER 8
DOCILE WOMEN?

Pin Money, Homemaking, and Class Conflict

Women have held an uncertain place in the class consciousness debates. The traditional stereotype has questioned women's commitment to class struggle; it has regarded their employment as a source of "pin money" and concluded that their grievances are either borne patiently (because temporary) or avoided by withdrawal. Women have long been reputed to be poor candidates for union organization and, once organized, to have dubious staying power during strikes. Their class affiliations have generally been thought to derive from their husbands' or fathers' occupational positions. All of these unsubstantiated but widely held impressions add up to the stereotype of a docile worker.

The facts have shown otherwise. When tested, women have played no less heroic a role than men in American labor struggles. From the early organization of the New York garment workers with their 1909 strike oath ("If I turn traitor to the cause I now pledge, may this hand wither from the arm I now raise," Levine, 1924:154; Laslett, 1970:121), through the Wobblies' great 1912 victory in the Lawrence textile mills (Dubofsky, 1969), to the Women's Emergency Brigade defense of the 1937 General Motors sit-down strike (Fine, 1969) and, most recently, the expansion of public sector unionism, women have disproved the notion of their docility. And well before women achieved prominence in most other fields, radicals such as Mary Harris ("Mother Jones") and Elizabeth Gurley Flynn were organizing workers, men and women alike, against industrial capitalism; today Crystal Lee Jordan ("Norma Rae") and Karen Silkwood may have won similar places in the popular culture. (On the other side of the class divide, women protagonists—though less common—have proved no less militant: Katherine Graham's *Washington Post* faced down the newspaper crafts where her archrival, the *New York Times*, had flinched.)

We must remember that for women, too, class consciousness can de-

181

velop out of class conflict and does not necessarily precede it. One of the leaders in the Women's Emergency Brigade has described the conversion to militancy among the Michigan housewives: "A new type of woman was born in the strike. Women who only yesterday were horrified at unionism, who felt inferior to the task of organizing, speaking, leading, have as if overnight, become the spearhead in the battle of unionism" (Fine, 1969: 201). "Women . . . horrified at unionism" are hardly the models of class consciousness that we would expect to play the decisive role in the critical labor conflict of the Depression, to insert themselves between police and their husbands barricaded in the Chevrolet engine plant. And yet these same women, when faced with a situation testing their class allegiance, took the decisive step that propelled the class struggle forward, taking them along with it. Their class allegiance may have been a necessary precondition, but a politically elaborated ideology was not.

The image of docile women as an obstacle to working-class consciousness survives in spite of these dramatic events. Reductionist fallacies again tend to blame working-class women for their own oppression. Gender differences in class conflict are routinely attributed to different psychologies rather than to the different situations that confront men and women workers.

Unionization

It is a fact that women have always had lower unionization rates than men; in 1977 only 11 percent of female private-sector employees were unionized, compared with 27 percent of men (Freeman and Medoff, 1984: 27).[1] These low rates are routinely attributed to women's weak class consciousness. Women are said to be unreceptive to union organization because they lack a commitment to their jobs, because they are too submissive to challenge their bosses, or because labor conflict would appear unfeminine. "Let's face the fact," one (male) AFL-CIO unionist declared in 1959, "women are, in the main, unorganizable. They are more emotional than men and they simply lack the necessary staying power to build effective

1. The restriction to private-sector employees exaggerates the gender difference. Statistics for all employed workers in 1985 report 13 percent unionization for women and 22 percent unionization for men (U.S. Bureau of Labor Statistics, 1986).

unions" (quoted in Foner, 1980:419). His words echoed Gompers's pessimistic advice to New England telephone operators 40 years earlier: "You're only girls and such strikes have an awful record" (Foner, 1980:111). Fortunately, the "girls" didn't listen. They struck—and promptly won union recognition and wage increases.

Strictly structural factors may account for the low unionization rates. Women are segregated into the least-skilled, lowest-paid jobs in the economy, precisely those jobs that are most difficult to organize, whether held by men or women. Meredith Tax, in her study of the women's labor movement in the late nineteenth century, points to just these structural factors:

> In fact, they were unorganized because they had just become workers; because they had so much work to do at home that they could hardly move; because their husbands, boyfriends, and fathers did not let them go to meetings; because they earned so little that they could not afford to take risks; and because no one would organize them. And when anyone tried, women often showed that despite all these barriers they were raring to go. (1980:32)

Today, we can examine the gender differences in unionization rates more quantitatively; the results point to the same structural differences in the position of women workers. By far the largest part of the reason for women's lower unionization is the type of jobs they are segregated into. Clerical and service workers are less unionized than skilled and semiskilled workers; trade and service industries are less unionized than transportation and construction. This is true for both men and women in those jobs— although men have the good fortune to be more often skilled craftsmen and operatives working in transportation and construction (and therefore unionized), while women are stuck as clerks and service workers in retail trade and personal services (and therefore nonunion). When we compare men and women working in the same occupation in the same-sized firm in the same industry, the 16 percent difference in unionization rates reduces to just 6 percent (Freeman and Medoff, 1984:28).[2]

Although we have hard evidence to show that these structural factors are

2. Another study of 1976 unionization rates (Antos, Chandler, and Mellow, 1980) showed that the 15.4 percent lower female unionization reduces to a 12.7 percent difference when regional and personal factors such as part-time employment are controlled, and to just 5.5 percent after applying even crude controls (seven and nine categories) for occupation and industry.

important, there is little evidence pointing to gender differences in class consciousness. In fact, what attitudinal evidence we do have suggests exactly the opposite. Attitude surveys document that women are more favorable to unions than men (see Table 8.1). In a 1982 ABC News/*Washington Post* poll (ICPSR, 1983), more women (62 percent) than men (52 percent) reported that they would join a union if they had not already done so.[3] Women are also more sympathetic with labor than with business, disapprove more of the air traffic controller (PATCO) firings, and agree more often that workers are better off in unions. In our GSS samples, 74 percent of working women say they have some or a great deal of confidence in organized labor; only 64 percent of working men report that confidence.

These direct investigations of union attitudes do not find the psychological differences that are commonly inferred from different behavior. Instead, they indicate that the different behavior (low unionization) results from the different structural position of women (segregation into low-skill positions), not from different attitudes (hostility toward unions or weaker class consciousness). The structural obstacles that women workers face are imposing enough; they hardly need the additional burden of a gratuitous stigma that they are lacking in class consciousness.[4]

Class Perceptions

Still, suspicions persist about women's class consciousness: that women do not see themselves divided into sharply defined classes, that their work experiences are less central to their class perceptions than is true of men. This is a variant of the "pin money" thesis: since women do not have the

3. The slightly different wording of this question in the 1977 Quality of Employment survey (Freeman and Medoff, 1984) produces lower levels of agreement but the same gender difference favoring women. If current union members are added back into the totals as favoring joining a union, the difference reduces to women 67 percent, men 62 percent in the ABC News/*Washington Post* poll—a statistically nonsignificant five percentage points.

4. Nancy Seifer (1973:40–41) records a different psychological disadvantage that women may suffer from: she suggests that "perhaps more than any other single factor it is women's lack of self-confidence which mitigates against organizing." She cites a remark by a (female) labor official that "long years of discrimination have convinced many of them the effort will be fruitless."

TABLE 8.1. Gender differences in attitudes toward unions

Survey Question	Response	Women	Men
1982 ABC News/Washington Post Poll (ICPSR, 1983)			
Current union member?	member	12%	21%*[a]
If you were working on a job where you could join a labor union, do you think you would join, or not? (not asked of union members)	join	62%	52%*
In general, do you approve or disapprove of labor unions?	approve	72%	69%
Would you say you personally are more sympathetic to business or labor in the United States?	labor	64%	53%*
As you know, Reagan fired all the air traffic controllers who went on strike last summer. Did you approve or disapprove of his firing them?	disapprove	54%	38%*
Do you agree or disagree that most workers who are not in management jobs would be better off belonging to a union than not belonging to one?	agree	65%	56%*
Approximate sample size		546	455

TABLE 8.1. *continued*

Survey Question	Response	Women	Men
1977 Quality of Employment Survey (Freeman and Medoff, 1984)			
Current union member	member	11%	27%
If an election were held with secret ballots, would you vote for or against having a union or employees' association represent you?	vote for	41%	27%*
General Social Surveys			
As far as the people running organized labor are concerned, would you say you have a great deal of confidence, only some confidence, or hardly any confidence at all in them?	great deal or some	73%	62%*

NOTE: [a]* = statistically significant difference, $p < .05$

same lifetime commitment to work, it figures less strongly in their perceptions of their own class position.

Although women's self-perceptions of class do not differ in the aggregate from men's (51 percent of white women place themselves in the middle class; 52 percent of white men), the *process* by which women arrive at their class placement is different. We have already seen (in Chapter 4) that women's jobs do not determine their class placements as much as men's jobs determine men's placements.

One explanation might be that women depend on their husbands' jobs for their class placements so that their own jobs have less influence. This was the point of view of the early literature on family status (see, for example, Parsons, 1943; Centers, 1949:35). The assumption was—and it was little more than an assumption—that the entire family's status was determined by the husband's achievements; once she was married, a woman's employment was irrelevant.

Fortunately, women's class perceptions have now received considerable research attention.[5] The first results challenged the traditional stereotype; in placing themselves in the class structure, working wives appeared to use their own occupations and education, although their husbands' occupations and education were also important (Ritter and Hargens, 1975; Hiller and Philliber, 1978; Van Velsor and Beeghley, 1979). In contrast, the men ignore their wives' attainments (Felson and Knoke, 1974; Van Velsor and Beeghley, 1979).[6]

5. As recently as 1973, Joan Acker quite correctly complained that American sociology had too often ignored women; e.g., Centers's original research investigated only men's class identification. His admonition (1949:35) that women's class psychology must be studied next went largely unheeded during more than a quarter-century of American research. The early exemplars of class-identification research, the studies by Hodge and Treiman (1968) and by Jackman and Jackman (1973), subsumed most women's class placements under their husband's occupational attainments.

6. There are many methodological problems in this research. The Ritter and Hargens (1975) and Hiller and Philliber (1978) studies of the relative importance of husbands' and wives' jobs fail to include any controls for educational attainments, controls that in our data eliminate the significant occupation effects they report (see also Jackman and Jackman, 1983). Nor do the data from the studies always support their conclusions. The Van Velsor and Beeghley analysis, the most thorough of the group, shows a nonsignificant coefficient for the effect of husband's occupation on the wife's class placement, and yet it claims (1979:775) that "the data . . . indicate the importance of *both* husband's and respondent's own occupational characteristics" (emphasis added). The Felson and Knoke (1974) analysis depends on an inappropriate partitioning of variance that precludes a direct assessment of the effects of husband's

Still later research by Jackman and Jackman (1983) has now challenged the revisionist interpretation and reasserted the traditional model. In their data, women seem to use *only* the status of their husbands' occupations in choosing a class label; their own jobs do not appear to alter their class placements. The Jackmans attribute the earlier revisionist results to methodological problems. But their research has problems of its own: their analysis includes women who work only part time (31 percent of the sample). Our data, as one might expect, show that women with part-time employment do rely entirely on their husbands' jobs in choosing a class label.

But the main problem with all the earlier research is that it does not take into account two very important factors. First, women's class perceptions differ from men's because women tend to adopt a maximizing strategy: if *either* a woman *or* her husband holds a mangerial position, she claims a middle-class position. Second, women's jobs differ from men's jobs in systematic ways that tend to obscure class divisions. This second explanation says nothing about women or men themselves; it is their jobs that differ, not their psychology. For both men and women in typically "female" jobs, the manager-worker class division does not produce much difference in class perception. Because this second explanation focuses on the characteristics of work, not of "consciousness," it parallels the explanations given above for women's low unionization rates: the gender differences in class conflict result from the different structural positions in which women workers find themselves more than from different reactions to a similar structural position.

To compare men's and women's class perceptions, we must first broaden the research design. The past interest in working wives crowded out two groups that ought not to be ignored: single women and housewives. Excluding these two groups removes the majority of women from the research.[7]

---

and wife's occupation and thus renders the results equivocal. Nevertheless, these authors discount the one direct test of wife's status that they do make—a test inconveniently yielding positive results that contradict most of their main conclusions.

7. It also ignores some important research questions. For instance, as Acker (1973:177) has pointed out, even the traditional stratification models accepted the importance of a single woman's job ("women determine their own social status only when they are not attached to a man"). But according to the traditional models, marriage will reduce or eliminate the status relevance of a woman's job and education. A theoretically interesting comparison, therefore, is between the importance to class placements of single women's jobs and married women's

TABLE 8.2. Sample sizes: combinations of gender, marital status, and spouse's class

	Not Employed	Worker	Manager
Women			
Unmarried	—	284	161
Spouse = not employed	—	—	—
Spouse = worker	907	283	69
Spouse = manager	542	94	122
Men			
Unmarried	—	206	170
Spouse = not employed	—	794	501
Spouse = worker	—	264	111
Spouse = manager	—	74	121

SOURCE: General Social Surveys.

The role of the spouse's class position

We divide the GSS sample of women into eight categories whose class placements we would like to estimate. The design is most easily understood in Table 8.2, which reports the sample sizes for each of the eight categories. A comparable design for men also has eight categories, although only six are directly comparable.[8]

---

jobs. The traditional stereotype of women would predict that single women's jobs are more important to single women's class perceptions than married women's jobs are to theirs. As yet, this comparison has not been made because the sample is restricted to married women.

8. To simplify the analysis somewhat, we have dropped cases of single women who are not working or married women whose husbands are not working. Since these are usually stu-

The class placements in the eight cells are estimated after adjustments for differences in family income, age (since the married–not married differences compare respondents of quite different ages), the education of the respondent and (if married) of the spouse. The adjusted middle-class placements of the eight categories are reported in Table 8.3. Inspection of this table reveals a major reason previous estimates of the effects of women's work were so low: managerial positions do not matter for women who are married to managerial husbands. If the husband is himself managerial, then it makes little difference whether the wife is employed in a working-class or a managerial position; she already sees herself as quite middle class. Similarly, the *husband's job makes little difference to a woman who is herself managerial*; again, she already sees herself as quite middle class. This is the maximizing strategy suggested above: either a woman's own position or her husband's position as a manager is sufficient to justify a middle-class placement.

In contrast to the women's maximizing strategy, men follow a markedly egocentric strategy in relating objective class position to perceived class placement: they simply ignore their wives' jobs. Men with managerial wives are no more likely to see themselves as middle class than men with working-class wives. Thus, the men do indeed fit the traditional family stereotypes (developed by men, incidentally); their class perceptions depend almost entirely on their own jobs.

Three other comparisons are important to notice in these results: the effects of marriage, of the wife's not working, and of both wife and husband in managerial positions. First, the traditional model suggests that marriage completely alters the social significance of a woman's job: while single, her job may determine her class placement; once she is married, it is her husband's job that is important. The results disprove this model. Not only single women but women married to working-class husbands use their own jobs in placing themselves in the class structure. The effect of mana-

---

dents or retirees (or wives of students or retirees), we have also restricted the sample to women between the ages of 25 and 60, when such omissions are inconsequential. Nor have we adjusted the estimated class placements for occupational prestige, since to be consistent we would then have to adjust for the effects of the respondent's and spouse's occupational prestige; the analysis would become so complex and the problems of multicolinearity so pervasive that the results would be impossible to interpret meaningfully. Most of the job effects are captured by the managerial-nonmanagerial differences, and the omission of occupational prestige reduces the overall fit only slightly. Managers are defined as all the census classifications of managers and professionals except technicians.

TABLE 8.3. Joint effects of own and spouse's position on class perceptions

	Adjusted Percentage Middle-Class Self-Placements		
	Not Employed	*Worker*	*Manager*
Women			
Unmarried	—	38%	54%
Spouse = not employed	—	—	—
Spouse = worker	40%	34%	53%
Spouse = manager	60%	48%	41%
Men			
Unmarried	—	38%	57%
Spouse = not employed	—	35%	64%
Spouse = worker	—	29%	59%
Spouse = manager	—	29%	60%

SOURCE: General Social Surveys.
NOTE: Adjusted percentages are calculated after controls for respondent's and spouse's education, family income, and age (see Table 8.D).

gerial position for single women is + 16 percent; the effect for women with working-class husbands is + 19 percent—about the same within the limits of our surveys.[9]

9. The GSS and Election Sample are quite consistent, although several of the effects are stronger in the GSS. The Election Sample results are presented in the chapter appendix (Tables 8.A–8.D).

Second, more housewives see themselves as middle class than do equivalently placed women who have working-class jobs. The experience of a subordinate role at work seems to reinforce a woman's recognition of herself as working class. The housewife role is more ambiguous in class terms.

Finally, women who have managerial jobs themselves and who are married to husbands with managerial jobs—a stereotypically dual-career household that we would expect to be most middle class—are, in fact, less middle class than couples with only one managerial spouse. This curious anomaly occurs in both the GSS and the Election Sample, and despite many additional tests we have not been able to explain it.[10] It remains a mystery.

To summarize these results: the relevance of husbands' managerial jobs accounts for a large part of the difference between men's and women's class perceptions. A man ignores the occupation of his wife even if she is a manager; he uses only his own occupation to place himself (an egocentric strategy). A woman will use her husband's managerial position to place herself in the middle class and ignore her own working-class job (a maximizing strategy). If we exclude from the comparison men and women married to managerial spouses, then the gender difference in class perception is much less noticeable. In the GSS, a managerial position increases women's middle-class placement by an average of 17.9 percent and men's by an average of 25.9 percent. In the Election Sample, the difference is almost erased: the increase is 15.5 percent for women and 18.8 percent for men.

The gender composition of men's and women's occupations

Thus far, we have explained part of the difference between men's and women's class perceptions by their different responses to being married to a managerial spouse. The second part of the explanation has nothing to do with the differences between men and women but is a result of the differ-

---

10. Before introducing controls for the other variables, the dual-manager cell is the most middle-class cell, although not much above the single-manager couples (see the appendix tables). We thought the controls for income might be lowering the middle-class placements in this cell especially; we thought it might be an interaction effect of college educations; we thought it might result from an age effect or age interaction with managerial position. Tests for all of these did not eliminate the anomaly.

ence between men's and women's *jobs*. It is well known that women are largely segregated in a narrow range of occupations that are almost entirely held by women: in nursing, teaching, clerical work, food service, and textile industries, for example (Oppenheimer, 1970). It may be that these kinds of work do not imply class membership as clearly as do the craft and administrative positions that men more often occupy. The division between managerial and nonmanagerial positions may be quite distinct among men's jobs but is more blurred and gradual among women's jobs (Glenn and Feldberg, 1977). If it is the jobs and not the people holding them that determine the perceived sharpness of the manager-worker gap, then we would expect that those (few) women in typically "male" occupations will perceive their class position much as men do: that is, with a sharp division between managers and workers. Conversely, those (few) men in typically "female" occupations will perceive their class position much as women do: that is, with a weak division between managers and workers.

We can test for the effects of job characteristics by scoring every occupation for its gender composition. Using census reports (U.S. Bureau of the Census, 1963:1–10, 1973b:1–11), we calculate the percentage of males in each occupational category; these scores are then assigned to each individual according to his or her occupation. Of course, men end up on the average with much higher scores (84.0 in the GSS) than women (34.4), but there is a range within both sexes, so that we can look at the effects of sex composition of occupations among women and among men. Do women in the more "male" occupations perceive their class position any differently from women in thoroughly "female" occupations?

Gender composition, by itself, is not related to middle- or working-class placement; male jobs are not seen as any more middle class than female jobs.[11] But we are interested in whether the managerial-class division is more decisive for class placements among male jobs than among female jobs. To answer this question, we estimate the difference between managers and workers at each level of occupational "maleness." The results provide good support for a sharper class division among typically male jobs than among typically female jobs.

Figure 8.1 displays the results of this analysis. Among women, the difference between managers and workers is enormous for those women in typically male occupations. But this difference shrinks as we look at

---

11. Male jobs, of course, tend to pay better than female jobs, so the extra income results in more middle-class placements. But if we control for income, there is no association of gender composition of the occupation with class placements.

FIGURE 8.1. Class perceptions by sex composition of
occupation and sex of worker

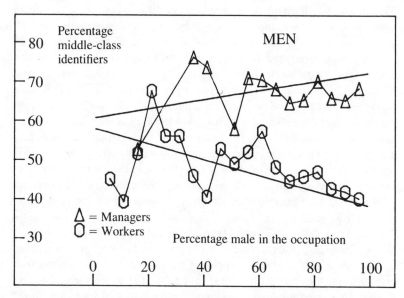

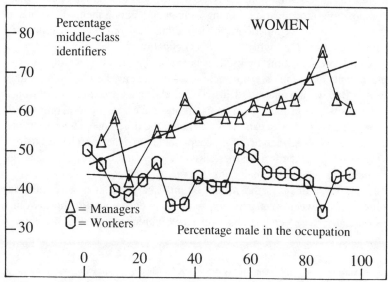

SOURCE: General Social Surveys.

women in more typically female occupations. For example, in jobs of 90 percent male composition, women managers are estimated to be 30.5 percent more middle class than are workers. But in jobs of only 10 percent male composition, the estimated self-placements differ by only 6.0 percent. Thus, part of the reason the managerial effect is weaker for women is that they are segregated into female occupations where the manager-worker difference is not a very sharp gap.

What strengthens this interpretation is that the same phenomenon is observed among men. For men too, the management-labor gap is more important among male occupations than among female occupations. In the GSS, for men in occupations of 90 percent male composition, managers are estimated to be 37.6 percent more middle class than workers; for men in occupations of only 10 percent male composition, the class placements differ by only 8.6 percent. Since men are more often in male jobs, the manager-worker division seems quite important; that is, men are more often found on the right side of Figure 8.1, where the gap in class perceptions is large, and women more often on the left side where the gap is small. But if we hold constant the "maleness" of the occupation, there is no difference in the size of the managerial division. Thus, the gender composition of jobs explains all the remaining difference between men's and women's class perceptions.[12]

What is it about "female" jobs that makes them less relevant for class perception? We might find some answers in the growing body of feminist psychology that studies gender differences in levels of moral development (Gilligan, 1982). Because women are socialized to preserve the family and to take primary responsibility for child care, they attend more to interpersonal relations. This attention to affiliative ties and the needs of others is replicated in the expectations set for women working within the paid labor force in such roles as domestics, secretaries, sales clerks, and teachers. In those positions, as well as in those where tending to the personal needs of others is not explicitly included in the job definition (as in textile and

---

12. The Election Sample data are not quite as clear, but again women perceive class differences between managerial and nonmanagerial jobs as readily as men do when we control for sex composition. But for women there is a slight deviation from the standard pattern. The women in the Election Sample still perceive a difference between managers and workers even in typically female occupations—perhaps less difference than do women in male occupations but still a difference. Nevertheless, the central point is still supported: the gender composition of the job determines the importance of the manager-worker division.

light factory work), interpersonal attachments remain more important to women; thus, they may face a greater barrier to identifying major divisions between themselves and their bosses.

But despite the internal conflicts and the importance of interpersonal attachments, class divisions are perceived. In Ellen Goodman's (1979) study of how people confront and move through changes in their lives, one respondent was a Black woman who achieved a managerial position after spending 30 years as a secretary. She describes the strong feelings of attachment to her bosses that evolved over the years but never loses sight of the differences in their positions—even acknowledging that secretaries can be "office maids":

> You can have a personal attachment for somebody you're working for. At least I did. I had worked with two really fine men, which is one of the hazards of a secretarial job. You may work for truly fine people. You get so identified with them that you don't know that you have a career that's your own.
>
> If you work for a person, as I did, who has some respect for your mind, you're not really an office maid. The personal attachment is there. It's one of the reasons why you like coming to work. And yet, that makes it very difficult to leave. So when I thought about leaving, there was something sad in it for me and yet something I wanted. (1979:49–50)

We suspect that the interpersonal attachments of women's jobs may explain their lack of class relevance. We do not have the data to test such an explanation; more information on interpersonal relationships at work would be helpful. But with more research attention now focusing on the effects of gender segregation at work, perhaps such data will eventually become available.

Summary

We have made some progress in explaining why women seem to perceive their work less in class terms than men do. Two factors are important: the first individual, the second more structural. Women married to managerial husbands do not use their own jobs in determining their class placement; men married to managerial wives do. It is mainly among this subset of men and women that men are the more "class conscious." For the remaining types, who are the bulk of the labor force, the differences between men and women are accounted for largely by the differences between men's and women's jobs, not by anything intrinsic to men and women themselves. The perceived class division between managers and workers is relatively weak in "female" jobs, whereas there is a clearly perceived class division between managers and workers in "male" occupations. Since men are more often in male occupations, men appear more class conscious on the average, but women in these male occupations are just as class conscious as the men are. Conversely, men in largely female occupations do not see as great a gap between managers and workers; they have as difficult a time as women do in translating their "objective" class position into a class perception. But because there are relatively few men in these female jobs, they don't affect the overall averages much. Since women are concentrated in just these occupations where the manager-worker distinction is not seen as a major class division, women as a group seem to be less class conscious.

Appendix

TABLE 8.A. Sample sizes: combinations of gender, marital status, and spouse's class

	Not Employed	Worker	Manager
Women			
Unmarried	—	267	121
Spouse = not employed	—	—	—
Spouse = worker	596	246	55
Spouse = manager	407	117	99
Men			
Unmarried	—	156	137
Spouse = not employed	—	551	393
Spouse = worker	—	331	112
Spouse = manager	—	55	93

SOURCE: American Election Surveys.

TABLE 8.B. Joint effects of own and spouse's position on class perceptions

	Adjusted Percentage Middle-Class Self-Placements		
	Not Employed	*Worker*	*Manager*
Women			
Unmarried	—	41%	55%
Spouse = not employed	—	—	—
Spouse = worker	47%	35%	54%
Spouse = manager	57%	52%	44%
Men			
Unmarried	—	39%	46%
Spouse = not employed	—	37%	62%
Spouse = worker	—	34%	50%
Spouse = manager	—	36%	45%

SOURCE: American Election Surveys.
NOTE: Adjusted percentages are calculated after controls for respondents and spouse's education, family income, and age (see Table 8.D.).

TABLE 8.C. Unadjusted middle-class placements

	Women			Men		
	Not Employed	Worker	Manager	Not Employed	Worker	Manager
General Social Surveys						
Unmarried	—	30%	68%	—	36%	76%
Spouse = not employed	—	—	—	—	33%	79%
Spouse = worker	38%	34%	64%	—	31%	72%
Spouse = manager	78%	64%	72%	—	43%	84%
American Election Surveys						
Unmarried	—	34%	70%	—	33%	67%
Spouse = not employed	—	—	—	—	31%	79%
Spouse = worker	44%	35%	67%	—	32%	61%
Spouse = manager	76%	63%	74%	—	48%	77%

TABLE 8.D. Probit analyses of class perceptions with all spouse interaction terms

Variable	Women		Men	
	Probit Coefficient	T-Ratio	Probit Coefficient	T-Ratio
	General Social Surveys			
Respondent's class	.383	3.96	.748	10.47
Spouse's class	.527	7.06	-.015	-0.11
R Class X Sp Class	-.534	-2.98	.064	0.29
R Class X Single	.254	1.16	-.089	0.54
Wife in 1f X Husb class	-.180	-1.02	-.015	-0.08
Respondent's education	.077	6.40	.095	9.37
Spouse's education	.085	6.90	.047	2.84
Marital status: single	.060	0.76	.104	1.27
Wife in labor force	-.155	-2.28	-.145	-2.02
Family income	.496	9.96	.600	10.34
Age	.007	2.47	-.048	-15.87
Age squared	.001	1.70	.069	2.18
Likelihood chi-square	638.0	(df = 12)	730.9	(df = 12)

TABLE 8.D. *continued*

Variable	Women		Men	
	Probit Coefficient	T-Ratio	Probit Coefficient	T-Ratio
	American Election Surveys			
Respondent's class	.404	3.75	.632	8.06
Spouse's class	.309	3.70	.035	0.23
R Class X Sp Class	−.659	−3.23	−.123	−0.47
R Class X Single	−.027	−0.11	−.267	−1.46
Wife in 1f X Husb class	.111	0.62	−.243	−1.30
Respondent's education	.167	10.90	.148	11.53
Spouse's education	.055	3.73	.059	2.95
Marital status: single	.116	1.31	.053	0.58
Wife in labor force	−.282	−3.76	−.074	−0.98
Family income	.433	7.70	.519	7.88
Age	.003	0.97	−.011	−3.17
Age squared	.000	1.40	.000	0.55
Likelihood chi-square	478.9	(df = 12)	620.7	(df = 12)

CHAPTER 9
FEAR AND LOATHING?

Ethnic Hostility and Working-Class Consciousness

Within the Left, the most common explanation of American exceptionalism has been the ethnic diversity of the American working class: the differences among native-born, immigrant, and slave descendant; among Protestant, Catholic, and Jew; among Irish, Italian, German, and Slav— all these have stymied any movement toward class solidarity. In this view, the many pieces of the American working-class puzzle would not fit together. Working-class culture, even its language, was a melange of separate identities, each attached to a primordial national heritage rather than to a universalistic class consciousness. As a result, instead of fighting the common class enemy, workers too easily dissipated their energies in fighting each other.

In an 1892 letter (Marx and Engels, 1953:242), Engels notes the "great obstacle" of the divisions between the native-born American labor "aristocracy" and the badly paid immigrants; what's more, the immigrant groups themselves, he says, were divided into "different nationalities which understand neither one another nor, for the most part, the language of the country."[1] In the next decade, the leading German socialist Karl Kautsky (1905, cited in Moore, 1970:117–20) again blamed American ethnic heterogeneity for crippling working-class solidarity.

Initially, the Left jumped at the ethnicity explanation because ethnic divisions would pose only a temporary obstacle to class conflict. Most believed with Engels that working-class solidarity "in the end overcomes all minor troubles; ere long the struggling and squabbling battalions will be

---

1. See also his December 2, 1893, letter to Sorge (Marx and Engels, 1953:258) in which he again mentions the division between the native born and the immigrants. However, neither Marx nor Engels studied American workers carefully, so they never substantiated their remarks with much specific evidence.

formed in a long line of battle array, presenting to the enemy a well-ordered front" (1887, in Marx and Engels, 1953:290). But even by Kautsky's time, the ethnicity explanation had already worn a little thin (Moore, 1970:121), and many wondered when the inevitable economic forces would break through the ethnic restraints.

Despite the failed prophecy, leftist scholarship still emphasizes ethnic divisions.[2] Writing in the *Socialist Register*, Jerome Karabel (1979:215) faults Sombart for his neglect of the ethnic hostilities that "fragmented the proletariat into a bewildering array of mutually suspicious nationality groups."[3] The American socialist Michael Harrington (1976:xi) singles out the antisocialism of Irish Catholics to explain the conservatism of the AFL.[4] More recently, Mike Davis (1980), in a *New Left Review* article, blamed the "racism and nativism" of American workers for subverting successive waves of working-class struggles.

Marxists may favor the ethnicity explanation of American exceptionalism because it permits them to sidestep questions about the economic inevitability of socialist movements.[5] It is also natural to look for explanations of American exceptionalism among any distinctive characteristics of the United States. Ethnic divisions are both characteristically American and a

---

2. Besides the citations noted in the text, see Gramsci ([1948] 1971:287), Coser (1956:77), Bottomore (1966:54), Aronowitz (1973:140), Burnham (1974:655), Parenti (1978:97), and in a more qualified and potentially insightful way, Katznelson (1981:6–19). Some non-Marxists have agreed on the importance of ethnicity in explaining weak class consciousness. Parkin (1979:4–5), in fact, makes the inability of Marxism to explain ethnic solidarity a major feature of his revision of class theory. American historians John Commons (1908) and Oscar Handlin (1951) stressed American immigrants' conservatism as the key to American exceptionalism. Selig Perlman (1928:168), on the other hand, regarded the native-born workers' hostility to the immigrants as the second most important factor (after affluence) in the weakening of American labor solidarity.

3. Karabel's critique echoed the misgivings of Sombart's editor and translator, C. T. Husbands (1976:xxvii). Kautsky also had offered ethnic heterogeneity as an alternative to Sombart's emphasis on working-class affluence (see Moore, 1970:117–20).

4. See also Perlman (1928:168) for a similar assertion of the incompatibility of American Catholicism and working-class radicalism. But see Dawley (1976:138) for an assertion that Irish-Catholics were just as militant as Yankee Protestants. Laslett (1970:54) also points to several examples of radicalism among Irish Catholics in the United States (e.g., the Molly Maguires).

5. Non-Marxists have not so much denied the relevance of ethnic diversity as ignored the issue. It has never played a significant role in Lipset's analyses (1963, 1977). The original edition of the Laslett and Lipset (1974) reader *Failure of a Dream?* had no selection on ethnicity or race, a shortcoming that the authors corrected in the revised (1984) edition.

plausible immediate cause of working-class weakness. "Divide and con-quer" is surely one of the oldest maxims of social conflict. We are left with a neat syllogism:

Ethnic divisions within the working class weaken class solidarity.

The American working class is one of the most ethnically heteroge-neous classes in all capitalism.

Therefore, the American working class is bound to have weak class solidarity.

We examine this reasoning by challenging its major premise. First, we need to scrutinize the historical evidence that ethnic and racial divisions have undermined class solidarity. What specific working-class struggles were subverted by ethnic hostility? Are these instances balanced by other examples of working-class solidarity where ethnic and racial loyalties actu-ally helped to mobilize working-class movements? Second, we question on psychological grounds the supposed incompatibility of class and ethnic identifications. We suggest a plausible case for exactly the reverse: that ethnic loyalties can serve to bridge the gap between individual workers and a broader class consciousness. At the least, we should consider class and ethnic identities as *independent* dimensions, not as mutually exclusive al-ternatives.

Ethnic Competition in Labor Struggles

Despite the Left's repeated emphasis on ethnicity, there are few docu-mented instances of the divisive effects of ethnic loyalties being crucial for the failure of working-class protest. Ethnic and racial conflicts are more of-ten the consequence than the cause of working-class failures. Only after class-based mobilization proves fruitless do ethnic cleavages appear. When workers lose strikes, some sections of the working class inevitably prove to be less persistent than others, thus bringing attention to the intraclass divisions. But most of these strikes would have been lost in any case because of the intransigence of the employers and their vast economic and political resources. In fact, ethnic loyalties can be not only compatible with but even supportive of class mobilization.

Ethnic support for class solidarity

South Chicago. William Kornblum (1974) describes how South Chicago steelworkers expand their ethnic ties into a larger *class* solidarity. The steelworkers first develop ethnic loyalties within their families and neighborhoods, but these separate group identifications are aggregated into a common class-based movement by union and party politics: "The preoccupation of South Chicago unionists with ethnic and racial politics can hardly be dismissed as "false consciousness." Rather it is part of the overall political process whereby common class interests are eventually identified" (1974:90).

Kornblum discovered that the new Mexican working-class leaders gained a foothold in union organizations on a base of their prominence within an ethnic community. In the unions, Mexicans have taken their place beside Serbian, Polish, and Croatian leaders who won their positions by the same process of ethnic mobility. The Mexicans' identification with their community sometimes creates conflict with the earlier ethnic groups, but if the Mexicans are to secure a place in the power structure of South Chicago, their ethnic differences must eventually be negotiated, and the community base broadened to a class-oriented political program.[6]

Lordstown. Even when workers seem hopelessly divided into warring ethnic factions, class consciousness may unite them against their employers. Stanley Aronowitz's (1973) study of the Lordstown Chevrolet strike showed that ethnic conflicts can coexist with a shared hostility toward the corporation. In Lordstown, Blacks distrusted whites; native Ohioans snubbed the immigrant "hillbillies" from the South, who were suspected of being company stooges because they seemed willing to do any work and suffer any conditions in order to keep their jobs. Yet none of these ethnic hostilities prevented the strike. The southerners surprised everybody by leading the slowdowns and sabotage against General Motors. Workers did not forget their ethnic loyalties, but they put them aside in the fight with GM management (Aronowitz, 1973:29).

6. Using similar logic, Craig Calhoun (1982:129–31) argues that preindustrial community ties were important in the early history of building solidarity among the English working class.

Immigrants

The sudden class solidarity of the Lordstown "hillbillies" fits a pattern often observed throughout U.S. labor history: precisely those ethnic groups suspected of disloyalty to their class comrades have proved to be the *most* militant and persistent soldiers in the class struggle.

It was the turn-of-the-century consensus that immigrant workers would never develop an appropriate working-class consciousness. Managers and trade unionists alike dismissed immigrants as a docile labor force well suited to their degrading jobs. Gompers's patronizing attitude was indicative: "Born in lands of oppression [the immigrants] reached manhood without that full mental development which makes for independence and self-preservation" (cited in Brody, 1965:43).

Theories of immigrant conservatism. Everybody buttressed disdain for the immigrants with plausible theories as to why immigration undermined working-class consciousness, though not all these theories were so crude as Gompers's assertion that immigrants lacked "full mental development." A few accused specific institutions, especially the Catholic Church, of conspiring with employers against the unions (e.g., Interchurch World Movement, 1920:150; Handlin, 1951:217).[7] Most analyzed the immigrants' social psychology and thus blamed the victims for their oppression.

One theory claimed that to immigrant workers of impoverished origins, even their modest pay looked like a windfall. In other words, immigrants remained conservative because they felt no deprivation relative to their standard of comparison (cf. Pettigrew, 1967).

A second theory blamed the immigrants' conservatism on their temporary status. Many were "sojourners" who sought a capital hoard in America to take back home (Rosenblum, 1973:33–37, 123–26; Karabel, 1979:215–16). To accumulate savings they needed steady employment, not strikes that would interrupt their earning and eat away at their savings

---

7. If the Catholic Church did side with employers, it was little different from other churches. Irving Bernstein (1960:8) reports that in the South, "religion was a branch of the textile industry" and quotes one South Carolina mill manager: "We had a young fellow from an Eastern seminary down here as pastor . . . and the young fool went around saying that we helped pay the preachers' salaries in order to control them. That was a damn lie—and we got rid of him."

(Handlin, 1951:75; Brody, 1960:136–37). Those immigrants who expected to return home (Thomas and Znaniecki, 1927:1493) could regard
the most degrading working conditions as only a temporary hardship.
Many did return to Europe, especially during economic recessions. Emi-
gration, therefore, became an alternative to protest.

Gerald Rosenblum (1973) has developed a third theory, that the European immigrants could accept better the discontinuities of early industrialization because they never knew the preexisting American social order. The
old social contract had been based on the Jeffersonian ideal of an independent citizenry, and native-born workers felt betrayed when the new industrial order disrupted those expectations; it appeared not only harsh but ille-
gitimate. Immigrants, on the other hand, had left their prior expectations
back in Europe. The hardships of American life could be deplored, but
there was no sense of illegitimacy. Rosenblum's theory looks promising
because it explains not only immigrant conservatism but the fact that the
early stages of industrialization run the greatest risk of protest and revolution.

Immigrant militance. The problem with all these theories, however, is
that subsequent events proved immigrant docility to be fictitious. After the
turn of the century, one outbreak of labor unrest after another found immigrants not only joining but leading the struggle (Higham, 1955:225). For
instance, in the Great Steel Strike of 1919 (Brody, 1960 and 1965) the immigrants organized first and held out longest. The strike was far more
widespread than anybody had anticipated because the union organizers
were able to convert ethnic loyalties into class solidarity. "Strikes had the
force of communal action among immigrants. . . . To violate the community will peculiarly disturb the immigrant, for he identified himself, not
primarily as an individual in the American manner but as a member of a
group" (Brody, 1965:157).

Immigrant workers everywhere translated their ethnic ties into class solidarity (see Gutman, 1976:61–66). The successful United Mine Workers
(UMW) strikes were based on the strong sense of community solidarity
among Slavic miners (Greene, 1968). The oath taken in the 1909 garment
workers' strike, "If I turn traitor to the cause I now pledge, may this hand
wither from the arm I now raise," was an old Jewish ritual oath that the
striking women repeated in Yiddish. Slavic steelworkers in Indiana in
1910 took a similar oath against scabbing by kissing a crucifix. In the successful 1912 strike of the Lawrence textile mills, the IWW organized sepa-

rate meetings according to language, where workers' support for the strike was reinforced within the familiar setting of the ethnic community (Dubofsky, 1969:241–42). Even Gompers, despite his professed dislike for unskilled immigrants, was quick to come to their aid once effective strikes were underway; he assisted the New York cloakmakers in 1910, the furriers in 1912, and other garment workers in 1913 and 1916 (Dubofsky, 1968:70). In each of these organizing drives, ties to the ethnic communities more often reinforced class solidarity than divided workers.

Though union defeats were once blamed on immigrant workers, careful research has shown solidarity across native-born and immigrant groups alike. For example, the loss of the Long Strike of 1877 in the Pennsylvania anthracite coal region was sometimes attributed to the mass importation of Slavic laborers, but no such migration occurred in the numbers imagined, nor was it so ethnically distinct. And support for the union was as strong in the heavily Slavic areas as in the native-born English-speaking areas (Greene, 1968:66–67). The failure of the strike is more appropriately attributed to the employers' intransigence: they instigated it by aggressively forcing wage cuts on workers in the entire region, and they were determined to wait out the strike in order to break the union, no matter how unified the workers remained.

Much of the ethnic hostility that did occur was the result of employers' attempts to pit one group against another.[8] By casting one ethnic community in the role of strikebreaker, employers tried to create opposing ties to class and ethnic solidarity. For example, in the 1919 steel strike, a labor spy was instructed to "stir up as much bad feeling as you possibly can between the Serbians and the Italians. Spread data among the Serbians that the Italians are going back to work. . . . Urge them to go back to work or the Italians will get their jobs" (Interchurch World Movement, 1920:230). Yet as cunning as such appeals might seem, these divide-and-conquer strategies did not always succeed. Employers were often inept precisely because of the class barrier that separated them from the workers. Kornblum (1974:97) notes that the labor spy given those instructions probably

---

8. Engels had earlier noted U.S. capitalists' deliberate use of ethnicity to divide workers: "Your bourgeoisie knows much better even than the Austrian government how to play off one nationality against the other: Jews, Italians, Bohemians, etc., against Germans and Irish, and each one against the other, so that differences in workers' standards of living exist, I believe, in New York to an extent unheard of elsewhere" (1892, in Marx and Engels, 1953:242). This theme has been repeated more recently by Karabel (1979:218).

had little success, since the main ethnic division among the striking workers was between Poles and northern Europeans!

Ethnicity also reinforced militance when immigrant groups brought a European radicalism with them to American shores. Engels regularly complained about the New York socialists who maintained their German language along with their socialist purity (Marx and Engels, [1893], 1953: 257–58; [1894] 1953:262–63), but the radical heritage of the mostly German brewery workers made their union a resolutely socialist bastion within Gompers's AFL (Laslett, 1970:45). The Jewish garment workers in New York had brought with them from Russia a tradition of revolutionary opposition to the existing order (Dubofsky, 1968; Laslett, 1970:134); Hungarians and Finns were also said to be "Socialist by tradition" (Interchurch World Movement, 1920:150). These ethnic communities nurtured a radicalism that demonstrates once again not only the compatibility of ethnicity and class consciousness but their mutual reinforcement.

Nativism. Such militancy forced Americans to reevaluate the role of immigrants in American exceptionalism. But the reevaluation did not abandon the ethnic explanation; it merely stood it on its head: if the Germans, Jews, Slavs, and Italians turned out to be such working-class militants, it must be the native-born Americans whose class consciousness was suspect. By World War I, business leaders themselves were calling for a halt to immigration (Higham, 1955:50–52).[9] According to the new reasoning, *nativist* sentiment was the better protection against working-class solidarity, because the native-born Protestant workers shared with their employers a common language, a cultural heritage, and often a contempt for the impoverished and unskilled "hunky."

The nativist theory is as plausible as the immigrant explanation, but again, the actual labor history does not fit well. Except in a few cases, ethnic divisions did not drive native-born American workers closer to their employers. American workers were never trapped into the position of white South African or Ulster Protestant workers (cf., Parkin, 1979:4–5). They might distrust the immigrant laborers as unreliable allies, but rarely to an extent that clouded their awareness of who the enemy was.

---

9. Business interest in restricting immigration waxed and waned in cycle with labor unrest. Once the post–World War I strike wave had been thoroughly defeated, industrialists rediscovered the advantages of cheap immigrant labor and lobbied *against* any restriction of immigration (Higham, 1955:232).

American workers built solidarity at the workplace in the face of well-orchestrated campaigns of patriotic nativism and strident anti-Catholicism. After the Civil War the electorate was divided between Protestants and Catholics, but the labor movement was united. When these early unions were crushed following the "Great Upheaval" of 1877, the Knights of Labor rose up to rejoin Protestant and Catholic, native-born and immigrant. The Knights suffered from many weaknesses, for which they eventually paid dearly, but ethnic divisions were not a major problem (Dawley, 1976: 190–91). And these divisions were overcome despite a wave of nativist resurgence throughout the country at the time. When the Industrial Workers of the World again attempted a mass-based working-class movement, after the Knights declined, they found little difficulty in organizing native-born, immigrant, and Black workers into "One Big Union." Even the conservative AFL, perhaps because of its mixed immigrant and native-born membership, was at first unreceptive to the nativist appeals that periodically swept the country (Higham, 1955:49,72).[10]

The Great Steel Strike. The 1919 steel strike again provides a case in point. When the immigrants surprised everybody by becoming militant strikers, employers appealed instead to the "Americanism" of their native-born workers (Higham, 1955:226). The strike coincided with a Red scare claiming that Bolshevism had entered America in the persons of its unskilled immigrant work force. But the nativist appeals were only marginally successful. In the end, it was the skilled (that is, predominantly native-born) workers who first broke ranks and returned to work, but the strike was already a lost cause by the time the native-immigrant division broke into a major cleavage. The steel corporations had marshaled their economic and political resources to break the strike, and they simply refused to negotiate.

A contemporary report rejected ethnic and nativist explanations of the strike's failure and instead pinned the blame on the strength of capital:

> The first cause of failure was the size of the Steel Corporation. The United States Steel Corporation was too big to be beaten by 300,000 workingmen. It had too large a cash surplus, too many allies among other businesses, too much

---

10. After the turn of the century—and especially in light of the IWW threat—the AFL more actively sought immigration restrictions and became more recognizably nativist (Higham, 1955:305).

support from government officers, local and national, too strong influence with
social institutions such as the press and the pulpit. (Interchurch World Movement, 1920:177)

Led by Judge Elbert Gary of U.S. Steel, the companies refused even to
meet with union leaders; they also avoided the intervention of third-party
church and government leaders. Pennsylvania police banned public meetings and arrested union men without warrants. In Gary, Indiana, the U.S.
Army imposed martial law, broke up the picket lines, and arrested union
officers. The press likewise rallied to the support of the corporations. Pittsburgh papers reported full production in Cleveland; Cleveland papers reported full production in Pittsburgh. At the height of its power, U.S. Steel
was simply too strong and too intransigent to be defeated by any feasible
working-class movement.

Patriotism and class consciousness. Not only have nativist appeals been
overrated as a divisive force, but patriotism has often been used to *promote*
working-class solidarity. The U.S. Steel chairman was regularly portrayed
as "Kaiser" Gary. If Americans had fought a war to make the world safe
for democracy, why should workers tolerate corporate despots who refused
even to talk with a union delegation? Mother Jones, then 89, played this
theme to the hilt: "Our Kaisers sit up and smoke seventy-five cent cigars
and have lackeys with knee pants bring them champagne while you starve,
while you grow old at forty, stoking their furnaces. . . . If Gary wants to
work twelve hours a day let him go in the blooming mill and work" (Jones,
1925:211–12). And one native-born American, a skilled worker in
Youngstown, equated Americanism with the union effort:

> I had relatives in the Revolutionary War, I fought for freedom in the Philippines
> myself, and I had three boys in the army fighting for democracy in France. One
> of them is lying in the Argonne Forest now. If my boy could give his life
> fighting for free democracy in Europe, I guess I can stand it to fight this battle
> through to the end. I am going to help my fellow workmen show Judge Gary
> that he can't act as if he was a king or kaiser. (Interchurch World Movement,
> 1920:132–33)

Workers saw no reason to consider patriotism incompatible with class
consciousness. They saw the labor movement as the truly American cause.
They carried American flags as standard props in protest marches. To

them, industrial conflict was part of the tradition of the American Revolution (Dawley, 1976:226 and passim). The 1877 railroad strikers were, according to a Massachusetts clergyman, "the lineal descendents of Samuel Adams, John Hancock, and the Massachusetts yeomen who began so great a disturbance a hundred years ago . . . only now the kings are money kings and then they were political kings" (quoted in Gutman, 1976:52). Eugene Debs used to compare the Pinkerton men at Homestead to the British at Lexington and Concord (Debs, 1970:224).

Thus, history provides little support for the supposedly debilitating effect of either ethnicity or nativism on working-class movements. However plausible, the theories do not stand up under close examination. Certainly if either factor—the immigrant's peasant conservatism or the native-born worker's racist hostility—had been the crucial obstacle to class consciousness, we would expect by now to have witnessed increased class conflict. Working-class immigration halted for the most part, but native workers did not then turn their hostility toward their employers. Second- and third-generation Americans have had no greater success in class conflict than their forebears. Yet both ethnic and nativist explanations of American exceptionalism survive today, immune from the criticism of a disconfirming history.

The Consistency of Ethnic
and Class Consciousness

Social theorists often indulge in such polar dichotomies as class versus ethnic consciousness.[11] This penchant for contrast often obscures the mutually reinforcing nature of the two poles. What first appear to be mutually exclusive opposites turn out to be parts of the same process. As we have seen in polyethnic America, ethnic loyalties often provide the foundation

---

11. This problem is not unique to the study of class consciousness. In a similar analysis half a world away, Lloyd and Susanne Rudolph (1967) showed that the supposed opposites of modernity and tradition were not opposite at all but closely linked. The most traditional of all ties, those within the castes of India,were used as the primary basis for mobilizing participation in the "modern" process of democratic politics. Modernity, instead of sweeping tradition away, reinforced it and formalized it in chartered caste associations. We believe that ethnicity and class mobilization share a similar symbiotic relationship.

for building a broader class consciousness, rather than inhibiting class solidarity.

The idea that ethnicity divides the American working class often rests on an implicit assumption that ethnic identifications are *psychologically* incompatible with class consciousness—as if workers could have only one strong social commitment. This view seems to suggest that if workers invest their emotional energy in an attachment to an ethnic community, they have no energy left for the class struggle.

There is no known law of psychology that says people are limited to a single social identification. On the contrary, it is clear that people can and do combine many strong identifications that are appropriate in different contexts.[12] Family, community, work, party, religion, ethnic group, nation—each can command a sense of attachment independent of the others. The individual who has a strong identification with any one such group is no less inclined toward a strong identification with any other. Indeed, as a psychological regularity, we might expect strong identifications to be positively correlated; the major contrast may be between the committed individual who is closely enmeshed in networks of both class and community, and the isolated individual who has little identification with any group.

There is little evidence from recent survey research that ethnic and class identifications are psychologically incompatible. The 1972 American National Election Study (ICPSR, 1975) asked respondents to select the groups in society that they "feel particularly close to—people who are most like you in their ideas and interests and feelings about things." The respondents chose from a list handed to them by the interviewer that included "Catholics," "Protestants," and "Jews"—a weak proxy for ethnic identification but one that defines the broadest boundaries of ethnicity. Some class-relevant groups were also listed: "businessmen," "middle-class people," and "workingmen."[13] Again, these are not unambiguous class categories, so we must be doubly cautious in suggesting that the questions

---

12. Frank Parkin (1979:21) criticizes the "either/or" assumption and argues, in a clever paraphrase of Marx, that man can "think of himself as an industrial worker in the morning, a Black in the afternoon, and an American in the evening, without ever thinking of himself wholly as a worker, a Black, or an American." See also our discussion in Chapter 3 of people's multiple images of the social structure and their place within it.

13. It is perhaps revealing of American social science that the authors of these questions could not quite bring themselves to inquire about the working *class*. Instead they substituted the innocuous and perhaps meaningless "workingmen"—a term that is, in addition, sexist.

TABLE 9.1. Closeness to workingmen among working-class Protestants
and Catholics

	Working-Class Catholics		Working-Class Protestants	
	Close to Catholics	*Not Close to Catholics*	*Close to Protestants*	*Not Close to Protestants*
Close to workingmen	56%	43%	62%	45%
Not close to workingmen	44%	57%	38%	55%
N	134	123	488	236

SOURCE: American Election Surveys, 1972.

tapped class and ethnic identifications. And we can only suppose that the
respondents interpreted the question of "feeling close to" as an indicator of
group identification. There is little research evidence on what meaning respondents impart to such questions, or with what other attitudes or behaviors any questions of "closeness" are associated.

Admitting all these reservations, we still find it interesting that the results show only positive relationships between class and religious "closeness": the closer people felt to their religious group, the closer they felt to
their class. For instance, among working-class (nonmanagerial) Catholics,
those who reported feeling close to other Catholics were more likely to report themselves as close to "workingmen" (see Table 9.1). The correlation
of closeness to Catholics and closeness to workingmen is moderately *positive* (Yule's Q = + 0.27); among working-class Protestants, the working-
men-Protestant correlation is also positive (Yule's Q = + 0.34). If ethnic
and class loyalties were competing, one might expect to find negative relationships between the two attitudes: respondents would be close to either
the religious or the class group, but not both. The results indicated instead
that respondents tended to feel close to both or to neither.

FIGURE 9.1. Class placements among 18 ethnic groups

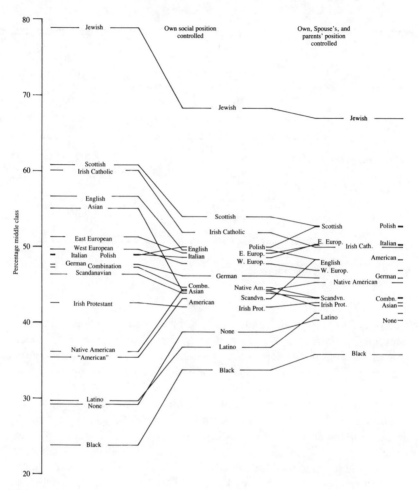

SOURCE: General Social Surveys.

It is more plausible, and more consistent with the data, to think of ethnic and class commitments as *independent* of each other, at least psychologically. They are separate realms of social life for most Americans. A person's class and ethnicity are distinct ties to the larger society, and Americans do not confuse them easily. When Americans think about class divisions, they do not worry about their ethnic heritage; they do not consider how recently their families came to these shores, nor where they came from, nor—for the most part—what religion they happened to bring with them. These considerations are irrelevant to a determination of class position or class interests.

This independence is confirmed by an analysis of the relationship of ethnicity to the subjective class placements analyzed in Chapter 4. With only a few exceptions, members of different ethnic groups respond quite similarly to the working-class—middle-class placement question. It is true that Americans from English stock think of themselves as middle class more often than do, for instance, Americans of Polish or Italian extraction—although the difference is smaller than many might expect—but this is irrelevant for evaluating the impact of ethnicity on working-class solidarity. Americans of English background are more often managers, earn larger incomes, and have had somewhat more schooling. Although their advantages are relatively minor, their structural position entirely explains their more frequent middle-class placement. When we compare, say, a Polish-American machinist making $20,000 and having a high school diploma with a similar "English-stock" machinist, both are equally likely to call themselves working class. Ethnicity is largely unrelated to class placements once the "objective" class characteristics are held constant.

Figure 9.1 demonstrates the general unimportance of ethnicity for class placements. The graphs begin with simple proportions of each ethnic group who report middle-class self-placement.[14] Next, they show the esti-

---

14. Our ethnicity coding is based primarily on the respondents' own reports of what countries their ancestors came from. If more than one country was named, respondents were asked to choose the country they felt closest to. A few were unable to make this choice, so we have added a residual "combination" category. Two other residual categories are also included: a large group that could not name any country of ancestry, and a smaller group that insisted on naming "America" or some region within the United States. Two exceptions were made to the country-of-ancestry basis: Jews and Blacks were given their own categories, based on the respondents' religion and race, respectively. In addition, to get samples of sufficient size for estimating "average" class placements reliably, we collapsed some of the specific national categories into broader groups: e.g., Czechs, Greeks, Hungarians, Russians, Lithuanians, Yugoslavians, and Rumanians all merit separate categories in the original data but are combined here into East European. This process loses some detail, but given the pattern of results where such single-nation detail *is* available, we doubt that the conclusions we draw are much affected by the broader scope of our classifications. These procedures created 18 separate ethnic categories in both the GSS and the Election Sample. See Table 9.A for sample sizes.

mated proportions after controls for the "basic model" variables—the person's managerial class, occupational prestige, years of school, and family income. They then recalculate the estimated proportions after additional controls for spouse and parental characteristics. Ethnicity is closely bound to these family contexts, and specifying controls for spouse and family background will help us to sort what part of the ethnic differences in class placements can be attributed to the respondents' own positions, what part to their family's positions, and what part to the more general ethnic community.

Two general conclusions are illustrated by these graphs. First, the extent of ethnic difference in class placements is greatly reduced by the personal and family controls; most ethnic differences become negligible by the time all the controls are entered. Second, there are two notable exceptions to this pattern: Blacks and Jews, especially, retain their distinctiveness after all controls, and it shows up in each of the samples.

Beginning with the exceptions, the class placements of minority groups are often distinctive in ways that cannot be explained by the respondents' own or their family's position in U.S. society. On the one hand, Jews stand out as remarkably middle class; on the other, Blacks and (to a lesser extent) Latinos and Native Americans tend to be exceptionally working class. Of course, Jews *are* more middle class than the rest of the population: 52 percent of the GSS sample of Jews hold managerial positions, compared with only 27 percent of the rest of the population; 64 percent of Jews went to college, but only 34 percent of the rest of the sample did. And Blacks are more working class than whites: 87 percent have nonmanagerial positions, versus 71 percent of whites; 74 percent never went to college, versus 65 percent of whites. But these differences cannot explain the ultimate positions in the graphs, since the *individual* socioeconomic positions are held constant. The controls reduce the distinctiveness of Jews, Blacks, Latinos, and Native Americans, but they do not eliminate the differences. The class placements of Blacks and Jews, at least, are still quite distinctive and are likely to remain so, no matter how extensive a set of controls we might include. Black managers with college degrees more often assert a working-class identity than equivalent white managers; Jewish factory workers who dropped out of high school more often assume a middle-class placement than their Gentile counterparts. Apparently, at least at these extremes, Americans "borrow" class characteristics from their ethnic communities even if they do not as individuals fit the class labels.

We will postpone a more detailed consideration of the racial differences until the next chapter. Racial conflict has played such a recurrent role in explaining American working-class exceptionalism that it deserves separate treatment. But these ethnic/racial characteristics are relevant for class perceptions only at the extremes. For the vast majority of white non-Jewish Americans, ethnic affiliations do not enter into class perceptions. If we set aside the five "minority" groups—Jews, Blacks, Latinos, Native Americans, and non-European (primarily Asian) immigrants—the differences among the remaining 13 categories (81 percent of the samples) are negligible. These groups all crowd the middle of Figure 9.1 with little seeming order.

We can compute a composite "beta" statistic that expresses the total amount of variation in middle-class placements associated with the ethnic categories and then test whether the coefficient is statistically different from chance expectations. Table 9.2 reports these statistics for both the 18- and 13-category classifications. The 18-category classification produces small (in comparison with the controls) but statistically significant beta statistics. The size of the ethnic "effect" diminishes greatly with controls, as illustrated in Figure 9.1, but the coefficient remaining after applying all controls is still statistically significant. When the five minority categories are removed from the analysis, however, the size of the ethnicity effect diminishes to virtual irrelevance; we could expect by chance alone to find such differences among these 13 ethnic groups.[15]

Moreover, the 13 groups array themselves in no particular order. Northern Europeans are no more middle class than eastern and southern Europeans. Typically Protestant groups are no more middle-class than typically Catholic ethnics. The ultimate position of the 13 groups in Figure 9.1 is unrelated to any identifiable characteristic; their positions are uncorrelated with the groups' average class, income, or educational position; the results from the GSS samples are uncorrelated with the results from the Election Sample. In short, the best conclusion to be drawn from the middle-class placements of the 13 groups is that they fall into an essentially random order.[16]

15. The increment to the chi-square resulting from the 18 ethnic categories is 68.8—statistically significant with 17 degrees of freedom. The increment to the chi-square resulting from the 13 ethnic categories is only 19.5, not significant at the 0.05 level with 12 degrees of freedom.

16. Despite this randomness, one category may be worthy of at least passing note. Americans who cannot or will not report any ethnic affiliation are among the most working class of

220

Fear and Loathing?

TABLE 9.2. Strength of ethnic effects on class perceptions, before and after controls for class position and socioeconomic status

	Equation with 18 Ethnic Categories (N = 7,794)				Equation with 13 Ethnic Categories (N = 6,293)
	No Controls	*Own Position*	*Own & Spouse's Position*	*Own, Spouse's & Parents' Position*	*Own, Spouse's, & Parents' Position*
Composite effects of					
Ethnicity	.314	.161	.151	.140	.078
Own position[a]		.589	.510	.469	.521
Spouse's position[b]			.225	.203	.194
Parents' position[c]				.158	.144

SOURCE: General Social Surveys.
NOTES:
[a]Own position variables include labor force status, manager (mental labor), occupational prestige, education, family income, and sex.
[b]Spouse's position variables include a marital status dummy, labor force status, manager (mental labor), occupational prestige, and education.
[c]Parents' position variables include mother's education and a dummy variable for missing data on mother's education, father's education and a dummy variable for missing data on father's education, father's managerial (mental labor) position, father's farm occupation, father's occupational prestige, and a dummy variable for missing data on father's occupation.

all groups. This is true for both the GSS (where only Blacks are more working class) and the Election Sample (where only Irish Protestants among the nonminority groups, together with Blacks and Native Americans, are more working class). All other groups, both the so-called ethnics and the more "establishment" northern Europeans are more middle class. These non-ethnics, presumably the more "native-stock" Americans, are also more objectively working class, but they remain more subjectively working class even when compared with ethnics of equivalent social position.

Nor are other aspects of ethnicity much related to class placement. The distinction between "ethnic" and "native stock" is sometimes a proxy for a Catholic-Protestant distinction, and in many ways religion is the most significant ethnic division remaining within white America. According to the so-called triple melting-pot thesis (Kennedy, 1944; Herberg, 1955), the simpler religious divisions have outlasted the more diverse set of national origins. Catholicism in particular is alleged to have stifled working-class consciousness in the United States (Perlman, 1928:168; Harrington, 1976: xi).

We have already noted the distinctive middle-class position of Jews. To test for further religious differences, we repeated the analysis using only the Catholic-Protestant dichotomy, omitting all "minority" respondents from the analysis. As might be expected from the previous results, we found religion unrelated to class self-placement. After we control for the "basic model" variables, 46 percent of Catholic men and 47 percent of Protestant men identify as middle class. Similarly, 46 percent of Catholic women and 43 percent of Protestant women identify as middle class. Such small differences were repeated in an analysis of the Election Sample and were statistically nonsignificant in each case.

Similarly, recentness of immigration does not enter into the working-class–middle-class placements. By the time of these surveys, a majority of adults were fourth-generation Americans; still, a significant minority had at least one immigrant grandparent or even parent, and an even smaller number were immigrants themselves. In both surveys, middle-class placements do not differ among these generations once personal and family socioeconomic position are controlled.

One possibility remains of a way in which ethnicity could interfere with class perception. Certain ethnic groups—especially, we might guess, those with strong ethnic attachments—might be more "confused" about their class placements. Class divisions may simply be less relevant among such groups, so that they perceive class position less clearly. In such cases there would be a weaker relationship between actual class location and the subjective class perception: more managers would choose the working-class label, but they would be balanced by more workers choosing a middle-class label. Overall, the group ends up with an average frequency of middle-class and working-class placements, but there is less consistency between objective and subjective class position.

We test this possibility by calculating the difference in class placements between managers and workers within each of the 18 ethnic groups, within the Protestant and Catholic categories, and within each immigrant genera-

TABLE 9.3. Manager-nonmanager differences in class
perceptions among Protestants and Catholics

| | Adjusted Percentage Middle-Class Self-Placement | |
	Catholics	*Protestants*
Managers	57%	61%
	(431)	(995)
Workers	41%	38%
	(1,034)	(2,070)
Difference	16%	22%

SOURCE: General Social Surveys.
NOTE: Sample sizes are presented in parentheses. Women and men are pooled
because results were similar. All percentages are adjusted to means on occupational prestige, respondent's education, and family income. Managers are defined
as all the census classifications of managers and professionals except technicians.

tion. If any group blurs the division between classes, then the difference
between managers and nonmanagers should be smaller for that group. We
found no systematic pattern across ethnic groups in how clearly they perceive the manager-worker division. The differences between managers and
workers vary somewhat from one group to the next, but there is no pattern
to these differences. Nor are they very large; we could expect such differences to arise entirely by chance. The separate class placements among
Protestants and Catholics are displayed in Table 9.3. The class division
appears slightly stronger among Protestants than among Catholics. However, the difference is no greater than we would expect by chance; in fact,
in the American Election Sample (not shown), the manager-worker division is slightly larger for the Catholics.

In sum, we have been unable to detect any substantial effect of ethnicity
on the class perception process. With the exception of Blacks and Jews,
ethnic groups in the same class and status position have the same propor-

tion of working- and middle-class placements. Nor is there any evidence that ethnicity interferes in the translation of objective class into subjective class. At the psychological level, at least, class and ethnicity are distinct phenomena in American society.

Appendix

TABLE 9.A. Sample sizes of 18 ethnic groups

Ethnicity	N	%
English	903	11.6
Scottish	195	2.5
Scandinavian	374	4.8
German	1331	17.1
Other West European	436	5.6
Irish Protestant	467	6.0
Irish Catholic	296	3.8
Polish	187	2.4
Other East European	280	3.6
Combination	786	10.1
American only	86	1.1
Other	101	1.3
Jewish	179	2.3
Hispanic	288	3.7
Native American	171	2.2
Black	763	9.8
None	553	7.1

SOURCE: General Social Surveys.

CHAPTER 10
MILITANT BLACKS?

The Persistent Significance of Class

For most of this century, Black people have been kept on the lowest rungs of the social structure and segregated from the dominant culture. The castelike nature of the racial barrier has frequently allowed white social science to ignore variations in social class, lifestyle, life chances, and social differentiations of any sort within the Black community. Even as the formal legal barriers between races began to erode with the civil rights movement, social science research on Blacks in the 1950s and 1960s most often either ignored class differentiations or focused on lower-class Blacks, often generalizing their conditions to the entire Black population (Billingsley, 1968; Rainwater and Yancey, 1967). Furthermore, research on class perceptions has tended to exclude Blacks altogether or to identify differences whose theoretical significance gets lost in a broader study of whites' perceptions. Not surprisingly, the empirical results and theoretical generalizations about the relationship of the experience of racial oppression to perceptions of class structure have frequently been inconsistent and contradictory.

Who is Black and Middle Class?

As early as 1899, W. E. B. Du Bois (1967:310) cautioned: "There is no surer way of misunderstanding the Negro or of being misunderstood by him than by ignoring manifest differences of condition and power." Since the 1930s and 1940s, students of Black life have investigated class in the Black community—from its structural sources to its social, economic, and psychological implications (Dollard, 1937; Frazier, 1939; Drake and Cayton, 1945; Cox, 1948). More recently, there has been much research

225

and popular attention directed to the Black middle class (e.g., Wilson, 1978; Willie, 1979; Collins, 1983). That work generally acknowledges the growth of the Black middle class since World War II, even as a debate escalates over who is Black and middle class and what it means to be Black and middle class (e.g., Hare, 1973; Wilson, 1978; Higginbotham, 1981; Newby, 1981; Collins, 1983). Throughout this literature, there seems to be agreement on at least one issue: being Black and middle class is different from being white and middle class. For our purpose—to explore the subjective class identifications of Blacks—two important themes in this literature are especially relevant.

Middle class as "middle mass"

One thread in the literature is that the Black middle class is typically defined more broadly than the white middle class. The comments of Hare and Billingsley illustrate this theme:

> Objectively, just where the Black middle class begins and ends is anybody's guess. It clearly includes professionals, white collar workers and skilled workers. But what is middle class for whites may not be the standard that Blacks will use. The Black middle class includes the semi-skilled. Bus drivers would be middle class for Blacks as would be almost any homeowner. A policeman or mail carrier might be lower middle class for whites but might rank much higher among Blacks. A physician, or even a teacher, might be "upper class" in some Black social circles. (Hare, 1973:45)

> The indices of social class which have been developed in social science research are relatively more reliable when used within white ethnic groups, where they were developed, than when used unmodified with Negro groups. For example, the family of a high school principal in a white community may be considered middle class. In a Negro community, however, in all probability, the Negro high school principal's family will be considered upper class. (Billingsley, 1968:122–23)

Wilson (1978), like others before him (Frazier, 1957; Billingsley, 1968; Hare, 1973), has employed a definition of the Black middle class that encompasses all white-collar workers and skilled blue-collar workers. It derives from Weber's (1921) notion that classes reflect shared economic "life chances" largely determined by market relations. According to Wilson's view of the Black community, life chances most sharply diverge between the white-collar and skilled-worker middle class on the one hand and the semiskilled and unskilled working class on the other.

This inclusive "middle-mass" view of the Black middle class is put forth at a time when even the more restrictive blue-collar–white-collar dichotomy (also frequently employed as an operationalization of Weber's notion of class) is generally dismissed as too broadly defined to represent the middle class among whites.

Figure 10.1 summarizes key differences among Wilson's "middle-mass" view of the Black class structure, a traditional "blue-collar–white-collar" dichotomy, and Braverman's "professional/managerial-class–working-class" dichotomy. With minor exceptions these occupational groupings represent traditional operationalizations of the three different views of the class structure.[1] It is apparent that Wilson's view of the Black middle class is the most inclusive, whereas the two versions of the class structure that have not focused specifically on the Black community view the middle class as a more restricted group.

The middle class as "respected community members"

A second prominent theme in the post–World War II scholarship on class in the Black community suggests that Black people see themselves and others as middle class on the basis of criteria that are relatively independent of the material realities of their lives. That is, they do not see the middle class in relation to an objective position in the class structure or the prestige hierarchy of the society at large. Instead, they see class as a primarily nonmaterial, ideological phenomenon. In the Black community, to consider oneself and to be considered by others as middle class requires that one display middle-class behaviors, such as maintaining stable family relationships, being active in community and church affairs, and spending money and dressing in particular ways. Typical of this approach are the positions of Frazier and Billingsley:

---

1. The primary difference between these broad occupational categories and the operationalization of the class categories involves the case of foremen, who are blue collar (and thus working class) according to the Weberian dichotomy. Due to their role in managing and controlling the activities of workers, however, Braverman (1974) classifies foremen in the professional/managerial class: i.e., the "middle class."

FIGURE 10.1. Three models of class structure in the
Black community

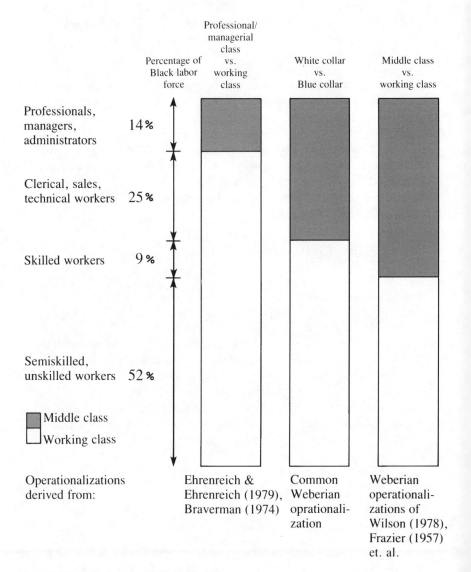

SOURCE: U.S. Census, 1980, Table 279.

In this segregated world, especially in cities, a class structure slowly emerged
which was based upon social distinctions such as education and conventional
behavior, rather than upon occupation and income. At the top of the social pyra-
mid there was a small upper class. The superior status of this class was due
chiefly to its differentiation from the great mass of the Negro population because
of a family heritage which resulted partly from its mixed ancestry. (Frazier,
1957:20)

Not only do absolute levels of education, income, and occupation take on somewhat different meanings in the Negro community, but factors other than these,
including respectability and community activity, loom large in the attribution of
social status. (Billingsley, 1968:122–23)

In addition to displaying middle-class behavior, individuals must maintain middle-class values and place a high value on education as a mobility
channel:

The middle class is marked off from the lower class by a pattern of behavior expressed in stable family and associational relationships, in great concern with
"front" and "respectability," and in a drive for "getting ahead." All this finds an
objective measure in standard of living — the way people spend their money and
in "public behavior." (Drake and Cayton, 1945:661–62)

According to this view, a retail sales clerk who values education highly,
works hard, is a stable community member, and attends church might be
viewed as middle class in the Black community. Her middle-class position
would be recognized despite her low educational attainment; despite the
low value placed on her work (with its related low earnings and prestige)
by the wider (white) society; and despite the lack of authority, power, or
control vested in her position. In this view, the Black middle class is substantially within the grasp of most individuals, separate from their relationship to the system of production. Class is viewed as a function of attitude,
behavior, and personal character; it is independent of power in the wider
society or the character of one's occupation.

Views such as this focus attention on the alternate visions of the social
system that are developed by superexploited groups. They illustrate how
Black people validate themselves and their people, in the face of racist
assaults on their culture, by setting internal community standards for
evaluating worth. For example, recent research (Higginbotham, 1985)
identifies two values explicitly taught in many Black homes: "There is no
such thing as a lowly occupation," and "Do the best you can, whatever you

do." Such teachings clearly imply that a person should be judged not by the type of work he or she does (something over which one has little control in a racist society) but rather by the quality of his or her performance in the role (something over which one has more control). In short, one's worth in the society should not be determined by one's place in the restricted occupational spheres to which Blacks are relegated in a racist society.

The presence of a different value system for judging self-worth and esteem does not necessarily mean that the material conditions of life are ignored when Blacks evaluate their position in the *class* structure. To return to the earlier example, the retail sales clerk who attends church, strives to get ahead, works hard, and behaves appropriately may have earned a level of respect and esteem in the Black community that would be unattainable for a similarly situated white woman. But the essential question here is whether the same criteria that seem to play a major role in the assignment of respect or esteem also determine perceptions of position in the objective class structure. If so, we would not expect that position in the objective class structure would predict Blacks' class identifications, because middle-class self-identification would rest on internal community value and behavior, separate from class position in the broader society. The following analysis explores the relationship of objective class and class self-placements among Blacks.

Managerial-class division

Our data indicate that the division between the professional/managerial class (mental labor) and the working class (manual labor) does represent a meaningful class distinction in the minds of Black Americans (see Table 10.1). Middle-class self-placements are reported by 22 percent of the men, and 19 percent of the working women. Further, managers and workers differ greatly in their middle-class self-placement. Choosing the middle-class label among men were 53 percent of the managers and only 18 percent of the workers; among working women, 39 percent of the managers and 16 percent of the workers. For Black men and working women, these are differences of 36 percent and 24 percent respectively, in the middle-class self-placements of managers and workers.

These gross differences do not represent conclusive evidence of class-based perceptions. The gaps may merely reflect the higher income, education, and prestige associated with mental labor. Table 10.2 displays the data after adjustments for these status factors (see appendix, Table 10.A,

TABLE 10.1. Black sample sizes and middle-class
self-placements

	Men	Women
N (unweighted)	728	777
N (weighted)	661.2	661
% Middle Class		
Total Sample	21.8%	19.3%
Managers	53%	39%
Workers	18%	16%
Difference	36%	24%

SOURCES: General Social Surveys and American Election Surveys.

for equations). Among men, the 36 percent difference between managers and workers remains a 25 percent gap after controlling for income, education, and occupational prestige. For working women, status differences account for 11 of the 24 percentage points separating managers and workers, and class perceptions for the remaining 13 points of the mental-manual gap in middle-class self-placements.

The effect of mental labor on Blacks' choice of the middle-class label is twice as large for Black men as for Black working women. This finding is consistent with the results previously presented for white women: class divisions are not as sharply defined and perceived by women or by workers in female-dominated occupations. Of course, the sex-segregated nature of occupations is even more pronounced for Black women. Racial oppression has historically placed them in a classic double-bind situation. On the one hand, racist institutions devalued and exploited Black men's labor so that the survival of Black families—the women's domain—would depend on Black women's employment outside the home. Thus, during the first half of the twentieth century, labor force participation rates among Black women ranged from 37 to 50 percent (U.S. Bureau of the Census, 1973a). However, Black women were pushed into the same racially restricted labor

TABLE 10.2. Effects of managerial position on
            Black class perceptions

	Adjusted Percentage Middle-Class Self-Placement	
	Men	*Women*
Managers	42	29
Workers	17	16
Class difference	25	13
Status difference	12	11

SOURCES: General Social Surveys and American Election Surveys.
NOTE: Percentages represent middle-class placement at mean values of education, income, and occupational prestige. Class difference = the effect of class net of all status variables; status difference = the effect of all status variables combined net of the class variable. The probit equation is in Table 10.A.

market, so that paid employment options were limited to the least desirable and dirtiest of "women's jobs." Until 1960 approximately 60 percent of employed Black women worked as domestics in private households (U.S. Bureau of Census, 1973a). More recently, Black women have entered jobs formerly held by white women just as those jobs were becoming proletarianized, routinized, deskilled, and devalued—as is the case with clerical work (Braverman, 1974; Higginbotham, 1983).

Despite the way that race and gender oppression have produced a uniquely restricted set of work and family options for Black women, the data indicate that the managerial class distinction is meaningful to Black women's as well as Black men's view of themselves in the class system. Perhaps as striking as the apparent strength of the mental-manual division is the undeniable weakness of the status factors for predicting Blacks' class self-placements. Neither education, income, nor occupational prestige affects the class identifications of men, and among working women, only additional education produces more middle-class self-placements.

Previous studies of class identification have typically ignored Blacks, but Jackman and Jackman (1973) and Evers (1976) concluded that income alone (not education, occupational prestige, or collar color) has a significant impact on Blacks' perceptions of class. In their more extensive study of class identification, Jackman and Jackman (1983:86) find that even income doesn't predict class identification among the Black working or middle classes. They conclude that racial identity overwhelms the impact of "socioeconomic achievements" in Black consciousness. Our results suggest that class identity is quite strong among Blacks but that it is shaped by the mental-manual class division, not by "socioeconomic achievements." Additional increments in income, education, or prestige—factors that may be important in the interpersonal realm (for self-esteem, respectability, and the like)—do not alter Blacks' perceptions of their position in the broader social class system.

Other class divisions: collar color, middle mass

While the managerial division is an important class distinction among Blacks, it may not be the only—or even the most meaningful—class system they perceived. We will examine two alternative conceptions of class that have been preferred by some Black scholars (e.g., Frazier, 1957; Willie, 1976; Wilson, 1978).

Figure 10.2 summarizes the results of tests of the middle-mass and manual-nonmanual class divisions (see Table 10.B for equations). The middle-mass division suggests that the critical class boundaries are those separating skilled manual laborers from unskilled and semiskilled workers. The data are presented so that we can evaluate the middle-mass and collar-color divisions and a close approximation of the managerial division in the same model. This is done by identifying the increment in the percentage of middle-class identifiers from semiskilled and unskilled workers to three other occupational groupings: (1) skilled workers (the middle-mass model); (2) lower white-collar, clerical, and sales workers (the manual-nonmanual model); and (3) managers and professionals (the professional/managerial model).

The middle-mass class model is not supported by these data: there is no significant difference in the middle-class identifications of skilled craftsmen and semi- and unskilled workers. The lifestyle and social rank differences between skilled workers and other blue-collar workers that have

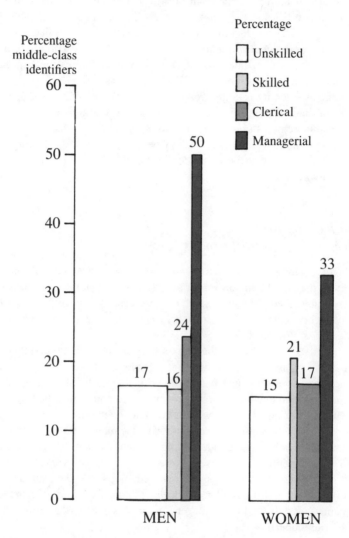

FIGURE 10.2. Effects of several class divisions on middle-class placements

SOURCES: General Social Surveys and American Election Surveys.

been noted by Black scholars (e.g., Frazier, 1957; Billingsley, 1968; Hare, 1973) may affect a worker's esteem in the Black community, but they are not interpreted as *class* boundaries.

The next occupational grouping—clerical and sales work—is also one that means little for class identification. Other than the greater middle-class self-placements produced by the higher education, income, and prestige of the work, clerical and sales workers are no more likely to identify as middle class than are unskilled and semiskilled workers. Among Black men, most of these clerical workers are postal clerks, file clerks, mail carriers, and the like. However, one might expect this division to produce the greatest increment in middle-class identification for the working women, since the nature of race and gender segregation has meant that even today a negligible number of Black women have been able to secure skilled crafts positions (Westcott, 1982). So the first sizable group of Black women above such low-status manual laborer positions as domestic and service workers, farm workers, clothing pressers and ironers, and other operatives are in clerical and sales work. But even for Black women, clerical work does not appear to increase middle-class identifications beyond those of manual laborers. Black women in clerical and sales positions clearly see themselves as working class and more closely aligned with domestic workers' standing than with the professionals and managers for whom they work.

In many areas of life—for example, occupational health and safety— being a clerical worker or salesperson rather than a manual laborer may mean facing different risks, stresses, opportunities, and challenges. But when Black women assess their standing in the class structure, they see that the jobs are still created and controlled by others, people are still supervised, and power is still vested in the "bosses." Slightly higher income may mean more control over other aspects of their lives but does not place those women in a position to fully shape their own lives.

These data clearly reinforce other findings that the critical class division perceived is the one between managers and workers. Even when we compare skilled workers and managers who have similar levels of education, income, and prestige, managers are 26.4 percent more likely to identify themselves as middle class (see Figure 10.2). The differences are not as great for women, but 15.8 percent more women managers than clerical workers identify as middle class at the same status levels.[2] In short, the

---

2. We also examined the role of authority and self-employment in Blacks' class perceptions. Neither factor was significantly related to middle-class identification once the mental-

mental-manual dichotomy is by far the most meaningful dimension in determining who is seen as middle class in the Black community.

Comparisons of Blacks and Whites

To this point, the data suggest that the perceived criterion for inclusion in
the middle class is the same among Blacks as among whites—managerial
position. But we have not yet directly compared the class identification
process for Blacks and whites. Although the arguments of Frazier, (1957)
Willie (1976), Wilson (1978), and others seem to suggest that Blacks are
less class conscious—and more status conscious—than whites, such
a conclusion is not self-evident. In fact, several researchers have rather
forcefully contended that the Black working class is *more* class conscious,
has a stronger sense of social injustice, and is more militant than the white
working class (Leggett, 1968; Geschwender, 1977; Robinson and Bell,
1978; Schlozman and Verba, 1979; Gurin et al., 1980; and Schulman et
al., 1983). Bonacich's (1980:16) summary statement is typical of this perspective: "Black workers in the United States, despite their subproletarian
status (or perhaps more accurately, because of it) are undoubtedly more
class conscious and ready for socialist revolution than the white working
class."

Some of the research on Blacks has shown a tendency to draw such conclusions from demonstrations of militant behavior; for example, Geschwender (1977) takes incidents of Black worker militancy as evidence that
Black workers are more class conscious than white workers. We have repeatedly cautioned against assuming that lack of successful worker mili-

---

manual and status variables were controlled. The test had limitations, however, that caution
against quickly dismissing these domains. Wives were excluded from the analysis because the
supervision question was not asked of spouse's occupation. Moreover, these samples are limited to GSS surveys, while the earlier analyses included the Election Sample. The sample
sizes remaining are men, 214; working women, 192. Statistically distinguishing the separate
effects of three class categories (mental labor, authority, and self-employment) while controlling the four status variables is especially problematic, since the numbers of Black self-
employed (men, 13; working women, 9) and supervisors are small. Further, the coefficients
for self-employment are fairly large even though not statistically significant. In sum, however, we believe that better data are required before we dismiss them as irrelevant class factors
in the Black community.

tancy or revolution is evidence of a lack of class consciousness. In this case, even though the conclusion is reversed—Blacks are deemed more, not less, class conscious—the inference is no less troublesome. Blacks' class consciousness must be assessed by direct examination, not inferred from militant acts.

Leggett's study of Detroit autoworkers and the study by Schulman and his colleagues of a Southern textile community are exceptions because they directly question both Black and white workers on class issues. In part, Leggett (1968:4) also tends to equate militancy with class consciousness: "Many American Negroes have displayed class consciousness by expressing militant views and by taking aggressive political action. The militant Negro is particularly common among blue-collar workers found in large urban ghettoes." But in Leggett's scale for measuring class consciousness, the highest levels—more frequently reported by Blacks—clearly indicate a willingness for social change; however, that may reflect a "race" rather than a "class" consciousness.[3] Fortunately, the study also provides us with a wealth of comments from Black workers that attest to a strong sense of class thinking in the Black community. Here, for example, are some Black responses to the question: "Who gets the profits when business booms in Detroit?"

> You know who gets the profits. The stockholders. The big wigs get the big fat bonuses the more they produce.

> The manufacturers. The worker just gets a living out of it. The profits go to the operators.

> The owners of big business. The rich man. He's the one that gets the profits. (Leggett, 1968:9, 100)

To explore whether Blacks are more or less likely than whites to perceive class divisions, we will examine two factors. First, since Blacks are

---

3. Specifically, "militancy" was measured by willingness to take action against a landlord, and "egalitarianism" by a willingness to distribute the wealth of the country evenly. Particularly in the case of the landlord issue, race consciousness could have been an equally strong motivation for Detroit Blacks—many of whom probably lived in white-owned buildings or houses, and all of whom were well aware of the restrictions on housing that derived from racial, not class, discrimination. Given the high levels of racial segregation, housing is not a good issue on which to discriminate between race and class consciousness among Black people.

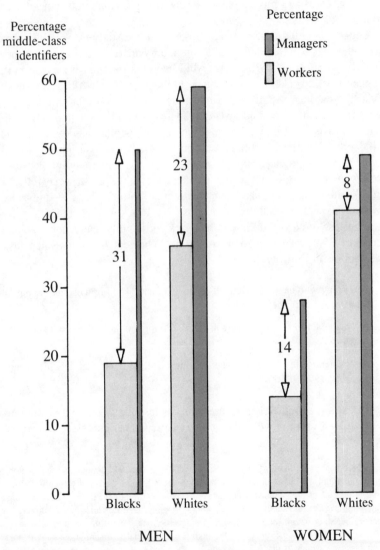

FIGURE 10.3. Black-white differences in class
self-placements

SOURCES: General Social Surveys and American Election Surveys.

more concentrated in the working class than whites, they should be more likely than whites to identify as working class. Second, if class divisions are more clearly perceived in the Black community, then the difference between Black managers and workers in the percentage of middle-class placements should be greater than the gap between white managers and workers.[4]

Figure 10.3 displays the data from the GSS and the Election Sample bearing on the two class questions (see Table 10.C for equations). First, even when comparing Black and white workers having equivalent levels of education, income, and prestige, 17 percent more white males (N = 6,544) and 27 percent more white females (N = 4,709) identify as working class than Black men (N = 679) and Black women (N = 698). Only 19 percent of all Black male workers but fully 36 percent of all white male workers identify as middle class. These differences are even more pronounced among working women, where only 14 percent of Blacks but 41 percent of whites identify with the middle class. Black workers seem more reluctant to take on the middle-class label than white workers. Although by a smaller margin, it is also the case that white managers and professionals are more likely to identify as middle class than their Black counterparts: among the men, 59 percent of white managers but 50 percent of Black managers; among working women, 49 percent of white managers but only 28 percent of Black managers.

Why do so many Black managers and professionals consider themselves working class? One common but, we believe, false explanation is that racial oppression diminishes the importance of class in a person's identity. For example, Jackman and Jackman (1983) cite attachment to race to explain the finding that Black class identifications were not related to prestige, income, or education. They discovered that Blacks who identified as

---

4. Past research on class self-placements is not particularly helpful in answering these questions. For the most part, differences in class thinking resulting from racial oppression were neither expected nor explored. The few notable exceptions unfortunately reached different conclusions. Evers (1976), Schlozman and Verba (1979), and Schulman et al. (1983) report that Blacks are more likely to identify as working class than are whites of equivalent social position. Hodge and Treiman (1968) find no such difference, and Jackman and Jackman (1983) report that Blacks are more likely to identify as poor. Some studies have focused on the impact of status characteristics on class identification but never directly on class. They provide some evidence of status identification (Jackman and Jackman, 1973; Evers, 1976) or the lack of status identification (Jackman and Jackman, 1983), but leave us without any understanding of class perceptions in the Black community.

middle or working class felt warmer toward "Blacks" than they did toward their own class. The Jackmans concluded that for middle- and working-class Blacks, class identity is secondary to racial identity, and "subordinate statuses are more personally compelling—people are not equally influenced by all their group memberships, as pluralists assume, but instead are most sensitive to those that give them a subordinate status" (1983: 86).

A key problem with this line of reasoning is its assumption that human beings rank-order their multiple statuses. An emerging body of Black feminist thought makes clear that Black women (a group with the additional subordinate status of gender) do not rank the multiple dimensions of their oppression (e.g., Dill, 1983). Furthermore, Black feminists contend that the pressure to rank statuses is externally imposed and is actively resisted by Black women, who employ the concept of simultaneity of oppression to represent their experience (Smith, 1983). Collins points to the absurdity of such a ranking from the point of view of Black women themselves:

> For Black women, subordinate status attached to an array of dichotomies (e.g., race, class, sex) is a personally experienced, culturally based contradiction that means, in a fundamental sense, if one were to rank oppressions, one is denying part of oneself. Thus, Black feminist thought has been concerned with the connections between systems of oppression, and with finding out exactly what holds this interlocking system together. (forthcoming: 10)

There are avenues for further investigation that might yield information about the greater working-class content in the work situations of Black professionals and managers. Black professionals and managers are less likely to be self-employed (Newby, 1983; Collins, 1983) or to wield significant authority, and are generally to be found in the public sector in relatively powerless positions (Higginbotham, forthcoming). Sharon Collins (1983) notes that middle-class Blacks in both the public and private sectors tend to work in jobs with "segregated functions"—administering to the Black working class in programs designed to ensure their continued dependency. Many who hold jobs in the public sector are "street level bureaucrats" (Lipsky, 1980). These professionals administer social services in schools, social welfare agencies, and other public-sector spheres to a clientele that is increasingly composed of minorities. The current crisis of capitalism has been particularly harsh on these workers. All too frequently they are caught between a bureaucracy facing retrenchment and a growing population of needy clients. Despite its professional nature, the work becomes highly routinized, and workers retain little control over its shape.

Likewise, neither are Black workers likely to be found in the skilled and more desirable working-class occupations, or in positions that retain authority over others. They are more likely to be "ghettoized" into the most menial, least stable, and least desirable of working-class jobs.

In addition to the characteristics of the jobs that Blacks do, a greater working-class identification among Blacks may reflect the impact of the more working-class family origins of Black workers and managers. The castelike nature of the racial barrier during most of this century has meant that Blacks have only recently begun to enter the managerial class and are more likely than whites to have been raised in working-class or "under class" families (Wilson, 1978). As we shall see in Chapter 11, there is evidence among the white samples that the class of the family of origin exerts a continuing influence on people's current class perceptions.

Despite the greater working-class identification among Black managers, the data also suggest that the perceived class gap between Black managers and Black workers is greater than between white managers and white workers, whether they are working women or men. Among men having the same status characteristics, Black managers are 31 percent more likely than Black workers to identify as middle class, while white managers are only 23 percent more middle class than white workers. For working women, the perceived class divisions are also greater among Blacks than among whites: Black women managers are 14 percent more likely than Black workers to identify as middle class; white managerial women, only 8 percent more likely than white workers. In short, the weight of the evidence comparing Black and white class divisions seems to suggest that managerial class boundaries are more clearly perceived in the Black community than among whites.

But if Blacks are more class conscious than whites, they also appear to be less status conscious. A comparison of average Black and white workers shows that each additional year of education for Black male workers increases middle-class self-placements by 0.83 percent; the same year produces 4.35 percent more middle-class identifiers among whites. A 10 percent increase in average income produces a 1.5 percent increase in middle-class placements for white workers but only a 0.3 percent increase for Black workers. The fact that occupational prestige is not significant for Blacks or whites suggests that it is unimportant to the class identifications of either group.

For working women, each additional year of education among Blacks becomes a 2.4 percent increase in middle-class self-placements; for whites, 5.8 percent. A 10 percent increase in income for working women produces 1.2 percent more white middle-class identifiers but a nonsignificant decrease of 1.0 percent in Black middle-class placements. As was the case for men, occupational prestige is unimportant to both Black and white working women's class perceptions.

In sum, the data consistently assert that Black people are less likely than whites to translate status differences into different class orientations. This is in no way to suggest that Black people are oblivious to status distinctions. Recall that several Black researchers have carefully documented the attention paid to status in the Black community, especially among the Black middle class (Frazier, 1957). Status variations may be critical to such interpersonal issues as self-esteem, honor, and friendship choices or such lifestyle issues as consumption patterns and preferences. However, those influences must be clearly distinguished from the perception of class. Status divisions may be no less important in the Black community for determining how one spends one's money, but differences in income or in education are less likely to be confused with true class boundaries among Blacks than among whites. These data support the conclusions of Leggett (1968) and Geschwender (1977) that Blacks are indeed more class conscious than whites.

Trends in Class Self-Placement

It is difficult to discuss the class positions or perceptions of Black Americans without a historical perspective—even more problematic than for whites—although ahistorical empiricism makes little sense in any case. Most scholars agree that only since World War II has a Black class structure developed that in any way resembles the white class structure. Since that time, such dramatic changes have taken place in the stratification of the Black community that it is important to investigate not only the current perceptions but also the post–World War II alterations in the class structure and class perceptions of Black Americans (Cannon, 1984).

The civil rights movement, the breakdown of segregationist barriers, and the expansive post–World War II economy all enabled the Black class structure to begin to take on some of the characteristics of the white class structure (Wilson, 1978). During the postwar period, the castelike nature of the racial barrier began to dissolve with gains in average constant-dollar family income and personal earnings, educational attainment, and occupational standing (Farley, 1977; Wilson, 1978; Burstein, 1979). These status gains accompanied significant shifts in the percentage of the Black community employed in professional, technical, managerial, and administrative occupations. Newman et al. (1978:62) report that in 1940 only 4 percent of employed Blacks occupied such positions. By 1980 that group had increased almost fourfold, to 15 percent of all employed Black workers (Wescott, 1982).[5]

Newby (1983) finds a similar rise of Black employment in the "primary independent" sector of the labor force where the work is not routinized and the workers have supervisory authority and decision-making power but are not themselves directly supervised. He reports that the percentage of employed Black males in these jobs more than tripled, from 3.9 percent in 1960 to 12.8 percent in 1980. Among Black females, gains were also great, from 7.3 percent in 1960 to 15.5 percent of employed Black women in 1980. Simultaneously, shifts occurred in the private sector and in self-employment: by 1980, 75 percent of Black males were so employed. These trends lead Newby to conclude that "the relationship of Blacks to the overall political economy has been shifting dramatically over the last two decades. In fact, the change suggests that Blacks are no longer "outside" the class structure but becoming more integral to it in both the "middle layers" and the working class" (1983:16).

William Wilson (1978) goes even further to suggest that the growing post–World War II class divisions in the Black community signaled the declining significance of race in determining Blacks' life chances.

> As the Black middle class rides on the wave of political and social changes, benefiting from the growth of employment opportunities in the growing corporate and government sectors of the economy, the Black underclass falls behind the larger society in every conceivable respect. The economic and political systems in the United States have demonstrated remarkable flexibility in allowing talented Blacks to fill positions of prestige and influence at the same time that these systems have shown persistent rigidity in handling the problems of lower-class Blacks. As a result, for the first time in American history class issues can meaningfully compete with race issues in the way Blacks develop or maintain a sense of group position. (Wilson, 1978:22)

---

5. During the same period, white employment in these occupations increased at a slower rate, from 17 percent of all employed white workers in 1940 to 28.5 percent in 1980 (Newman, 1978; Wescott, 1982).

Unlike Wilson, Newby (1983) stops short of concluding that the changes in the Black class structure can be taken as "fundamental" or "permanent." Others too suggest that the changes highlighted by Wilson should not be taken as evidence of a fundamental shift in racism or in the Black class structure (e.g., Newman, 1979; Pettigrew, 1979; Willie, 1979). Analytically, these critiques tend to take one of two tacks: pointing to the fragility, tenuousness, and marginality of the new Black middle class, or highlighting the worsening conditions of life for the Black poor and the growth of the Black underclass.[6]

Typical of the first perspective is recent work by Sharon Collins (1983: 374). She suggests that the Black middle class is not integrated into the market economy because its members are predominantly working in positions created by government policies, not by consumer-generated market forces; thus the Black middle class is in a uniquely tenuous position, and the withdrawal of federal supports would erode this class position. Newman (1979:95) similarly points to the weak position of the Black middle class: "The Black underclass is but a stone's throw from its middle class in our still segregated society, and not much farther, either in distance or riches, from its wealthy. Few Black families are truly rich in the traditional sense."

Debate has centered on the extent of change in the Black community and on the social significance of the changes for many aspects of Black life, but there has been no research on the subjective meaning of the observable objective trends; no research has addressed the question of the importance of changes by asking whether the Black community actually sees itself differently. If, as Newman suggests, the new Black middle class remains a mere "stone's throw" from the Black underclass, then we would not expect their class self-placements to be all that different. In such a case, our longitudinal data would document the increased percentage of Blacks in the managerial class, and the improvements in average education, earnings, and occupational prestige but not necessarily a greater subjective sense of belonging to the middle class.

The cross-sectional analysis presented earlier hints that Blacks have perceived some of the changes in class and status. But there are important questions that cannot be answered by this still-shot of social reality at one

---

6. E.g., Newman (1979:93) reports the income gap between middle class and underclass is much smaller for Blacks than for whites. Hill (1979:78) reminds us that Black unemployment was at its highest level ever by 1978 and more than 2.3 times the white ratio.

historical moment. For example, have middle-class self-placements steadily risen throughout the post–World War II period in direct proportion to the status gains and growth in the Black middle class? Or could the strong class perceptions observed above merely reflect the thinking of the 1970s, and could it have supplanted a greater orientation to status distinctions in the 1950s or 1960s? In short, what has been the relation between the perception of class position and actual change in the class structure of the Black community since World War II? We examine these and other related trends in Blacks' class self-placements between 1952 and 1978, and thus bring additional evidence to bear on the clarity of Blacks' class images.

Data were taken from the 12 election surveys between 1952 and 1978, and variables were operationalized in the same way as for the time-trend analysis presented in Chapter 6. For purposes of these analyses, data are presented for a pooled sample of employed male heads of households and wives of household heads.[7] The total sample size for all years combined is 1,235; after weighting, this yields an effective 1,086.9.

Let us first document the growth in the managerial class and the improved status rankings experienced by the Blacks in these election surveys. The means of the status and class variables show improvements in each of these indicators over the period (see Table 10.3). However, since sample sizes in some years are small, year-to-year variations in the indicators may be unstable. Thus, four separate regressions—including all respondents in all years—were used to obtain for each indicator a single measure that summarizes the extent of change in that factor over the 26-year period. Those measures are presented at the bottom of Table 10.3 as the slopes (i.e., the understandardized regression coefficients) of the four bivariate linear regressions, where each socioeconomic variable was taken as the dependent variable, and the time-period variable was treated as independent. In this way, the slope for time period merely captures the yearly change in each class or status variable and, when multiplied by 26, indicates the esti-

7. Prior to 1966, the surveys contained head of household's occupational information but no data on respondent's occupation. Since we could not know a working woman's own occupation when she was married, continuing with that sample was not feasible for the time-trend analysis. Although results are not presented in the text, analyses of the smaller sample of female heads of households indicated an increase in middle-class identification from 6.6 percent in 1952 to 21 percent in 1978. That increase was only partly explained by the class and status factors, none of which had a statistically significant impact on middle-class self-placements. The sample of female heads of household was also characterized by a small number of managers (never more than seven in a year) and lower status rankings.

TABLE 10.3. Changes in social position of Blacks, 1952–78

Year	Occupational Prestige	Family Income (1967 $)	Education (Years)	Percentage Managerial	N
1952	31.8	3,504	8.4	8.8	91
1956	27.4	3,669	8.4	5.2	97
1958	30.0	3,693	8.5	9.9	81
1960	32.1	4,625	9.0	6.8	59
1964	31.8	5,905	9.8	10.0	230
1966	30.9	5,802	10.2	5.3	76
1968	33.4	6,712	10.6	13.5	126
1970	31.1	6,436	9.8	9.0	111
1972	34.3	7,650	11.1	14.0	121
1974	33.4	7,417	11.2	8.5	59
1976	33.2	7,214	11.7	9.8	92
1978	34.3	6,951	11.4	14.1	92
Slope	.1705[a]	.1777[b]	.1412	.0019	
	(4.06)	(11.67)	(11.45)	(1.73)	

SOURCE: American Election Surveys.
NOTES:
[a]T-values are parenthesized below the unstandardized slopes for time (year of interview). Weighted N for each equation = 1,086.9. Sample combines male heads of households and wives of household heads.
[b]Income values were coded in constant $1,000 units.

mated gains in each of the indicators from 1952 to 1978. In sum, these data show significant increases of 4.4 prestige points, 3.7 years of education, $4,620 constant dollars, and a nonsignificant increase of 4.9 in the percentage of workers employed in professional and managerial occupations.

Have middle-class self-placements steadily risen throughout the post–World War II period in direct proportion to Blacks' improved status rankings and expanded managerial class? Figure 10.4 also presents the percentage of middle-class self-placements for each year. Although there are short-term fluctuations, a significant overall increase in middle-class identification is documented in the probit analysis results (see appendix, Table 10.D, column 1). As in the regressions above, the probit analysis takes time (i.e., the year of the interview) as the independent variable and the middle- or working-class self-placements of individuals as dependent. The statistically significant time coefficient summarizes the yearly change in middle-class self-placements for the 1,086.9 individuals. When the coefficient is translated into percentage-point predictions, it reveals that middle-class identification *more than doubles* over the 26-year period, from 10 percent of the sample identifying as middle class to 22 percent.

The fact that objective class and status gains occurred at the same time as increased middle-class self-placements hints that the one change produced the other, but only a direct test can determine whether it was the increased percentage of managerial and high-status Blacks and not a heightened false consciousness among the working class that produced more middle-class self-placements. This question is addressed by adding the status and class variables to the simple model including only the time-period variable.

The results (see column 2 of Table 10.D) indicate that the probit coefficient for time is reduced to zero ($B = 0.0074$; $t = 1.22$) when the class and status variables are controlled. Controlling the class and status variables effectively compares Blacks who have the same class and status characteristics at different points in time. Since the time variable is reduced to zero, this indicates that individuals in 1952 were no less likely to identify as middle class than their equal status and class counterparts in 1978.[8]

___

8. Column 3 of appendix Table 10.D reports the interactions of time period with the class and status variables. Only the occupational prestige interaction is statistically significant, and it is negative—indicating that prestige differences are less important determinants of Blacks' class identifications now than they were in the past. The nonsignificant interactions for managerial class position, education, and income suggest that these factors were important deter-

FIGURE 10.4. Changes in Black class placements

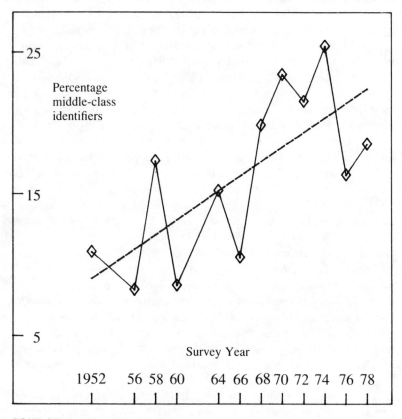

SOURCE: American Election Surveys.

Thus, the 12-point increase—or doubling—of middle-class identifiers among Blacks between 1952 and 1978 was produced by the concomitant upgrading of the Black class and status structure. More Blacks occupied managerial class and high status rankings, and they identified as middle class. In sum, the changes in the Black class structure noted by Wilson

minants of Blacks' class identifications in the early postwar period and remained so into the 1970s.

(1978), Newby (1983), and others clearly produced more self-consciously middle-class Blacks.

Conclusions

Scholarship on the Black community has highlighted the growing importance of class as a significant factor differentiating the experiences and defining the problems of Black Americans (Wilson, 1978). Organizations, such as the National Association for the Advancement of Colored People (NAACP) and the Urban League, have now broadened their focus to include institutionalized racism and other structural inequities linked to class. Today, these groups concentrate on such class and economic issues as low-income housing, health care, and jobs for the poor and working classes regardless of color.

Despite this recent thrust, very little was known about the way that class is perceived in the Black community.[9] Previous research has produced widely divergent pictures of the phenomenon. Some conceptions of the Black middle class (e.g., Frazier, 1957; Wilson, 1978) hold that it encompasses skilled workers and all white-collar workers ("middle mass" models); some hold that it includes only white-collar workers ("collar-color" models).

Some characterize the Black community as highly *status conscious*, emphasizing respect, prestige, and esteem as critical evaluative dimensions (e.g., Frazier, 1957; Drake and Cayton, 1962; Billingsley, 1968). They suggest that merely holding middle-class values (e.g., valuing education) or engaging in certain public behavior (e.g., attending cultural events) is what makes a person middle class. On the other hand, some politically leftist white scholars (e.g., Leggett, 1968; Geschwender, 1977) have presented an opposing image of Blacks as highly *class conscious*. Seen as having nothing to lose, Blacks in this picture are portrayed as the militant

---

9. In some ways, earlier analyses of the question of class consciousness in the Black community using national surveys could be considered premature, given the small size of the Black middle class. If virtually all members of the Black community were a part of the subproletariat, then race-caste thinking would be equivalent to class thinking, and separating the two analytically would be difficult if not impossible. Now, however, the Black middle class is large enough to allow meaningful differentiation between race and class.

vanguard of the modern proletariat.[10] Finally, a few scholars who have examined class identification among Blacks suggest that they are *neither class nor status conscious*. For all Blacks except the poor, "feelings of racial identity overwhelm the subjective significance of any socioeconomic achievements" (Jackman and Jackman, 1983:86; Hodge and Treiman, 1968).

The obvious contradictions in these viewpoints can be resolved only through research that directly examines class perceptions in the Black community. The data presented here on the class self-placements of Black Americans do not support the more middle-mass or collar-color definitions of the middle class in the Black community. Instead, they indicate that objective class divisions are indeed perceived in the Black community, and that (even more than among whites) it is the mental-manual dichotomy that best distinguishes those who see themselves as middle class from the remaining working class. Clerks, secretaries, postal carriers, and janitors alike tend to identify as working class.

Even as professional or managerial position is *more* important to the consciousness of Blacks than it is to whites, so status rankings are *less* critical to the class self-placements of Blacks than they are to whites. Thus, it is the dichotomous "them-versus-us," "mental-versus-manual" model rather than a continuous hierarchical prestige ladder that reflects the way Blacks identify themselves in the class system. Though "front," "respectability," and other status concerns may hold importance in some domains of Black life, status rankings do not blur Blacks' class perceptions. Previous research concluding that class is not perceived by most Blacks (e.g., Jackman and Jackman, 1973, 1983; Evers, 1976) erred by focusing solely on status measures or the blue-collar–white-collar dichotomy and omitting the critical mental–manual dimension.

In addition to the lesser impact of prestige on class self-placements for Blacks, these data show that Black people are—and have been—overwhelmingly working class, both objectively and subjectively. With this reality as a backdrop, however, the recent rise in middle-class identifiers—produced by the socioeconomic upgrading of the race—signifies a major change in class perceptions among Blacks. Now, there is a sizable segment

10. It should be noted that the Black scholars' concern with status reflected a similar trend in white middle-class scholarship at the time. And while white leftist scholarship may have portrayed an idealized radical image of Blacks, mainstream white scholarship ignored Blacks altogether.

of that population in middle-class positions who also *see* themselves in that way. This is in contrast to whites, who have been characterized by a relatively large proportion of middle-class identifiers throughout the post–World War II period. In fact, middle-class identification remains more than twice as high among whites as among Blacks.

A close look at the class identification process among Blacks reminds us that future research is needed that puts Blacks and other people of color at the center of the analysis. Most studies of class perceptions have not done that, so contradictory conclusions about Blacks and the class system have remained comfortably buried in larger studies of whites' perceptions. Findings about Blacks almost always diverge from white results but the discrepancies never really serve as the seeds of a new theory. New research on race, class, and gender is beginning to challenge these traditions. For example, Patricia Hill Collins (forthcoming), a Black feminist scholar, shows that when Black women are the starting point of any analysis, a holistic perspective is called for, which illuminates the interconnections of race, class, and gender in people's lives. Some of these new developments in research on this topic are discussed in Chapter 12.

Appendix

TABLE 10.A. Probit equations for mental-manual effects on
Blacks' middle-class self-placements

| | Probit Coefficients | |
	Men	*Women*
Professional		
managerial class	.8959*	.4941*
Prestige	.0015	.0025
Education	.0226	.0592*
Income	.0252	− .0523
Survey	− .3946*	.0763
Constant	− 1.1223	− 1.6667

SOURCES: General Social Surveys and American Election Surveys.
NOTE: * = $p < .05$. Education is years of schooling. Prestige is NORC occupational prestige score. Income is log of constant 1980 dollars family income. Survey is 0 = GSS; 1 = American Election Surveys.

TABLE 10.B. Probit coefficients for effects of several class divisions on Blacks' middle-class self-placements

	Probit Coefficients	
	Men	*Women*
Professional managerial	.97*	.59*
Clerical and sales	.25	.08
Skilled	− .02	.21
N (unweighted)	728	777
N (weighted)	656.1	666.8

SOURCES: General Social Surveys and American Election Surveys.
NOTE: * = $p < .05$. These coefficients represent those for each occupational category controlling for education, income, and prestige. These analyses were also conducted separately for the GSS and American Election samples, and the results are replicated within each subsample.

TABLE 10.C. Probit analyses of class perceptions by race

	Men		Women	
	Black	*White*	*Black*	*White*
Probit coefficients				
Professional managerial				
class	.8866	.5771$^+$	.4941	.1865*
Occupational prestige	−.0001	.0080	.0022	.0057
Education	.0211	.1098*	.0604	.1464*
Income	.0783	.3736*	−.0338	.2993*
Survey year	.0446		.2198*	
Race: Black	−.5375		−.8591	
Constant	−.3508		−.2235	

NOTE: $^+$ indicates $p = .065$; * = $p < .05$. Coefficients that are significantly different for Blacks and whites are starred.

TABLE 10.D. Explaining changes in Blacks' middle-class self-placements

	Equations		
	(1)	(2)	(3)
Time	.0202	.0074	.0637
	(3.47)	(1.22)	(10.40)
Occupational prestige		.0094	.0371
		(1.45)	(5.67)
Years of education		.0419	.0646
		(2.34)	(3.63)
Family income		.1836	−.0065
(log of constant $)		(2.85)	(−0.10)
Managerial dichotomy		.4289	.0704
		(3.06)	(0.50)
Time × prestige			−.0018
			(−2.17)
Time × education			−.0016
			(−0.72)
Time × income			.0126
			(1.56)
Time × managers			.0235
			(1.34)
Constant	−1.3026	−2.2043	−3.0619
Likelihood X^2	11.77	85.36	93.13

SOURCE: American Election Surveys
NOTE: T-values are parenthesized below the unstandardized probit coefficients. Weighted N for each equation = 1,086.9.

255

CHAPTER 11
THE AMERICAN DREAM

More than any nation, America has celebrated itself as the land of opportunity. Immigrants came to the New World to escape European class barriers. In America, wealth and position were to be organized differently—open to every person of talent and hard work. The frontier beckoned to those seeking a new chance. The fabulous wealth of the continent promised abundance for all who were willing to work. It was the natural setting for an ideology of individualism.

The roots of the American Dream can be found in colonial America; it gave *Poor Richard's Almanac* its distinctive American character. But it was especially during the rise of industrialization in the late nineteenth century that the imagery of upward mobility came to dominate America's discussions of itself (Thernstrom, 1964:57–59). It is certainly no accident that just as a massive industrial proletariat was being created on these shores, America worked hardest at convincing itself of its openness and classlessness.

The American Dream seemed the perfect immunization against the dangers of a militant class consciousness. It promised a common vision to all Americans—workers and bosses, the poor as well as the rich. In an open America, class struggle would be unnecessary. Discontent with one's position would inspire workers to change their positions within the system, rather than trying to change the system itself.[1]

Class struggle, if not unnecessary, would at least be crippled by the indi-

---

1. Among many possible expressions of this view, Tom Bottomore's is typical: "America was the 'land of opportunity,' a vast, unexplored and unexploited country in which it was always possible, or seemed possible, to escape from economic want or subjection by moving to a new place, acquiring land or some other property, and adding to it by personal effort and talent" (1966:49). See also Lipset, 1960:253, 1963:193–233.

vidualistic pursuit of gain. To the extent that workers succeeded in getting ahead, their mobility deprived the working class of its ablest leaders. To the extent that workers failed, they were left blaming themselves for their own deprivations (Lane, 1962; Sennett and Cobb, 1972). Either way, the struggle to get ahead fragmented workers and prevented them from developing a collective class consciousness. In this way, the American Dream reinforced the class system and protected it from the challenges of a radical working class.

The image of America as the Land of Promise is such an indelible part of the national heritage that it has been a favorite explanation for the failure of American class consciousness. Americans both believed in individual opportunity and lacked a radical working-class consciousness; the two characteristics must surely be linked as cause and effect.[2] The pieces of the theory fit so well together that research often neglected to look for rigorous evidence, convinced that closer scrutiny would only demonstrate the obvious.

There were some objections. American Dream theories especially outraged European Marxists (Moore, 1970).[3] According to Marxian theory, the spectacular development of American capitalism implied that American workers should be especially impoverished. Therefore, Marxists quickly challenged the reality of the American Dream. Sometimes they based their objections on little more than anecdotes describing individual cases of poverty or on travelogues of visiting Europeans.[4] Sometimes they undertook more rigorous compilations of wage rates, cost-of-living estimates, and standard-of-living comparisons (Kautsky, 1905–6, cited in Moore, 1970:118).

2. Usually, the causal linkage is implicit; only a few have attempted to formalize it into a general theory. The most interesting effort comes from the inventive economist Albert Hirschman (1970), who links mobility and revolt to the choice of Exit, Voice, or Loyalty. The discontented (those who reject Loyalty) are left with two alternatives: Voice (protest) and Exit (mobility). Hirschman, however, points out that Voice and Exit are sometimes complementary processes: workers seeking individual mobility may be precisely the ones who also lead collective protest.

3. However, a few European Marxists were impressed by American conditions. Wilhelm Liebknecht, a founder of the German Social Democratic Party, claimed that "generally the badly paid worker here [in the United States] is better off than our well-paid worker" (1887, cited in Moore, 1970:28–30).

4. Marx's daughter Eleanor and her husband, Edward Aveling, reported on their 1886 trip to the United States: "At the one end of the scale is the millionaire, openly, remorselessly crushing out all rivals, swallowing up all the feebler folk. At the other end is the helpless, starving proletarian" (cited in Moore, 1970:31).

But the Marxist dissent seemed, even then, more the desperate defense of a prophet that failed than an analysis of actual American conditions. The American Dream had more resilience than complex wage calculations could dislodge. The country's founders had passed down a faith in the opportunities of the New World, and the elite consensus simply dismissed the carping of radical critics as biased political ideology.

Latter-day academics with better tools, though hardly the same radical purpose, have taken up a similar line of questioning. Are American workers really more prosperous than their European contemporaries? Do they really have more chances to advance to the middle class? Or is the American Dream only a mirage that obscures the existing class divisions?

The prevalence of these empirical inquiries could easily distract us from the more fundamental question of the *relevance* of opportunity or affluence for working-class consciousness. Even if American workers were more mobile or prosperous, would that necessarily make them less class conscious? What is the connection between "objective" realities such as mobility rates and "subjective" reactions such as class consciousness? The theory that mobility or prosperity deters class consciousness is plausible enough, but nobody has adequately tested it.[5] Stephan Thernstrom, after two major histories of American mobility (1964, 1973), leaves to "future research" the question whether that mobility actually "impeded the formation of class-based protest movements" (1973:259). But this, of course, is the fundamental question.

Again, the exercise of constructing the opposite hypothesis is instructive (see Katznelson, 1981:12–13). Perhaps mobility promotes *dissension* rather than stability. After all, mobility disrupts the existing pattern of personal ties that usually keep subordinates in their place. Mobility raises expectations that were never imagined in traditional societies. The new expectations aggravate the sense of deprivation of those workers left behind. And the relative success of the few who succeed provides them also with greater resources with which to challenge those still above them.

Such destabilizing consequences of mobility are as plausible as the more conservative theory. A more Durkheimian theory that change creates unrest would explain why the early stages of industrialization are the most

---

5. Melvyn Dubofsky has made the same complaint: "One major assumption is that the possession of property in the form of homes or savings satisfies individuals with their place in the existing social order. Another premise assumes that limited occupational mobility for the parent and somewhat greater opportunity for the children tends to the same effect. Both assumptions seem logical but remain untested" (1975:12–13).

dangerous for capitalism. The great modern revolutions, the French, Russian, and Chinese, erupted not in advanced industrial economies but during capitalism's first stirrings. It is in the first stages that change is most severe and workers are freed from traditional restraints.

Clever reasoning could perhaps reconcile the two theories: perhaps both mobility and stability weaken working-class consciousness. Our purpose in raising the countertheory is to question a facile assumption that opportunity and wealth always weaken working-class consciousness. We would like proof and are disturbed by how little evidence has been mustered on behalf of such a theory.

Our contribution to this debate is quite modest. We merely wish to show that individual opportunity plays little part in obscuring the perception of class in the United States. American workers know who is working class, and the American Dream does not delude them into imagining that they are anything more or less than they are.

The American Dream concept provides at least three distinct explanations of American exceptionalism: the frontier, social mobility, and wealth. There is even a rough progression through history in the popularity of these three theories. The first explanations focused on the frontier as the outlet for working-class discontent. But as the frontier closed and the working class remained impotent, other explanations had to be sought.[6] The new theories equated the social mobility of industrial society with the geographic mobility of the old frontier (Thernstrom, 1964:61): the opportunity to move up replaced the opportunity to move West. And throughout our history but especially after World War II, various theorists have cited the American workers' affluence as the guarantor of working-class conservatism: it was not only the promise of mobility to the few but the reality of generous incomes for the many that forestalled any sense of mass injustice. We shall discuss each of these three theories in turn, distinguishing them for separate analysis, but recognizing that they form an interrelated set of explanations about how the American Dream has anesthetized working-class consciousness.

6. "In American thought an ingenuous faith in the open road westward had long supported belief in an open road upward. The [1880s] cast a shadow over both ideas at the same time. A new sense of 'closed space' compounded the emerging fears of a closed society" (Higham, 1955:38).

Geography

The Frontier

For Frederick Jackson Turner (1920) the American frontier explained weak American class consciousness. According to Turner's theory, the frontier was a great outlet that drained away the most discontented and reinforced an individualistic ideology of achievement. Class consciousness—not to mention class warfare—required a stable working class stuck in its position with little hope of escape.[7] The frontier opened up the escape valves and prevented the urban industrial pressure cooker from building up too much steam. The solidarities forged in the crowded cities of the East were dissipated in the great open spaces of the West.

In fact, the frontier thesis ignores some of the most violent battles in American labor history.[8] Most of the disorder in the 1894 Pullman strike occurred in the West (Taft and Ross, 1969:286). At Coeur d'Alene, Idaho, dynamite twice became the medium of exchange between striking miners and mine owners (Jensen, 1950). The Western Federation of Miners emerged from these conflicts as one of the most radical unions in American history, the progenitor of the Industrial Workers of the World (see Dubofsky, 1969). The Wobblies had their greatest strength in the West and fought some of their most violent conflicts there. Besides the IWW, the Pacific coast longshoremen's union has long distinguished itself as the major Communist-led union in the country.

Colorado probably exceeds all other states for the most violent labor

7. Even earlier, Engels (Marx and Engels [1894], 1953:294) had endorsed a similar view: "*Land* is the basis for speculation, and the American speculative mania and speculative opportunity are the chief levers that hold the native-born worker in bondage to the bourgeoisie. Only when there is a generation of native-born workers that cannot expect *anything* from speculation *any more*, will we have a solid foothold in America." In a letter to Sorge on January 16, 1895, he describes American class consciousness as zigzagging between "the mind of the industrial worker [and] that of the pioneering farmer" (Marx and Engels [1894], 1953: 270).

8. It also ignores the fact, as has long been noted, that not many eastern industrial workers ever migrated to the frontier (see Shannon, 1945). See the collection in Hofstadter and Lipset (1968) for other critiques of Turner. Some attempts to resurrect the frontier thesis have been based on the consequences for American economic growth (e.g., Simler, 1958; Murphy and Zellner, 1959; Karabel, 1979:214).

disputes. During the Colorado Labor War of 1904, violence killed 17 and wounded 23. Ten years later, coal strikes around Ludlow ended with 74 dead. In 1920, seven more died in a Denver street railway strike, and in 1927, eight were killed in another coal strike (Taft and Ross, 1969).

The West also pioneered the use of the general strike, often considered to be labor's most class-conscious weapon (see, for example, Luxemburg [1906], 1970; Brecher, 1972:233–63). By this standard, Seattle's general strike of 1919 was perhaps the most thorough demonstration of working-class solidarity in American history. At the time, the mayor called it a "Bolshevik insurrection" (Friedheim, 1964). General strikes were also called in Waco, Texas, and in Kansas City, Missouri, during World War I (Bing, 1921:30), and in San Francisco in 1934. In Billings, Montana, employers turned the tactic around and called a general lockout in 1918 (Bing, 1921:30).

All these labor battles were fought in the West, where the American frontier supposedly dissipated working-class consciousness. Despite the popularity of the thesis about the pacifying influence of the frontier, the historical data do not support it.

Nor do our survey data suggest any important regional differences in class perceptions (see Table 11.1). Western workers are about 3 percentage points *more* likely to see themselves as working class than workers elsewhere in the country. This difference is in the opposite direction from an expectation of weaker working-class consciousness. Moreover, managers in the West are also about 3 points *less* likely to see themselves as middle class, so the gap between managers and workers is almost exactly the same size in each region of the country: class divisions are no more or less clear in the West than in the more industrialized areas of the country.[9]

The South

If any region is known for its weak working-class movement today, it is the South, not the West. Low rates of unionization have combined with antiunion politics to reduce southern workers to the most poorly paid and weakest sector of American labor. In 1977 only 13 percent of southern

---

9. Further examination of the distinctiveness of the West reveals that only people who were raised there are more working class. Both managers and workers raised in the West are about 4 percentage points more likely to take a working-class label—a somewhat bigger difference than among current residents but still a trivial result.

TABLE 11.1. Adjusted regional differences in class
perceptions

	Adjusted Percentage Middle-Class Self-Placement			
	Northeast	*Central*	*South*	*West*
Managers	52%	52%	52%	49%
	(724)	(724)	(741)	(500)
Workers	32%	33%	33%	29%
	(1,275)	(1,766)	(1,974)	(948)
Difference	20%	19%	19%	20%

SOURCE: General Social Surveys.
NOTE: Sample sizes are in parentheses. Percentages are calculated after controlling for five dummy variables for urbanism of residence, own education, family income, own labor force status, gender, managerial class, spouse's occupational prestige, spouse's education, mother's education and a dummy variable for
missing data on mother's education, father's education, father's managerial class,
father's farm occupation, father's occupational prestige, and a dummy variable
for missing data on father's occupation. Regions follow the U.S. Census classification.

workers belonged to unions, compared to 24 percent in the rest of the
country (Freeman and Medoff, 1984:27).

Labor's weakness in the South cannot be blamed on weak working-class
consciousness. As Table 11.1 shows, southern workers perceive the working-class division in exactly the same way as do workers in the northeast
and north-central regions. Moreover, southern workers may want unions
as much as workers elsewhere. Freeman and Medoff (1984:29) report that
southern blue-collar workers not yet in unions are more likely (46 percent)
to say they would vote for a union than would similar workers in other regions (28 to 38 percent). (The ABC/*Washington Post* poll, however, found
no regional differences among nonunion blue-collar workers in their will-

ingness to join a union.) The attitudinal evidence, therefore, suggests that low unionization in the South may more reasonably be attributed to the hostility of management in low-profit southern industry and such barriers as the right-to-work laws prevalent in the South.

Internal migration

Nineteenth-century workers moved not only to the frontier but within the eastern metropolises as well. Boston in the 1880s underwent a "dizzying" turnover rate of 64 percent (Thernstrom, 1973:221).[10] Footloose workers rarely put down roots long enough to build a stable working-class movement. A continually fluctuating population obstructs labor organization, no matter how class conscious the workers are.[11]

Geographic movement has also been thought to encourage a psychology of individual achievement rather than a class-conscious solidarity, to reduce the sense of common class experience that creates strong working-class loyalties. Neighborhoods become less stable and work groups more temporary. As mobility severs the ties between one worker and another, it offers the hope of individual advancement.[12]

Neither the historical nor the attitudinal evidence supports this otherwise plausible theory. Migratory workers, such as loggers and maritime workers, have created some of the most radical and militant unions in the United States.

Our survey data also provide no support for any linkage between physi-

---

10. Our GSS data confirm substantial geographic mobility—they show 56 percent of the sample living in places other than those they were raised in, 30 percent in different states—but not Thernstrom's 64 percent turnover rate *per decade*.

11. "The extreme transiency of the urban masses must have severely limited the possibilities of mobilizing them politically and socially, and have facilitated control by more stable and prosperous elements of the population. Effective organization demands some continuity of membership, and this was glaringly absent among the poorest city dwellers of nineteenth- and early-twentieth-century America" (Thernstrom, 1973:232. See also Karabel, 1977:213.)

12. "The cause of this lack of psychological cohesiveness in American labor is the absence, by and large, of a completely 'settled' wage earning class. The opportunity of the 'West' has never ceased. In this vast country, several historical industrial stages are found existing side by side, though in demarcated areas. There is, therefore, the opportunity to migrate from older to newer and less developed sections, in which a person without much or any inherited property may still find the race for economic independence a free and open race" (Perlman, 1922:166). See also Lee (1961), who emphasizes all geographic migration as the true safety valve.

TABLE 11.2. Effects of geographic mobility on class perceptions

| | Adjusted Percentage Middle-Class Self-Placement | | | |
| | Men | | Women | |
	Movers	Stayers	Movers	Stayers
Managers	67%	64%	59%	61%
	(707)	(370)	(400)	(200)
Workers	42%	37%	48%	50%
	(937)	(943)	(831)	(673)
Difference	25%	27%	11%	11%

SOURCE: General Social Surveys.
NOTE: Sample sizes are in parentheses. Percentages follow controls for occupational prestige, years of education, and family income. Geographical mobility is defined as living in another town or city than at age 16.

cal mobility and weak working-class consciousness. Of course the interviews are all contemporary, whereas the geographic mobility theories developed from the early industrialization of the nineteenth century. If workers' reactions to geographic mobility were different then than they are now, we have almost no way of finding out what they were.

Should this movement have any effect on people's class perceptions? It is hard to predict its impact. The fluidity theory might suggest that class perceptions would be less stable for the movers. Compared to those settled in the same place all their lives, the movers might be less certain of their position in the class structure and therefore less class conscious. This greater uncertainty would be detected in our data as a less clear division between managers and workers.

In addition, geographic mobility itself may imply some middle-class status. In the contemporary United States, unlike in the nineteenth-century cities Thernstrom studied, geographic mobility is now associated with the middle class (Blau and Duncan, 1967).[13] People move out in order to move up. In our own sample, the managers are more often migrants: 66 percent of the managers are now living in places different from where they grew up, compared to 52 percent of workers. Migrants may therefore have some reason to assume a middle-class status even if their current jobs don't yet reflect middle-class positions.

There is little support for either of these possible implications of internal migration. "Movers" are slightly more middle class than "stayers" but by only a couple of percentage points (see Table 11.2). Both managers and workers who move show the same slight tendency to middle-class self-placement, so the gap between them is unaffected by migration. Thus there is no evidence at all that lifelong residents are any clearer about their class position than the transients. In sum, internal migration appears to be no more relevant than region in determining class perceptions.

Social Mobility

The frontier has long since ceased to be a significant factor in American class relations. Even geographic mobility is not the distinctive characteristic of the working class that it once was. As these outlets for class tensions became less available, more attention focused on a different kind of mobility—not physical movement across the country but social movement up the status ladder. The extent of this social mobility reinforced the image of America as the land of opportunity (Bottomore, 1966:50).

The rags-to-riches story has become the central element in the American Dream ideology. Even if most social mobility was only short-distance (rags-to-respectable-working-class, and working-class-to-small-proprietor), it still rewarded individual initiative and thus was believed to drain the American working class of the kind of collective resentment that created Old World militancy (de Tocqueville [1835, 1840], 1954 [vol. 2]:269;

---

13. Thernstrom reports that for nineteenth-century Newburyport (1964) and Boston (1973), those workers who could not find good jobs tended to move out; residents well established in middle-class positions tended to stay where their jobs were. Dawley (1976:155) confirms this negative relationship of migration and status for nineteenth-century Lynn. Thus, for this analysis, it would be especially hazardous to project the results back to earlier times.

Commons, 1908:760–61; Coser, 1956:36; Lipset, 1960:267; Lane, 1962: 218; Thernstrom, 1964:58, 1973:258; Sweezy, 1967: 160–61; Burawoy, 1979:106–7; Karabel, 1979:212). In Europe, workers were stuck in their lot in life and could turn only to collective protest for any hope of improving their position.

Arthur Shostak, for example, in his *Blue-Collar Life*, asserted—without offering any documented evidence—that in the United States,

> blue-collarites are further discouraged from class-conscious politics by the underrecognized presence in their ranks of two types of mobile individuals, those "displaced" workers skidding down from above, and those Horatio Alger types aspiring up and out. [The skidders], who either were raised in white-collar families or were once possessors of white-collar work . . . often remain optimistic about their chances to recoup status losses; as such they function to reduce working-class solidarity from below. . . . Blue-collarites who are busy making their way up and out of the ranks alternate ties among blue-collar peers, and in other ways undermine class cohesiveness. (Shostak, 1969:226)

Such assertions have never been systematically proven. Do skidders maintain middle-class values? Are potential mobiles less class conscious? American sociologists have not often asked about the *effects* of opportunity: does rapid mobility in fact reduce working-class consciousness?[14] Instead, they have questioned the *extent* of opportunity: do U.S. workers really have such great chances for advancement, and are they better chances than European workers have? Our main interest is in the *effects* of mobility although we can only begin to sketch an answer. But first we should look at what social science has learned about the rates of social mobility in the United States.

Rates of mobility

The verdict on American mobility rates is not yet in, despite vast amounts of research in the last two decades. The question proved more complicated than was first imagined. A number of false starts provided lessons about distinctions that must be made before we can compare mobility rates in the

14. Lopreato and Hazelrigg (1972:115, 442–55) claim that "mobility is the crucial variable interfering with the formation of classes" and provide some evidence that upwardly mobile Americans are more conservative and Republican. Design problems confound their conclusions, however.

United States with those of other industrial countries.[15] Much of American mobility into the new middle class is a consequence of the extraordinary growth of professional and managerial positions in the American occupational structure. As the percentage of middle-class positions increased from 15 to 30 percent in a generation, somebody had to fill those new positions. The openings thus created pulled up the children of working-class families. This kind of structural mobility was not a reflection of the openness of the system itself—that is, it did not reflect any of the equality of opportunity that Americans pride themselves upon. A society that guarantees middle-class positions to all the children of the middle class and accepts working-class children only in order to fill vacancies can hardly be judged to be very open and fluid. Therefore, the openness of the system—the degree of *circulation mobility*—came to be defined as all the residual movement up and down and social hierarchy once the mobility mandated by structural changes had been subtracted out.

The studies that separated structural from circulation mobility concluded that most American mobility was structurally required by the growth of middle-class positions (Hauser et al., 1975). With that growth-determined movement subtracted, U.S. rates of circulation mobility were above average but not exceptionally so, and gave every indication of being quite constant throughout history. One cross-national comparison of blue-collar–white-collar circulation mobility (Tyree, Semyonov, and Hodge, 1979) placed U.S. rates somewhat lower than Canada's and higher than Great Britain's.

Consequences of mobility

Our interest, however, is in the consequences of those mobility rates, and the study of these consequences has additional complications. The most important is the separation of the effects of mobility itself—the movement from one position to another—from the simple effects of destination and

---

15. The simplest distinction to be made is between *inter-* and *intra*generational mobility. Most studies have concentrated on intergenerational mobility—the changes between parental families and current positions. Intragenerational mobility—the career changes between first job and current position—has been less well studied, primarily for lack of adequate data. Our own research is forced into the same neglect, despite plausible arguments that the workers' own chances for advancement—not their children's—would have a more depressing effect on class conflict.

origin. The issues are necessarily intertwined, much like the age, period, and cohort effects discussed in Chapter 6.

We begin with a computation of working-class and middle-class placements for 20 separate categories according to four levels of the person's own occupation and five levels of the father's occupation. The divisions — professional/managerial, other white-collar, skilled blue-collar, other blue-collar, and farm (for fathers only) — incorporate the actual class divisions (manager-worker-farm) and the most often noted status distinctions within the working class. (More detailed breakdowns would be possible but would result in such small samples in some of the cells of the matrix that we would not get reliable estimates of their subjective class placements.)[16] The results of these calculations are presented in Table 11.3. The highlighted cells forming a diagonal in these tables represent the occupationally stable Americans whose work falls in the same broad category as their fathers'. Those above that diagonal are *upwardly mobile*: their occupational position has higher status than their fathers'.[17] They constitute 46–52 percent of the total sample, a large segment that reveals the structural shift upward between generations. The *downwardly mobile*, some 20–22 percent of the samples, are below the diagonal.

If we sort the 20 categories into these three broad groups, we find that the downwardly mobile are more working class than the stable, as we would expect. The upwardly mobile, however, are not more middle class than the stable; among women the upwardly mobile are notably less middle class than the stable. But these comparisons say little about the effects of mobility, because we cannot tell whether the class placements are determined by the direction of mobility or merely by the occupational destination. By definition, none of the downwardly mobile are managers, but substantial proportions of both the upwardly mobile and the stable currently hold managerial positions. Thus the upwardly mobile and the stable are

16. We have also computed all analyses of mobility with controls for the extraneous factors of age, education, income, and spouse's education and occupation, so that we can look directly at the effects of occupational position and mobility between those positions. Those adjusted results are reported in the chapter appendix, Tables 11.A–11.C. Because of the additional controls, the mobility effects are more muted in these tables; nevertheless, the same general conclusions may be drawn.

17. The determination of upward direction requires an assumption about the status level of farmers, whose position is otherwise ambiguous in an industrial order. We have placed them at the bottom, below the unskilled-semiskilled workers — a position that is justified by the resulting class placements of their children.

TABLE 11.3. Class perceptions by own and father's occupation

| | Percentage Middle-Class Self-Placement | | | |
	Unskilled	Skilled	White-Collar	Managerial/ Professional
		Men		
Father's occupation				
Farm	15% (246)	24% (159)	36% (48)	66% (121)
Unskilled	20% (377)	29% (242)	43% (107)	69% (222)
Skilled	27% (249)	33% (301)	50% (97)	78% (256)
White-collar	29% (42)	39% (31)	46% (31)	78% (87)
Managerial/professional	41% (118)	39% (121)	66% (111)	85% (485)
		Women		
Father's occupation				
Farm	20% (167)	39% (37)	37% (125)	56% (101)
Unskilled	23% (231)	25% (44)	37% (236)	53% (123)
Skilled	23% (164)	45% (32)	40% (277)	60% (120)
White-collar	35% (29)	40% (10)	35% (76)	58% (42)
Managerial/professional	35% (71)	62% (12)	58% (258)	74% (292)

SOURCE: General Social Surveys.

more middle class because they are more often managerial, not because they have been mobile.

What we have to do is look at the effects of mobility while holding constant the person's present position. For instance, we should compare the stable skilled workers with those who were upwardly mobile into skilled work and with those who were downwardly mobile into skilled work. It is obvious from Table 11.3 what the results of those comparisons would be. The upwardly mobile are *less* middle class than the stable; the stable are less middle class than the downwardly mobile. According to such an analysis, upward mobility makes people more working class and downward mobility makes people more middle class! But this result is also misleading because it is not the act of mobility per se that determines those class placements; it is the direct effect of parental origins. *All* persons with unskilled working-class fathers have more working-class identifications than people with skilled-worker fathers, regardless of their current positions; that is, there is a consistent (main) effect of father's occupation on class placement, regardless of the person's current position. Therefore, parental origin effects must also be subtracted from the mobility comparisons in order to determine the effects of movement itself. In other words, we must control for both parental origin and current occupation. To do this we have to estimate the effects of each of the "father's" and "own" categories, subtract these estimates from the observed percentages in Table 11.3, and *then* look at the differences due to mobility. These estimates are reported in Table 11.4. What is clear from this table is that mobility makes very little difference; virtually all the differences in Table 11.3 can be explained by the *overall* effects of "father's" and "own" occupation, beyond this, whether any mobility was entailed by the particular conjunction of the two is irrelevant.[18]

The conclusion about the effects of mobility is very similar to the conclusion about the rates of mobility: what matters is the *number* of middle-class and working-class positions, not the process by which people move into these positions. Working-class identifications will increase or decrease

---

18. An even more thorough test can be made by comparing how well the estimates for "father's" and "own" occupation reproduce all the cells in Table 11.3. In fact, summing the simple effects of both occupations will almost exactly reproduce each of the cells of the table. No cell is any different from what might be expected as a result of the two components. Adding additional coefficients to represent the individual cells increases the chi-square a negligible amount.

TABLE 11.4. Effects of upward, downward, and no
mobility on class perceptions

	Percentage Middle-Class Self-Placement		
	Upwardly Mobile	*Stable*	*Downwardly Mobile*
	No Controls		
Men	48%	50%	39%
	(1,585)	(1,194)	(672)
Women	41%	49%	43%
	(1,272)	(631)	(544)
	Control for Occupation		
Men	47%	45%	48%
Women	45%	44%	41%

SOURCE: General Social Surveys
NOTE: Sample sizes are in parentheses; they are the same for both uncontrolled and controlled percentages. Control for occupation = controls for own occupational group and father's occupational group. Upward mobility is defined as being in an occupational group higher than father's.

depending on the number of working-class positions and working-class (or farm) fathers. Mobility itself has little effect on subjective class placements.

The importance of one's own occupation is little more than a restatement of what we observed in Chapter 4: the person's position in the class structure is a primary determinant of class perceptions. We have now added a new component that requires some discussion: apparently one's father's position also has an effect on class perceptions. Those who had managerial fathers are especially likely to see themselves as middle class. Why is this? Why should family origin—removed by years or decades from the experience of most of our respondents—continue to have an effect on their subjective class placements? Granted, the parental effect is much weaker than that of the person's own job, but why should it remain at all? What relevance to positions in a *class* order could parental position have?

We suspect that the main reason the father's position affects class placement is that it also affects the chances for future advancement. We know from the status attainment research that the father's occupation continues to have an effect on the son's career mobility throughout the son's working life. Sons with middle-class fathers are likely to advance further than sons with working-class fathers. Perhaps the middle-class self-placements of the sons (and daughters) of middle-class parents anticipate this greater future advancement. The son may not have a truly middle-class position yet, but he can more realistically *anticipate* holding such a position if his father was middle-class.

Affluence

Sombart's best-known explanation of the lack of U.S. socialism was the affluence of the American worker:

> This much is certain: the American worker lives in comfortable circumstances. He is well fed. . . . He dresses like a gentleman and she like a lady and so he does not even outwardly become aware of the gap that separates him from the ruling class. It is no wonder if, in such a situation, any dissatisfaction with the "existing social order" finds difficulty in establishing itself in the mind of the worker. . . . All Socialist utopias came to nothing on roast beef and apple pie. (1906:105–6)

Countless defenders of the American Way have echoed this answer (Gulick and Bers, 1953:528; Potter, 1954; Lipset, 1963:203 and 1979:25; Wilensky, 1966; Laslett, 1970:135, 302; Wattenberg, 1974), and even some who are not such staunch defenders (Bottomore, 1966:53–55).[19]

19. Laslett repeatedly claims that affluence undermined labor militancy, but he rarely ties the historical facts together as cause and effect. For instance, he claims that the garment workers' gains after the 1910 Protocol of Peace had a conservative effect "over the long run," but then finds it difficult to explain why in the next union elections those workers chose an even more radical union leadership.

Two problems beset the affluence explanation. First, the facts about American workers' prosperity may be incorrect. Once historians incorporated cost-of-living adjustments into their calculations, the position of American workers looked less privileged. Phelps-Brown and Hopkins (1950) found that in the crucial period for labor organization between 1860 and 1913, the real wages of the U.S. worker rose less than the real wages of Swedish, German, British, or French workers.[20]

The second problem with the affluence explanation is more disturbing because it goes to the heart of our understanding of the causes of social protest. It turns out that social theorists have only *assumed* that affluence produces more conservative workers; rarely has anyone attempted to support the assumption with any evidence.[21] Nevertheless, the idea flourishes as if it were self-evident. For example, liberals implicitly accept it whenever they prescribe a dose of economic development as the best inoculation against Third World revolutions. The assumption is that poverty causes unrest and that eliminating poverty will eliminate the unrest.[22]

20. This was Kautsky's (1905-6) conclusion at the turn of the century. Husbands (1976: xxiv) has also attacked Sombart for his description of U.S. working-class affluence. Moreover, Sweden had the most rapidly improving standard of living in the Phelps-Brown and Hopkins (1950) study, and yet Sweden had one of the most radical labor movements (Rosenblum, 1973).

21. David Brody (1968) argues that the labor peace of the 1920s supports the assumption. The welfare capitalism that flourished during the decade (e.g., company insurance programs) failed only after the Depression, when the corporations were no longer able to keep the benefits coming. However, it seems more reasonable to explain the 1920s by the dramatic defeats of major strikes at the beginning of the decade (the coal strikes, the steel strike of 1919), a situation that turned around only during the New Deal, when the government ended its hostility toward unions.

22. Again, theory would be improved if we experimented with the opposite statement. Columnist George Will (1985) provides a convenient formulation—what he calls "Will's Law of Discontent" or the "Paradox of Prosperity"—that to us seems closer to the truth: "Discontent increases with the opportunities for acting on it. There is a lot of discontent going around among middle-aged people in the middle classes of affluent societies. These are people who have the ability to imagine other ways of living and the disposable income to act on their imaginings. A 13th-century peasant toiling from sunup to sundown behind an ox, in the shadow of a castle, tilling fields owned by the owner of the castle, never said to his spouse, 'Hey, let's chuck this and open a beer garden.'" Michael Harrington (1976:x), who probably agrees with George Will on little else, also questions the simple poverty-equals-unrest assumption. He points out that the great growth of the German Social Democrats before World War I coincided with working-class prosperity, and the student New Left in the 1960s was based on prosperous youth. And Howard Wachtel (1974:109, 119) argues that younger workers are now *more* militant because their incomes are more secure than were those of their Depression-burdened parents.

The fallacy in this theory, as Barrington Moore (1966) pointed out, is that poverty is as old as human society, but revolutions are rather rare events; indeed, they may be more common in the modern era, even though there is no evidence that poverty has grown. Moore reminds us of the obvious fact that revolutions are first and foremost struggles over *power*; it is the distribution of power, not the amount of wealth, that incites rebellion.

We have a similar objection to the affluence theory of American exceptionalism. Embourgeoisement arguments assume that affluence makes a difference—that workers who live comfortably enough will begin to see themselves as middle class even though they do not share any of the control over society that is characteristic of a true middle-class position. But this argument confuses status and power: affluence is a dimension of social status, and while it may be important for many things, it does not substitute for power. Workers will not, for the most part, be bought off by greater incomes; what makes them working class is their subordination, not their modest lifestyles. Again, one of Studs Terkel's workers expresses this as well as any sociologist:

> The almightly dollar is not the only thing in my estimation. There's more to it—how I'm treated. What I have to say about what I do, how I do it. It's more important than the almighty dollar. . . . I can concentrate on the social aspect, my rights. And I feel good all around when I'm able to stand up and speak for another guy's rights. That's how I got involved in this whole stinkin' mess. Fighting every day of my life. And I enjoy it. (1974:189–90)

We can test the affluence argument in two ways: first, by taking a closer look at the role that income plays in people's perceptions of their class position; second, by looking at the role of suburbanization. This is the only measure available to investigate directly the question of lifestyle—not just the amount of income earned but how it is spent to approximate a middle-class ideal. Fortunately, suburbanization has been a central item in the mythology of middle-class affluence. As Ben Wattenberg puts it in his celebration of the "massive majority middle class":

> For at least a quarter of a century, the idea of "middle class" in America has been associated with the idea of "suburbia." . . . It should come as no surprise to see . . . a massive increase in the rate and number of suburban dwellers. . . . There is no other nation in the world where suburbia has become the plurality lifestyle nor where it is moving, apparently inexorably, toward majority status. The case can be made, in fact, that the suburban lifestyle is the first new and major residential life pattern to emerge since the rapid growth of the cities during the early years of the Industrial Revolution. (1974:105–7)

This typically overblown statement suggests that suburbanization has weakened the class divisions that characterized industrial urban America.[23] But there are no data on suburbanization's effects; Wattenberg's data document the growth of suburbs, not their consequences. What we need to discover is whether suburbanization in particular and affluence in general really make any difference for workers who are otherwise thoroughly proletarian.[24]

In Chapter 4 we found that income is an important determinant of middle-class placements. In that sense the affluence argument is sustained: the more money one makes, the more likely one is to be middle class. But how important is income relative to class differences? Can workers *earn* their way into the middle class? Here the support for the affluence argument is more modest.[25] Figure 11.1 plots the proportions of middle-class placements separately for managers and workers (of equivalent education, occupational prestige, age, and so on). At all levels of income there is a substantial gap between managers and workers. In fact, workers making $16,000 would have to increase their income eight times before they had the same probability of being middle class as managers with $16,000 incomes. Thus, while higher incomes do tend to make workers more middle class, they do not make up for the basic class division that separates workers from managers.

Suburbanization does seem to have some effect on people's perception of their class position, but the effect is so modest that it is hardly worth the fuss that has been made over it. Relative to equivalent city and rural residents, suburbanites are 4 percent more likely to see themselves as middle class. The difference is larger than we could attribute to chance alone, but it cannot be of much substantive significance. Suburban workers are about 41 percent middle class; urban workers are 37 percent middle class. Equiv-

23. Eli Chinoy (1955:126) also emphasizes that possessions, particularly a home, convince his autoworkers that they are moving forward and thus have no need of collective protest. See also de Tocqueville [1835], 1954 [vol. 2]: 270; Lipset, 1960:269; and Lane, 1962: 80, 250.

24. Radical analyses (e.g., Parenti, 1978:101) have also blamed consumerism in the working class for falsely allying workers with property-owning capitalists.

25. We also do not know much of the income effect may be a proxy for differences in class position not captured by our three class indicators. In Chapter 4 we noted the weakness of the class indicators, especially the measure of authority. How much of the difference between a $30,000 truck dispatcher and a $15,000 truck dispatcher might be unmeasured differences in the class position of the two jobs (e.g., greater authority or more planning duties)?

FIGURE 11.1. Effects of income on class perceptions of
                    managers and workers

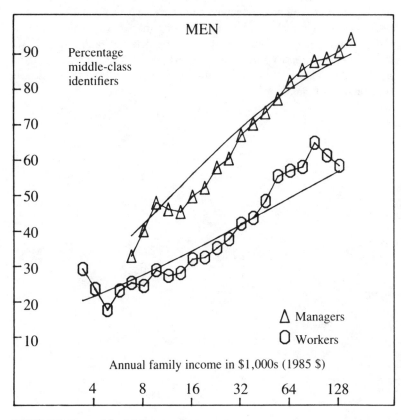

SOURCE: General Social Surveys.
NOTE: Fitted curve and plotted points are calculated after controls for occupational
prestige and years of education. Each point is a weighted average across ± 3 income categories.

alent managers are 60 percent and 55 percent middle class. Suburban
workers may appreciate the more open spaces and amenities of suburban
life, but they are not fooled into thinking they are middle class.

Our analyses therefore remind us again of the importance of the distinction between class and status to an understanding of how Americans see their society. Status differences such as income levels and lifestyles may be important to the way Americans rank themselves along a scale from low to high status, but they are less significant in the way Americans determine positions across the class division separating the working class from the middle class. That division, like the division between both those classes and capital, is primarily a division based on power. The American Dream, insofar as it includes visions of comfort and affluence, is largely irrelevant to the course of class conflicts.

TABLE 11.A. Adjusted class placements by own and father's occupation

| | Adjusted Percentage Middle-Class Self-Placement | | | |
	Unskilled	Skilled	White-Collar	Managerial/Professional
		Men		
Father's occupation				
Farm	22% (246)	26% (159)	34% (48)	57% (121)
Unskilled	22% (377)	28% (242)	39% (107)	57% (222)
Skilled	26% (249)	29% (301)	44% (97)	65% (256)
White-collar	26% (42)	33% (31)	36% (31)	63% (87)
Managerial/professional	37% (118)	32% (121)	55% (111)	67% (485)
		Women		
Father's occupation				
Farm	39% (167)	52% (37)	40% (125)	48% (101)
Unskilled	34% (231)	34% (44)	38% (236)	43% (123)
Skilled	30% (164)	46% (32)	39% (277)	46% (120)
White-collar	38% (29)	39% (10)	30% (76)	43% (42)
Managerial/professional	37% (71)	60% (12)	47% (258)	52% (292)

SOURCE: General Social Surveys.
NOTE: Controls were applied for own education, family income, a marital status dummy, spouse's labor force status, spouse's occupational group, spouse's education, mother's education, a dummy variable for missing data on mother's education, father's education, and a dummy variable for missing data on father's education.

TABLE 11.B. Adjusted class placements of the upwardly mobile, downwardly mobile, and stable

| | Adjusted Percentage Middle-Class Self-Placement | | |
	Upwardly Mobile	*Stable*	*Downwardly Mobile*
Men	39%	36%	30%
	(1,584)	(1,196)	(678)
Women	42%	42%	41%
	(1,266)	(636)	(552)

SOURCE: General Social Surveys.
NOTE: Sample sizes are in parentheses. Controls are for own education, family income, a marital status dummy variable, spouse's labor force status, spouse's occupational group, spouse's education, mother's education and a dummy variable for missing data on father's education. Upward mobility is defined as being in an occupational group higher than father's.

TABLE 11.C. Adjusted effects of upward, downward, and
no mobility

	Adjusted Percentage Middle-Class Self-Placement		
	Upwardly Mobile	Stable	Downwardly Mobile
Men	46%	45%	49%
	(1,584)	(1,196)	(678)
Women	42%	43%	44%
	(1,266)	(636)	(552)

SOURCE: General Social Surveys.
NOTE: Sample sizes are in parentheses. Controls are for own occupational group, father's occupational group, own education, family income, a marital status dummy, spouse's labor-force status, spouse's occupational group, spouse's education, mother's education, and a dummy variable for missing data on mother's education, father's education and a dummy variable for missing data on father's education. Upward mobility is defined as being in an occupational group higher than father's.

CHAPTER 12
REVERSING THE FOCUS

Capitalist Strength and Working-Class Consciousness

It is not the consciousness of men that determines their being, but, on the contrary, their social being determines their consciousness.—Karl Marx [1859], 1970:21

When we began working on American class perceptions, we were unsure of what we would find. What we discovered—over and over again—was that American workers are amazingly clear on the shape of the American class system and their place within it. We also discovered that our colleagues were often not pleased by our findings. The conventional wisdom that American workers were not class conscious had become ingrained in both the Left and the Right. As we continued to question other aspects of the paradigm of American exceptionalism, we were struck by how little hard evidence supported the conventional wisdom. In contrast, we were encouraged by the consistency of our results. The sum of the research adds up to a more convincing case than the parts taken singly.

First, Americans recognize class divisions. When they apply "middle class" and "working class" labels to themselves, they pay attention to where they fit in the dominance-subordination relations of production. If they supervise other workers, if they own their own productive property, and if they help plan the work or private lives of others, they are more likely to think of themselves as middle class. On the other hand, Americans do *not* assign class labels according to the prestige level of their occupations (Chapter 4). What matters is power, not status. Moreover, Americans recognize class divisions just as clearly as the British (Chapter 7), a society often assumed to be more sharply divided than the United States.

Working-class Americans are especially likely to recognize the class lines that divide them from the middle class. When they sort occupations into different social classes, the major line of division separates profession-

283

als and managers from all other workers. They are also more likely than middle-class Americans to isolate capitalists (i.e., big corporation executives) into a distinct category (Chapter 5). Middle-class Americans, on the other hand, are more likely to assimilate skilled and affluent blue-collar workers with themselves into a broad middle mass. This peculiarly middle-class image of society matches well the image drawn by much of American sociology. Workers have had a different image.

Moreover, Americans' clear perception of class divisions has not diminished over the years. True, postwar prosperity increased the size of the American middle class, but the division between it and the working class remains much where it always was (Chapter 6). Indeed, the gradual upward shift in middle-class self-perceptions matches almost exactly the objective changes in the social structure. The coordination of the subjective and objective changes suggests that Americans' models of class follow some absolute standard (i.e., the exercise of class power) and do not merely rank people along some relative scale of social status. The turning point in class perceptions has not been the postwar prosperity but may have been the Depression of the 1930s. That trauma apparently eliminated most pretensions to middle-class standing that were not grounded in objective conditions.

Second, most of the suggested causes of American exceptionalism do not seem to interfere with class perceptions. For example, Americans do not consider ethnic background relevant to determining class position. Italian-Americans are not less likely to think of themselves as middle class than are similarly placed native-born Americans of Anglo-Saxon origins (Chapter 9). Blacks (who are a partial exception to this rule in adopting unexpectedly high levels of working-class identification) draw their class dividing line just as white Americans do, placing professionals and managers in the middle class and others in the working class (Chapter 10). Living on the frontier or in the South (Chapter 11) makes little difference in class perceptions. And the upwardly mobile neither enjoy any special claims on middle-class standing nor support with special ardor a belief in the American Dream.

The accumulation of all this evidence requires a reconsideration of the prevailing wisdom about class consciousness in America. On what basis has previous work concluded that American workers lack class consciousness? How does their evidence differ from ours in a way that might explain the different conclusions? The first surprise we turned up in our search through the literature was that impressive evidence documenting the class consciousness of American workers was already on the record. Whether it was the "bitter feelings and fierce words" of a Newburyport worker, the Lynds' record of "Middletown" workers' contempt for but fear of "the business classes" (Chapter 2), or the New Haven mechanic's analysis of class structure (Chapter 4), evidence abounded that American workers clearly recognize the divisions that separate them from the owners and managers who dominate society. In dispute here is the interpretation of that evidence. Thernstrom dismisses the fierce words as "an elaborate game"; the Lynds concluded that Middletown workers were "individualists in an individualist culture"; Bakke's research has been neglected.

How could Thernstrom's and the Lynds' classic analyses of the American worker blithely dismiss their own evidence? And why had critics let them get away with it? Why was Bakke ignored? The problem originates, we believe, in the voluntaristic fallacy of explaining social outcomes with inferences about the psychology of the actors. American workers have not sponsored a socialist party with anywhere near the power of the European Left, and their union movement is a pale shadow of European unionism. These different outcomes led to the common inference of different psychological motivations—an inference so natural that not even critics noticed its psychological reductionism. Instead, debate flowed around the causes of this supposedly exceptional psychology: mobility, ethnic diversity, affluence, the lack of feudalism, and so on. Given so many possible explanations, nobody stopped to ask whether the phenomenon existed in the first place.

But there can be no simple one-to-one translation between workers' psychology and societal outcomes. Class subordination always interferes with workers' ability to realize their preferences. Inferences about workers' psychology led the American exceptionalism debates into a totally circular path: levels of class consciousness were inferred from the outward behavior; the class consciousness was then used to explain exactly the same behavior. The best way out of this circle is independent evidence on workers' class consciousness. But even where such direct investigations were undertaken, the conclusions were preordained: weak class consciousness was so obvious to all that interpretations of any new evidence were forced into the mold of the prevailing wisdom.

Blaming the American working class for its subordinate position pervades the theories of both the Left and the Right. The Left blames weak class consciousness among workers for the failure to lead a successful socialist movement. Conservatives contend that existing status differences are generally accepted as the just rewards due the privileged for their capital, hard work, motivation, and determination. In both cases, the blame for workers' subordinate position is placed squarely in the heads of the workers themselves.

The concept of victim blame has been well known to American sociology for two decades. Most introductory textbooks now contain descriptions of the functions performed by victim-blaming, who benefits, and how to identify such arguments. American sociology usually rejects the idea that women, minorities, and the poor are oppressed because they prefer subordinate status, don't work hard enough, have low self-esteem, and so on, yet it retains those types of arguments about the working class. Despite the longer history of social science research on class than on race or gender, blaming the victim still seems prevalent in much of the literature on the working class.

But what happens if we relinquish the victim-blaming approaches? If we accept the evidence for working-class consciousness in America, then the weak union movement and the failure of socialism still demand an explanation. Unfortunately, we have no easy or complete answers. We cannot offer a full-fledged alternative theory that will satisfy those who have come this far with us in questioning the conventional wisdom. That would require nothing less than another volume as large as this one. However, we can offer some suggestions about where to begin the search for solutions to the puzzle of American exceptionalism.

We believe that any attempt to understand the character of the American class struggle must focus on the exceptional character of American capitalists and on the resources that they bring to the struggle. It must also attend to the resources that workers have and to the battles they have already waged and continue to wage on a daily basis. In short, it is time to take a fresh look at both parties to class struggle in the United States.

The remainder of this chapter is divided into two parts. The first reports on new research that avoids victim-blaming and develops new insights into the daily character of class struggle as it is experienced by workers. To understand when, why, and how worker resistance takes place we look to this new research. The second focuses on the other party to class struggle and suggests some of the qualities that make American capital unique. To understand when, why, and how the resistance strategies of workers are successful, we should look to capitalist strength. In sum, the solution to the problem of American exceptionalism lies in the strength of capital as well as the consciousness and actions of the working class.

Resistance

The most promising fresh look at the working class comes from scholars investigating the intersection of class, race, and gender—a pursuit that springs from the new scholarship on women. This new research puts women and racial ethnic minorities at the center of our attention (Collins, forthcoming), rather than viewing them as either more radical (racial ethnics) or less radical (women) deviations from the "normal" white male worker. It is an approach increasingly called for, since women and minorities now constitute a majority of America's working class (Wright et al., 1982) and of its poor adults (Stallard et al., 1983). The theoretical value of focusing on women and minority workers is that it forces us to consider the interlocking connections between systems of oppression. As Rollins argues in her study of domestic workers:

> This is precisely the value of this study: the potential for the findings to have applicability to and thereby enhance our understanding of other kinds of relationships of domination, relationships in which the psychodynamics might be obscured by the more impersonal, institutionalized nature of the domination (as in bureaucracy) or by the emotional and social bonds between the parties (as in marriage) but in which they are just as powerful in contributing to the perpetuation of inequality. (1985:8)

Thus, research on race, class, and gender takes for granted that research on domestics, hospital ward secretaries, or jewelry-makers is research on the working class and must inform our visions of class in America.

These studies express no doubt about the class consciousness of the workers they observe. Black women workers resist oppression every day in myriad ways, some of which might be easily overlooked if attention were narrowly focused on the institutionalized resistance of white male union movements. Moreover as Collins (forthcoming) argues, it is apparent that oppositional consciousness is itself a form of resistance to the demands for deference and the direct assaults on their personhood that many Black women workers confront every day and that it can coexist with unfree and apparently conforming behavior. For example, recent research on Black women domestics (e.g., Dill, 1979; Rollins, 1985) documents their ways of preserving a positive view of self in the face of harsh daily treatment. Domestic work is precisely the kind of job that past research has seen as demeaning, full of the "hidden injuries of class" for those Americans who never made it up the ladder of opportunity (Sennett and Cobb, 1972; see also Chinoy, 1955:123–29). But domestic workers reject devaluation in three ways: they acquire intimate knowledge of their employers' lives that demystifies any ideology of superiority; they maintain values that contradict the white middle-class values of their employers (for example, they may measure a person's worth more by the quality of his or her interpersonal relationships and community standing than by material success); and they develop an "understanding of the meaning of class and race in America" that explains their subordinate position (Rollins, 1985:212–13). In the words of one respondent, "Domination. That's the name of the game. The more you know, the more you make the employer uneasy. . . . They want to dominate, exploit" (Rollins, 1985:227).

Participant observation in a costume jewelry factory identified three common forms of resistance practiced by the women workers (Shapiro-Perl, 1984:193–94). First, workers engaged in "pacing": that is, selectively hustling and idling to regulate their output to serve their own economic interests. Second, workers participated collectively in griping and antics to protest the pay and work situation; because everyone grumbled, supervisors could not single out any individual for retaliation, despite the stress it created for them. And finally, workers quit—the defiant act of withdrawing their labor power.

One incident on the shop floor illustrates their solidarity despite their weak position. As workers prepared to quit during a struggle over work conditions, an older woman worker counseled an appropriate orientation toward their jobs: "You learn these things. Not to get upset by this. Never take the job seriously. Just go from one factory to the next. Stand up for what you think is right. You wait for the right time to say things. You're young. You'll learn this" (Shapiro-Perl, 1984:204). These are not the words of a woman who is confused about her place in the class system. Rather, they come from a seasoned veteran who knows the game and maintains dignity by leaving one job for another when she must.

In a southern hospital, ward secretaries organized a more collective resistance by walking off the job after less formal means of protest proved ineffective (Sacks, 1984). And since World War II, retail sales workers across the nation have developed work groups that foster solidarity and counteract the competitiveness encouraged by management (Benson, 1984:119).

Each of these actions is familiar to students of industrial sociology. What is new is the interpretation: these investigators see them all as daily acts of class-conscious resistance. The resistance varies from individual quitting to collective walkouts or strikes, from minor fights to major challenges, from low-risk complaining to putting jobs on the line. Even the "mild" forms of low-risk resistance that pose no serious threat to management's power can validate the workers' role in the ongoing struggle. Shapiro-Perl (1984:195) contends that these workers' "conduct is no less than a calculated defense of class interests based on an experiential understanding of class struggle." To view worker militance only in terms of conventional actions like strikes or walkouts is to overlook informal but ongoing fight-back strategies that may contain the embryo of future worker organization. As these scholars see it, resistance is a way of life in communities of oppressed people, not an isolated incident or series of incidents in their history (Bookman and Morgen, forthcoming). In fact, survival itself is seen as a form of resistance when the oppression of workers and their families has been so severe as to endanger life and community (cf. Davis, 1981, on slave women's resistance; Dill, 1982; Schecter, 1982, on the battered women's movement).

Past observers of such resistance have dismissed it as either destructive of organizational goals (the establishment critique) or as a poor substitute for class struggle (the Marxist critique). Michael Burawoy (1978) is typical of the Marxist perspective. Burawoy criticizes Braverman (1974) for not sufficiently recognizing workers' struggles to resist management, and he documents the "games" that machine shop workers devise to win some control of their work routines. Yet rather than seeing these games as instances of class-conscious resistance, he draws the opposite conclusion: the games, he says, help to mystify the ongoing exploitation and produce *consent* to the power of management.

Why does Burawoy draw such a different conclusion from behavior that is quite similar to the actions reported in the studies of women workers? Part of the explanation lies in the conceptual baggage that researchers bring to their observations. Because the research on women grows out of a newly emerging field, researchers approach the study of class free from the weight of the theoretical perspectives that define and sometimes constrict the analysis of the working class. For Marxists, the shop floor games and the women's griping, pacing, and quitting are pale attempts at class struggle. Class consciousness, in their view, demands radical forms of resistance.

The women's research interprets shop-floor resistance as a more class-conscious struggle because it has a healthier respect for the power of management and owners. Recognizing that the balance of power rests with management, the investigators conclude that informal resistance may be the only alternative typically open to workers. For example, in their study of women workers in Silicon Valley, Katz and Kemnitzer (1984:214–15) observe:

> At this juncture the initiative is in the hands of employers and . . . the options open to workers are not of their own making. While in one way this formulation is true, and available options allow workers to find a livable strategy only within narrow limits, this does not give "the system" total dominance leaving no role for the perceptions, actions, and choices of real human beings. Indeed, quite the reverse is true; as we observed, individual workers quite knowingly take advantage of the contradictions and interstices of the situations they confront.

The "failure" to engage in more radical confrontations results from an awareness of management's power to stifle the protests by redesigning the workplace or firing all the protesters.

The researchers have no illusions about the limitations of informal means of resistance. The individualized choices workers can make have only the most limited potential for transforming the system. Quitting ultimately creates an industry with high turnover that robs the shop of its best leaders. After the successful walkout by ward secretaries, the hospital management took over the training of new ward secretaries in order to teach new workers "the right attitudes" and prevent worker self-training from developing solidarity among the secretaries (Sacks, 1984). Shapiro-Perl (1984:202) likewise points out how the pacing strategy of jewelry workers could be co-opted by management because of "the immense power management wields and the seemingly infinite ways it can step in to squelch worker resistance or turn it to its own ends."

The respect accorded to the power of management and owners by the scholars cited here may be more readily forthcoming when the research task is to simultaneously address the meaning of class, race, and gender oppression in people's lives.[1] Given this explicit objective (Collins, forth-

---

1. Despite its importance to understanding class in America, addressing the intersection of race, class, and gender is no easy task. For example, much of the new scholarship on women and patriarchy has replicated the exclusive tendencies of other fields and failed to incorporate

coming), it may be difficult to minimize the power of the oppressor in determining the success or failure of workers' resistance efforts.[2] In sum, our own research and this newly emerging body of work on race, class, and gender both point to the need to attend to the power of American capital if we hope to understand American exceptionalism.

Capitalist Strength

We believe it would be a worthwhile corrective to past mistakes to entertain a model of class conflict which assumes that working-class resistance is a constant feature of all capitalist societies and that the variation in class conflicts arises mostly from the differential resources that capital can bring to bear on workers.[3] Such a model denies the pluralist belief in the absence of a dominant class. It also reverses the usual order of priorities in the Marxist literature, which sees capital's domination as a constant feature, indeed a definitional axiom, of capitalist society. Marxists usually interpret variation in class conflicts as arising from workers' differential abilities — or worse, their differential predispositions — to overturn capitalist domination.

We do not pretend to be the first to think seriously about capital's

---

race and class into the analysis; see Baca Zinn et al. (1986) for a summary of these problems. Nevertheless, we feel that such work is likely to help us reformulate our visions of class in America.

2. However, we cannot ignore the fact that the Marxist dismissal of informal resistance is a white male interpretation and that race, class, and gender research is conducted by women and people of color. We suspect that because they are themselves members of oppressed groups, these researchers are far more aware of the vulnerability of workers to powerful bosses. Their own experience of oppression has taught them that consciousness and militancy do not always enable subordinate groups to overcome their oppression. What many white males see as a failure of class consciousness, some women and people of color recognize as the best possible outcome of active struggle against a more powerful oppressor. The workers do not lack class consciousness; they lack power.

3. Friends have warned us that this alternative model is too extreme: surely the truth lies somewhere in between, part capitalist strength, part working-class weakness. We have avoided such intellectual caution partly because we suspect that it could never dislodge the dominant paradigm. Also, the more we have used the capitalist strength model, the more impressed we are by how much it explains. More research remains to be done, but it seems to us, the more seriously we entertain this "extreme" model, the faster we will make progress.

strength. But on the one hand, establishment social science has been too
eager to minimize capital's power; on the other, the Marxist critique has
been too dogmatic in asserting capital's domination to be of much help in
explaining variations in capitalist strength. What we need is an appreciation of the power of capital as a *variable* feature of American society. We
need to explore capital's acquisition of power and its hold on society as a
dynamic process.

Revolutions

Early work on revolutionary potential did not always look in the right
places for its data. The first impulse was usually to examine workers. This
impulse derives from Marx's insistence that only the working class can deliver society from capitalist domination; it is the championing of workers'
struggles that sets Marxism apart from alternative "bourgeois" and "utopian" socialism. But acceptance of Marx's emphasis on working-class
struggles does not imply a belief that the only determinants of workers'
success lie within the workers' movement itself. That only traps us into the
victim-blaming fallacies we are trying to avoid.

Although the capital-worker relationship is central to the fate of capitalist societies, many of the determinants of that relationship lie outside the
capital-worker dyad. International wars and resistance from precapitalist
elites have weakened (and strengthened) capital in ways that determine its
vulnerability to challenges from subordinate groups (Therborn, 1977;
Skocpol, 1979). It is no accident that the Russian, Chinese, and Vietnamese revolutions followed immediately upon invasions by foreign armies.
These invasions weakened the hold of dominant classes without replacing
them with a permanent alternative. Revolutionary forces seize their opportunities when they can. The Russian, Chinese, and Vietnamese workers
and peasants made their revolutions, but not by themselves—not under
circumstances they themselves chose but under the "inherited circumstances they directly confronted" (Marx [1852], 1974: 146). There was not
enough that was exceptional about these forces to explain where and when
their revolutions succeeded. What was exceptional was the weakened and
disoriented opposition they faced.[4]

---

4. Lenin ([1920], 1975 [vol. 3]:343) acknowledges the dual prerequisites of successful
revolutions in his attack on "left-wing communism": "It is not enough for the exploited and
oppressed masses to realise the impossibility of living in the old way, and demand changes;

Jeffrey Paige's (1975) analysis of class conflicts in agrarian economies is another significant step in the direction of paying closer attention to dominant classes. Paige builds a four-celled table based on the strength or weakness of dominant and subordinate classes. The advantage of Paige's approach is that it assesses the strength of each class independently of the strength of the other class (cf. Korpi, 1978). Nevertheless, the distinction between revolutionary outbreaks and milder reformism is determined primarily by differences in the strength of the *dominant* class. Where the dominant class bases its power on the relatively strong resource of capital ownership, it is able to channel its labor opposition into the more manageable "reform-mongering" movements; but where the dominant class is weakened by its dependence on a fixed supply of land, it risks the outbreak of true revolution.

In contrast, the strength of the subordinate class affects only the type of revolution (peasant rebellions versus socialist/nationalist revolutions) or the oganizational structure of reformism (political action on commodity prices versus labor unions). It does not determine the more fundamental revolt or reform distinction. There may be a lesson here about the role of class consciousness in revolutions: class consciousness may be important not so much for destroying the old order (Moorhouse, 1976; Tilly and Tilly, 1981) as for the success of reconstructing society along truly socialist lines (Lukács [1922], 1971:70). After the revolution, a mobilized and class-conscious proletariat must resist the creation of new forms of privilege that threaten to subordinate workers once again (see Kraus, 1981 and 1983, on the Chinese case).

Finally, Mark Traugott's (1985) study of the Parisian insurrection of June 1848 again identifies dominant-class strength as the critical determinant of revolutionary outcomes. Traugott compares the social origins of the discontented workers from the National Workshops with the volunteers of the Mobile Guard who eventually repressed the revolution. He finds little class difference between the two armies; it was the organizational coherence of its officer corps that led the Mobile Guard into a reactionary role while the National Workshops dissolved into a revolutionary mob. Traugott interprets the failure of the 1848 insurrection as confirmation of Kath-

---

for a revolution to take place it is essential that the exploiters should not be able to live and rule in the old way. It is only when the ' *lower classes' do not want* to live in the old way and the 'upper classes' *cannot carry on in the old way* that the revolution can triumph."

erine Chorley's (1943) conclusion that no popular revolt can defeat a well-organized and properly trained military. Once again, it is the nature of the dominant forces, not the insurgents, that best explains revolutionary outcomes.

So too, in explaining American exceptionalism, we need to look first at American capital to explain the failures of the American Left. Rarely in the voluminous literature on American exceptionalism does one get the idea that capitalists might have had something to do with the failure of working-class movements. Yet participants in American class conflict have not neglected the strength of capital. In 1912, Samuel Gompers was quite clear about what made America exceptional:

> Nowhere in the civilized world is there such relentless, bitter, brutal war made upon the labor organization and the laboring men as here in the United States. In no country on the face of the globe is corporate wealth, the position of wealth, so powerful as it is here. (quoted in Dick, 1972:117)

The question that must be asked is not what weaknesses of workers undermined their protests but what resources of American capital gave it the capacity to thwart the challenges from below.

Economic resources

Foremost among these resources is American capital's economic strength (Tawney, 1942). We cannot forget that American workers mounted their challenge against a capitalist class that was then building its hegemony over the entire world economy. British industrial workers faced a declining world power; German workers, a capitalist class kept in check by nearby rivals who had arrived earlier; Swedish workers, a vibrant but small class whose size permitted it at best a marginal role in world capitalism. American capital, by contrast, not only dominated its own working class but overwhelmed its European competitors as well. The profits garnered by such massive growth provided an ample cushion against periodic challenges from below.

Strikes. One area in which these economic resources prove decisive is in industrial conflict. Insofar as strikes become a test of strength between capital and labor, economic resources enable capital to hold out for long-term advantages, despite any short-term cost.

Two facts are crucial for understanding U.S. strikes. First, American strikes remain among the *longest* in the world. While strikes have become shorter (and more widespread and frequent) in most other countries (Shorter and Tilly, 1974), the "shape" of U.S. strikes has remained remarkably constant (Edwards, 1981). There is little sign of the short "demonstration" walkout now typical of European industrial relations (Korpi and Shalev, 1980:315). U.S. strikes still produce the extended dramas that test the will of capital and labor over the unions' basic right to exist. Second, long strikes tend to be won by employers (Edwards, 1981:47). If management is going to capitulate, it tends to concede early in order to get back into the market. But if it wants a victory, it will hold out until the union breaks. In such a contest, U.S. capital rarely loses, partly because it has the financial resources to withstand enormous, if temporary, losses. This strategy would be self-destructive for weaker employers.

The great expansion of U.S. labor during the 1930s coincided with the lowest economic ebb of U.S. capital. Weakened already by declining markets and slashed stock values, capital had far less cushion with which to sustain prolonged shutdowns. One wonders also to what extent the economic disaster had demoralized American capital. The contrast with 1919 is instructive: then, U.S. Steel, still fattened by wartime profits, simply refused to consider any union demands.

Of course, the full story is more complex. Cyclical recessions, in contrast to the Great Depression, usually reinforce capital's grip over labor.[5] The 1930s may have reversed the usual order because of the government's new restraint in backing capital. But the theoretical import remains the same: the ups and downs of the U.S. labor movement result more from the environment in which labor finds itself than from any actions of unions or workers themselves.[6]

5. Econometric analyses confirm the decline of strike activity during periods of high unemployment (Ashenfelter and Johnson, 1969; Hibbs, 1976; Shalev, 1980). Despite the greater grievances of labor, unions are more vulnerable during recessions. Temporary shutdowns present no threat to a management already gearing down for slack demand. High unemployment also robs workers of alternative jobs, thus making them more cautious than when employment choices are more abundant.

6. The labor historian David Brody remarks: "The evident fact [is] that the decisive factors for union expansion lay outside the labor movement. . . . The political changes, together with the economic impact of the depression, cut down the defenses of capital. Even the mightiest of corporations became vulnerable to unionization during the thirties. The labor movement

Managerial control. U.S. capital's extraordinary economic surplus may also help to explain how American corporations developed a series of ingenious control mechanisms to keep labor in its place: scientific management, the assembly line, welfare capitalism, company unions, the human relations school, continuous process automation, computerization, and quality circles. Even an incomplete list impresses the observer with the variety of organizational controls that management has adopted in the course of the twentieth century.

The historic force of these controls is their steady onslaught, with each new managerial tactic replacing earlier attempts (Clawson, 1980). No tactic was decisive in its own right. Even the most overawed observers of Taylorism admit its limitations. The control won by many other innovations proved equally transitory: the employee benefits and company unions so popular in the 1920s quickly dissolved in the face of the militant unionism of the 1930s. Similarly, the new "bureaucratic control" and job ladders, which now seem so "totalitarian," will in the future have to be supplemented by further controls to maintain management's power (Edwards, 1979:152).

But new schemes keep management on the offensive. It is easy for critics to underestimate how difficult it is for bosses to maintain authority. Capital must learn how to dominate; it is not born with this knowledge. Melvin Dubofsky sees the turning point in the 1880s:

> At the start [in the 1870s] workers enjoyed a commanding position locally. Community merchants, professionals, and editors (clergy also) backed their working-class neighbors and customers in struggles against outside capitalists. Between 1877 and the next sharp outbreak of working-class violence in 1886, the balance of power between workers and their employers had tipped in favor of the industrialists. . . . Businesses grew in size and capital resources . . . many firms were in a stronger position to discipline their workers and to risk industrial warfare. In addition, many firms now operated more than a single plant. . . . Technological innovation also undercut the strength and security of workers. (1975:41)

John Commons, today considered a conservative labor historian, recognized in 1908 that U.S. corporations had further augmented their power to control labor:

---

was the beneficiary, not the agent, of the sudden turn in its fortunes" (1971:119,126). Brody also cites rank-and-file militancy as a contributing cause, but this seems to us to confuse cause and effect once more. Workers, like their union leaders, became more militant because the environment had become one in which successful confrontations were possible.

Strikes are successful mainly in the early stages when employers have not
learned the tactics of organization. After they have perfected their association,
after these associations have federated, and especially after employers have
consolidated in great corporations and trusts, their capacity for united action exceeds that of organized labor. . . . By wise promotions, watchful detectives, by
prompt discharge of agitators, by an all-around increase of wages when agita-
tion is active on the outside, by a reduction only when the menace has passed or
when work is slack, by shutting down a plant where unionism is taking root and
throwing orders to other plants, by establishing the so-called "open shop"—
these and other masterful strategems set up a problem quite different from what
unionism has heretofore met. (1908:280)

Of course, Commons mistook the growth of the giant trusts for a final cul-
mination of the class struggle, though it was actually only a stage in a continuing dialectical process; both sides continue to learn new strategems and
to deploy new weapons. But Commons did understand the fact that both
sides developed in the course of the conflict; it is not just a question of the
growth of class consciousness on labor's side.

The proletariat is simultaneously developing its strength for many of the
reasons Marx and Engels outlined:

With the development of industry the proletariat not only increases in number; it
becomes concentrated in greater masses, its strength grows, and it feels that
strength more. . . . This organisation of the proletarians into a class, and consequently into a political party, is continually being upset again by the competition among workers themselves. But it ever rises up again, stronger, firmer,
mightier. (Marx and Engels [1848], 1976:492–93)

But because capital has more resources at its disposal, its learning process
is faster, making the more advanced industrial economies less susceptible
to overthrow from below. Revolutions occur so often in the early phases of
capitalism (as in France in 1789, Russia in 1917), because it is then that
capitalists are most disorganized and most weakened by propertied rivals
abroad and at home. Despite the numerical and organizational weaknesses
of the early proletariat, it enjoys the advantage of a vulnerable moment in
history when less strength is required to topple the new regime.[7]

---

7. Alvin Gouldner (1980:141) has also explained the failures of working-class movements
in advanced capitalism as a consequence of the growing strength of capital. But he equates
capital's strength with its ideological hegemony over workers (i.e., the failure of working-
class consciousness). This is too narrow a way to consider capitalist strength and, as we have
argued throughout this book, is ultimately a form of blaming the victim.

A cross-national comparison of managerial control tactics would provide important evidence on the strength of U.S. capital. Some of these schemes originated in Europe or had European equivalents. But the wealth of U.S. capital may have permitted American corporations to invest more widely in new control mechanisms. Managerial controls are as much a capital investment as production machinery. Within the United States, it is monopoly capital firms that have usually pioneered in adopting new methods of controlling labor, from Rockefeller's welfare capitalism to Polaroid's bureaucratic controls (Edwards, 1979). They have had greater surpluses to experiment with a succession of plans devised to gain control of the workplace. American capital as a whole may have enjoyed the same economic advantage.

Political power

Repression. In 1912, Eugene Debs, the presidential candidate of the Socialist Party of America, increased his vote to 6 percent of the American electorate. By 1920, he was fighting his Democratic and Republican opponents from a jail in Atlanta, Georgia. Debs's treatment was perhaps mild in comparison to the fate of other political radicals. Anarchists were hanged in response to Chicago's Haymarket riot of 1886, and radicals were deported by the hundreds during the Red Scare of 1919–20.

Military intervention in strikes has been an effective weapon against labor for over a hundred years (see Table 12.1). In 1877, when a railroad strike blew out of the control of the various state militias that had been called up to suppress it, President Rutherford B. Hayes sent the United States Army to "restore order." In the process more than one hundred workers were killed and the strike was broken. After 1877 if the U.S. Army was not called in to quell a strike, it was often because state militias, the National Guard, or the local constabulary had already proved sufficient. One estimate counts 160 interventions by state and federal troops against striking workers (Taft and Ross, 1969:380).[8]

---

8. Leon Wolff, after noting the devastating effect of the state militia on the 1892 Homestead strike, lamented that "one searches in vain for a single case where the introduction of troops operated to the strikers' advantage" (Wolff, 1965:228). Actually, the record is not that bleak; at least three cases can be cited. In 1894, Populist Governor David Waite sent the state militia to Cripple Creek, Colorado, where it dispersed an army of sheriff's deputies and

TABLE 12.1. Use of federal troops to end strikes

Year	Location	Industry
1877	national	railroad (Great Upheaval)
1882	Omaha	smelting
1892	Coeur d'Alene, Idaho	metal mining
1894	national	railroad (Pullman)
1899	Coeur d'Alene, Idaho	metal mining
1907	Goldfield, Nevada	metal mining
1917	Pacific Northwest	lumber
1917	Montana and Arizona	copper
1919	national	steel
1919	Seattle	general strike
1919–22	national	coal mining
1920	Denver	streetcar
1941	Los Angeles	aviation
1944	Philadelphia	transit
1945	national	oil
1970	New York	postal
1981	national	air traffic controllers

SOURCES: Brecher, 1972; Goldstein, 1978.

forced a settlement on union terms (Jensen, 1950:38–53). In 1898, Governor John Tanner of Illinois sent National Guardsmen to the Virden coal mines to prevent strikebreakers from entering town (Taft and Ross, 1969:289). And in 1934, Farmer-Labor Governor Floyd Olson of Minnesota sent the National Guard to Minneapolis during a teamsters' strike and, after some hesitation, prevented the movement of most trucks (Walker, 1937; Bernstein, 1970:229–53). Nevertheless, one can be reasonably certain that the other 157 interventions in Ross and Taft's accounting ended up helping employers to break strikes. Capital learned quickly from exceptions and deliberately set about regaining control of the state and shoring up its support among the middle class (Dubofsky, 1969:37–38).

Government repression of the Left constitutes a long, if often poorly re-
membered, record in American history. And yet in cross-national perspec-
tive, has government repression in the United States been exceptional
(Dubofsky, 1975:100)? Debs was imprisoned for his antiwar politics, but
American socialists never faced the blanket outlawing that Bismarck
imposed on the German Social Democratic Party or Tsar Nicholas on
Lenin's Social Democrats. And, to overstate the point, Atlanta was not
Dachau.[9]

The comparative sociology of state repression has not yet been written,
but we doubt that the United States would score high in such an infamous
competition. Not all American governments were openly antilabor. Franklin D. Roosevelt's New Deal wrote a labor relations act that in theory at
least guaranteed the right of workers to unionize. The pivotal General Motors sit-down strike of 1936 succeeded only after the Michigan governor
refused to use the National Guard to evict strikers.

If far more severe state repression failed to extinguish workers' movements in Germany or Tsarist Russia, why did the U.S. Left wither after relatively mild government interference? Can we still maintain that dominant
class power explains failures of the Left? Our answer is twofold. First, despite the exceptions, state repression remains a powerful force. Second, repression is too narrow a definition of state power; it ignores the less coercive but often more effective means of controlling subordinate groups.

It would be foolish to underestimate the effectiveness of state repression
in controlling the Left. Although Lenin and the Bolsheviks survived Tsarist persecution, they triumphed only after the Russian state had been crippled by the German invasion. And although the German Social Democrats
emerged from their nineteenth-century proscription as a major party, a radical Left could not repeat this success after the Nazi decimation. In most
places, at most times, repression works—at least in the short run. Debs's
jailing and the federal troops at Coeur d'Alene made a difference. Any accounting of the problems of the American Left that neglects armed force
simply misses an important part of the story.

---

9. On the other hand, Europeans were truly shocked by the government repression following the Haymarket riots. An 1888 English commentator expressed this dismay: "Even in des-
potic Germany and enslaved Russia they would hardly venture to hang men for having written
articles and made speeches against the existing rule. It was left to the country whose political
institutions are the delight of so many of our Radical friends to commit this crime" (cited in
Moore, 1970:34).

This still does not explain why there appears to be a correlation between repression and socialist strength in the industrial world (Lipset, 1983). Nations that have most harshly repressed their labor movements have ended up with the strongest, most radical unions. The sooner workers are given the vote and collective bargaining, the more accommodating they are to capitalist domination. Thus, the United States, with early white male suffrage, has no true socialist party.[10] The correlation suggests that not only is repression ineffective; in the long run it backfires.

This may seem to be a great paradox. It implies that the dominant classes that have resorted to repression must have been very stupid, since their repression only strengthened and radicalized the opposition. The paradox is fictitious, however. It is not repression but the cessation of repression that benefits the Left. Repression works, but only so long as it can be maintained.

Repression can also be useful if it is combined with an offer to workers of more conservative alternatives. This is largely the history of the U.S. labor movement. The IWW was crushed, while the more conservative AFL received official government approval.[11] The Socialist Party was harassed, while the established parties opened themselves up to a mild reformism. American workers were left with a choice between a class-conscious but thoroughly defeated radical alternative and a conservative alternative that promised less but at least was permitted some successes.[12]

10. We are less sure of how Lipset categorizes the American labor movement as being legitimized at an "early" stage, since before the National Recovery Administration (NRA) was established, both capital and the state consistently resisted union organizing efforts whenever and wherever they appeared. Indeed, the whole measure of "economic citizenship" in Lipset's accounting seems more influenced by the eventual character of the left than by an independent assessment of the state's sanction of the labor movement (cf. Goldstein, 1983:56).

11. In 1917 the U.S. Department of Justice raided IWW headquarters across the country and arrested "almost the entire first and second-line leadership" (Dubofsky, 1975:125). On the other hand, Gompers's support of World War I won him access to President Wilson and some basic improvements in working-class life. Government-sponsored mediation boards settled labor disputes with a more evenhanded approach. The eight-hour day, equal pay for women, better working conditions, and higher wages accrued to the state-sanctioned AFL unions.

12. It bears repeating that in this environment the workers' decision to align themselves with the more successful AFL says little about their lack of class consciousness; it reflects only a simple rationality in the face of a given historical choice. Better to accept half a loaf now than to rely on great promises that would likely lead to the destruction of the union and dismissal from work. But the terms of the choice were dictated by the ruling class, not by the

Repression fails in the long run if it is not accompanied by the prospect of alternative benefits. Similarly, democratic reforms will lead to more radical demands if the Left is not repressed. Historical analyses must recognize *both* sides of this state intervention if they are to provide an accurate appraisal of the role of the state. Establishment social science focuses on the opening up of reformist alternatives and neglects the repression that went before; the Left reverses this bias.

The critical factor, therefore, is not repression; all capitalist states have repressed radical challenges that are sufficiently threatening. The critical factor is whether other benefits and other control mechanisms are simultaneously developed by dominant classes. The power of the dominant class determines its ability to develop these alternatives. Weak and hard-pressed capitalist classes do not (and cannot) develop alternative means of control. State repression is their last resort, and when this fails, the Left is released for explosive growth. But where capitalist classes are blessed with sufficient power, they have the political space to experiment with less harsh methods of control and the economic resources to entice workers to abandon more radical alternatives. We turn now to some of these less repressive types of control, which, although less violent, may be more effective.

Public policy. The surest test of power is not physical coercion or even open subordination. Power has another "face" (Bachrach and Baratz, 1962, 1963, and 1970), which can be detected not in what the powerful do but in what they leave undone—issues that are never raised, inequalities that are never challenged, injustices that are never questioned.[13] It was precisely this second face of power that the Lynds emphasized as the source of capitalist control in Muncie:

> It cannot be too often reiterated that the [Ball family—the largest capitalists] control of Middletown is for the most part unconscious rather than deliberate. People are not, when one gets beyond the immediate army of direct employees of the family, dictated to. It is rather the sort of control that makes men hesitant

---

workers. Workers were never allowed a choice between the AFL and a *successful* radical working-class movement. Even socialists who stayed within the AFL acknowledged that they did so not because they supported its conservative ideology but because the trade unions were their only viable alternative (Laslett, 1970:69).

13. The "third" face of power that Steven Lukes (1974) proposes, the ability to shape the consciousness of workers, is mainly another instance of blaming the victim.

about making decisions of importance unless these are in harmony with [Ball family] policies. Here we are witnessing the pervasiveness of the long fingers of capitalist ownership. (Lynd and Lynd, 1937:97)

Thus the fact that American labor is less often "dictated to" does not imply that American capital is any less powerful than elsewhere. Just the opposite may be the case: the infrequency of systematic state repression may indicate that capital is better able to mobilize the less coercive forms of power.[14]

To detect this second face of power, then, we must observe what is *not* done to supplement our understanding of what *is* done to control labor. Observing the unobservable is not so impossible as it may seem, especially if we bring a comparative perspective to the study of public policy. For example, labor law provides many crucial but (usually) nonviolent confrontations between workers and their government. We are handicapped by the lack of a systematic comparative sociology of labor policy, but we do know that these laws make a difference. State right-to-work laws reduce union organizing by about one-third (Ellwood and Fine, 1983). In contrast, Canadian labor laws restrain management's ability to obstruct union organizing; as a result, unions expand north of the border while they falter in the United States (Freeman and Medoff, 1984:242). The ALF-CIO insisted on U.S. labor law reform as a priority for the 1970s. Union leaders knew its importance; their problem was that they failed to achieve it. At least part of the subsequent decline in union membership can be attributed to the state hostility that this failure reflects.

Throughout the industrial era American capital has maintained control of a state that is outwardly democratic.[15] Much of Gompers's distrust of political reform can be traced to his recognition of the hostility of the state. Seemingly prolabor legislation was turned against unions (the Sherman Anti-Trust Act, for example); eight-hour laws proved to be ineffective;

14. Later, the Lynds acknowledged that coercion was sometimes necessary also, but "only in time of threatened labor trouble or political upheaval do those at the top bear down" (Lynd and Lynd, 1937:471).

15. Its power is not absolute; capital does not dictate the minutiae of all class politics. Compromises and setbacks can be readily identified but do not by themselves disprove the fact of political dominance. Critics of the neo-Marxist perspective sometimes like to think that a few counterexamples can refute the idea of capitalist control of the state. But dominant-class power, like all power, can be real without being omnipotent.

courts were consistently procapitalist. British workers, even well before
the rise of the Labour Party, experienced much less hostility (Dick,
1972:36). There, factory acts and trade union legislation benefited workers. We suspect that part of the reason for the lack of favorable labor legislation in the United States has been capital's more direct and more nearly
complete control of the state.

Mechanisms of state control

Postwar scholarship on political economy has swirled around the issue of
exactly how capital manages to maintain this control. Numerous mechanisms, from election laws to summer camps, have been suggested as contributing to capitalist control.[16] Without reviewing all of these avenues to
power, we would like to suggest that American capital enjoys greater access to several of them than does capital in most other Western nations.

   Elections. Liberals like to promote election law reform as their antidote
to the power of capital. (Eschewing an explicit class analysis, liberals
would merely point to the distortions caused by "wealth" and "special interests.") Elections cost too much, they point out, and the necessity of
hoarding campaign funds for the next election turns politicians into suppli-
cants at the feet of big money. To the extent that the need for campaign
financing biases politics in capital's favor, U.S. capital enjoys a bigger advantage than capital elsewhere. American elections cost more than elections anywhere else in the world. Campaigns are longer and depend more
heavily on expensive television advertising, which forces even the more
working-class-oriented Democrats into currying favor with capital.
   The result is that Republicans and Democrats divide the fractions of
capital between them. Republicans represent corporate oil; Democrats, independent oil. Republicans represent commercial finance; Democrats, the
savings and loan associations. In this competition for the pocketbooks of
the rich, the interests of the American working class do not enter the balance. Indeed, Elizabeth Drew reports a concern among Congressional

---

16. See Mills, 1956; Domhoff, 1967 and 1978. Our position in the debates about the
means of capitalist control is that no single avenue is decisive. Shutting off any one of them
could result in more political traffic flowing along the other routes. At the same time, political
struggles over these mechanisms of power are not meaningless. The more methods capital has
at its disposal for exercising power, the greater that power will be.

Democrats and Washington lobbyists that "we could end up with a dangerous situation in this country—where business is one party and labor the
other" (1983:43). This is precisely the "danger" that obtains in most other
Western democracies, without any undue consequences for the public
safety.

Government officials. When the head of the nation's largest stock bro-
kerage becomes secretary of the treasury and then the White House chief of
staff, it should be no mystery how capitalists exercise power. The practice
of bringing corporate executives into the government has been so widespread—in Democratic and Republican administrations alike—that
Donald Regan's appointment scarcely raised an eyebrow. Kennedy's and
Johnson's much-heralded secretary of defense, Robert McNamara, came
straight from the Ford Motor Company. What Americans sometimes forget
is how peculiar this custom is in international perspective. Where else
would the secretary of labor be a large employer whose main qualification
seems to have been sufficient wealth to become a major campaign contribu-
tor?

European cabinets rarely include corporate officials. The difference cannot be dismissed as merely the difference between parliamentary and presidential forms of government. That difference may explain why it is easier
for U.S. capital to penetrate the state, but it should not obscure the fact that
such direct penetration is much greater in the United States than elsewhere.[17]

Control of the economy. Recent neo-Marxist work on state power has
emphasized the importance of capital's control of the economy as the ultimate guarantor of its own political interests. The failure of "business
confidence" in a city, a state, or a nation quickly erodes new investment

17. We are not claiming that appointing capitalists as government officials is a sufficient or
even necessary factor in capital's control of the state. Such instrumentalist theories overlook
the importance of relatively autonomous states where capital "delegates" considerable power
to independent state officials. But recognizing relative autonomy should not lead us to neglect
the role of direct corporate penetration of the state. Instrumentalist theories were too limited;
that fault is not corrected by successor theories that disregard means of capitalist power already identified by the instrumentalists. Our contention, which is little more than a working
hypothesis now, is that—other things being equal—capital exerts even *greater* power in
those governments in which it is directly represented.

and, thus, the health of the economy. The result is the demeaning competition among elected leaders to provide a "suitable business climate" that will attract new industry and more jobs. No government official, no matter how Left-leaning or sympathetic to labor, can escape such competition. Capital exercises this power over the government without the need for any conspiracies or even any direct political role. It is, to borrow a phrase once popular in the 1960s, "part of the system."

Does capital in the United States benefit any more than that of other nations from its control of investment? We are not sure that capitalist economies vary along this dimension in any meaningful way. Nevertheless, a couple of factors suggest that, like other avenues to power, this one may be a little wider in the United States.

First, to reiterate a point we made in the first chapter, more of industry is in private hands in the United States than is typical elsewhere (see Table 1.1). Earlier, we used this fact as evidence of the weakness of the U.S. Left; now we must recognize that it may be both cause and consequence of that weakness. State ownership does not free a state from the constraints of an otherwise capitalist economy, but it may reduce the immediate leverage of private capital.

Second, geographic diversity and political fragmentation enable capital to play one jurisdiction against another in the contest for state concessions. The great expanse of the United States and its political federalism may give U.S. capital even more bargaining power than capital can wield elsewhere. Multinational expansion has further increased corporate flexibility in the postwar era. Northern states fear that their factories will flee to the Sun Belt, and Sun Belt states fear losses to the Third World (Bluestone and Harrison, 1982).

This economic leverage, because it is pervasive and *structural,* often defies recognition—much less measurement—in cross-national comparison. No money changes hands as in campaign financing, and no corporate officers switch seats to enter public office. But the political power that accrues to capital because of its control of jobs remains its most fundamental source of strength. Other avenues of access to the state may be shut off at some times in some places, but private capital always retains control over investment. The degree of control, however, varies from nation to nation; nowhere has capital's control been absolute. To a greater or lesser degree, capital's investment power has been checked by some compromises with the state or with other interests. In the United States, we suggest, these compromises have been minimal.

Ideology

The media have become everybody's favorite scapegoats for whatever they feel has gone wrong in society. Jesse Helms blames Dan Rather; women's groups attack pornography. All are struggling over the control of *ideas* as a way to change society.

The Left has adopted a similar approach in recent years. Its spokesmen cite easy reminders of corporate influence on the ideas of our times: corporate editorials on the op-ed page; Wall Street takeovers of the major networks; and elite policy discussion groups like the Trilateral Commission and the Business Roundtable. Gramsci's (1948) concept of "ideological hegemony" has won widespread acceptance as the explanation of capital's hold over society.

We are understandably skeptical about much of this analysis. Especially when it assumes that capital's ideological hegemony extends to the working class, we are unimpressed by the evidence of workers' acquiescence. It is not the working class that reads corporate op-ed pieces. It is not the working class that reads the reports—much less participates in the discussions—of the Trilateral Commission. When the "ideological hegemony" critique simply assumes a link between corporate control of the media and workers' attitudes, it falls prey to the psychological reductionism we have argued against so often.

Nevertheless, insofar as ideological hegemony refers to the *internal* cohesiveness of the dominant class and its hold over such closely allied groups as the middle class, it may explain some of the resilience of American capitalism. Forget workers, forget working-class consciousness: the real focus of study for the role of ideology should be the dominant groups. Max Weber, perhaps the first leading theorist of legitimacy, recognized why dominant groups need reassurance:

> The man of fortune is seldom satisfied with the fact of being fortunate. Beyond this he needs to know that he has a *right* to his good fortune. He wants to be convinced that he "deserves" it, and above all, that he deserves it in comparison with others. He wishes to be allowed the belief that the less fortunate also merely experience their due. Good fortune thus wants to be "legitimate" fortune. ([1915], 1946:271)

Here, the absence of a critical Left in the universities or in the media may contribute to American exceptionalism. The United States, which prides itself on its freedom of the press and freedom of speech, actually expresses a very narrow range of political opinion in its public discourse. The major debates occur well within the boundaries of conventional "bourgeois" economics. Marxist alternatives are dismissed with less attention than almost anywhere else in the industrialized world.

The conventionality of American political thought has its effect primarily within the dominant groups (not many workers attend lectures at Berkeley and Harvard, or at the Sorbonne or Cambridge), and its narrowness instills in the dominant classes a self-confidence in the legitimacy of bourgeois society that may be unparalleled in the world. Americans may debate reforms of this or that practice (environmentalism, consumerism, sexual morality) but not the fundamentals of the class system itself. Where few challenges are heard, dominant elites do not hesitate to make use of their power. The economic and political strength that capital can muster is thus reinforced by its conviction of its own "natural" right to organize society in its own interests.

The lack of feudalism

The source of this limited political thought lies partly in the failure of the Left itself. There is thus a danger of circularity in explaining bourgeois hegemony. But we can look in a second, more unlikely, place for an explanation of so thoroughgoing a bourgeois mentality. The United States, it has been often noted, was "born bourgeois." It lacks the feudal heritage that European capitalism had to overcome before it became dominant. This is, in fact, one of the most common themes in the explanations of American exceptionalism (Wells, 1906:72–76; Gramsci, [1948], 1971:286–87; Hartz, 1955; Bottomore, 1966:48; Burnham, 1974:718; Lipset, 1977 and 1983:2–6).[18] But most of the theorists supposed that the feudal heritage had its main effects on the working class, making them more conscious of class divisions (see especially Lipset, 1963:198–290). Instead, we suspect that it made its major impact on capitalists: the presence of an alternative elite weakened European capitalists in a way that American capital never experienced.[19]

---

18. Rosenblum (1973:19) complains that the feudalism explanation is not consistent with the similarly conservative labor movement in once-feudal Denmark, especially in comparison with the more radical and successful labor movements of Norway and Sweden, where feudalism had been weaker.

19. Although we emphasize here its enervating effect on *ideological* hegemony, the aristocratic heritage also diminished the *economic* and *political* strength of capital. Gramsci

.Among the legacies of the feudal-bourgeois conflict was an aristocratic tradition that tended to hold capitalism in contempt. The aristocracy eventually made its compromises with capitalism, but its sense of the sordidness of the scramble for wealth remains an underlying theme in European culture to a greater extent than in the United States. Bourgeois claims to ideological hegemony were far more contested in Europe than in the United States (Gramsci [1948], 1971:20; Burnham, 1980:42–43). The difference is not so much that bourgeois thought triumphed only in the United States—it triumphed everywhere—but that in the United States it barely faced a contest. Unchallenged by precapitalist ideals, it had scant reason to notice socialist thought either.[20]

A rethinking of ideological hegemony requires us to ask questions of what was previously taken for granted: capital's self-confidence in its own right to dominate. Michael Parenti, for instance, glosses over a very important question:

> Those who support the ongoing social order seem convinced that their claims, nor should it surprise us that persons, classes, and nations believe in their own virtue. . . . Even fascists are sincerely convinced of the virtue of their goals. What is significant is not whether the propagators of a dominant ideology believe in their own virtue—we may presume that they do—but that others do. (1978:85)

Perhaps we should not "presume" quite so hastily; there may be variation in the conviction with which dominant groups believe in their own virtue. To use Parenti's own example, it may have been the fervor with which fascists held their beliefs that gave them an advantage over bourgeois liberals in suppressing working-class resistance.

Conclusion

We began this research with a simple question. Do American workers perceive class? After extensive scrutiny of the responses of thousands of Americans to class questions, we came to the conclusion that they do. Our

---

([1948], 1971:285), e.g., notes that the "leaden burden" of unproductive precapitalist classes greatly hindered European capital accumulation.

20. Kenneth McNaught (1966) argues that a transition from liberal to socialist ideas was weakened by the lack of an aristocratic tradition of eccentricity and intellectual discipline. Consequently, the ideology of the American Left was especially vulnerable to attack as an alien doctrine.

finding contradicts taken-for-granted tenets that undergird most views of class and stratification in the United States. It is equally problematic for perspectives as divergent as neo-Marxism and neofunctionalism.

Accepting this conclusion enables us to raise many new questions about established views of the social order, what holds it together, and what challenges the existing power structure. In this last chapter we have suggested many hypotheses about the power of capital and the nature of class struggle in the United States. We recognize that in so doing we have moved far from the careful attention to data and the workers' own words that led us to this point. Nevertheless, we believe that such a theory offers the best possibility of making sense of many nagging anomalies in the existing treatments of American exceptionalism, such as the violence of American labor struggles, the political alienation of the working class, and low rates of unionization. We hope that others will also choose to raise old questions again and see what new light can be shed by attending to variations in the power of capital and by accepting the class consciousness and ongoing resistance of the American working class.

REFERENCES

Acker, Joan
1973   "Women and social stratification: A case of intellectual sexism." *American Journal of Sociology* 78 (January): 936–45.
Alford, Robert R.
1967   "Class voting in Anglo-American democracies." In *Party Systems and Voter Alignments,* edited by Seymour Martin Lipset and Stein Rokkan, 67–94. New York: Free Press.
Alves, Wayne M., and Peter H. Rossi
1978   "Who should get what? Fairness judgments of the distribution of earnings." *American Journal of Sociology* 84 (November): 541–64.
Antos, Joseph R.; Mark Chandler; and Wesley Mellow
1980   "Sex differences in union membership." *Industrial and Labor Relations Review* 33 (January): 162–69.
Aronowitz, Stanley
1973   *False Promises.* New York: McGraw-Hill.
1983   *Working Class Hero: A New Strategy for Labor.* New York: Adama.
Ashenfelter, Orley, and George E. Johnson
1969   "Bargaining theory, trade unions, and industrial strike activity." *American Economic Review* 59 (March): 35–49.
Aveling, Edward, and Eleanor Marx Aveling
[1888] 1969   *The Working Class Movement in America.* New York: Arno.
Baca Zinn, Maxine; Lynn W. Cannon; Elizabeth Higginbotham; and Bonnie T. Dill
1986   "The costs of exclusionary practices in women's studies." *Signs* 11 (Winter): 290–303.

311

Bachrach, Peter, and Morton S. Baratz
1962   "The two faces of power." *American Political Science Review* 56 (December): 947–52.
1963   "Decisions and nondecisions: An analytical framework." *American Political Science Review* 57 (September): 632–42.
1970   *Power and Poverty: Theory and Practice.* New York: Oxford University Press.
Bailey, Kenneth D.
1974   "Cluster analysis." In *Sociological Methodology, 1975*, edited by David R. Heise, 59–128. San Francisco: Jossey-Bass.
Bain, George Sayers, and Robert Price
1980   *Profiles of Union Growth: A Comparative Statistical Portrait of Eight Countries.* Oxford: Basil Blackwell.
Bakke, E. Wight
1940   *Citizens without Work: A Study of the Effects of Unemployment upon the Workers' Social Relations and Practices.* New Haven, Conn.: Yale University Press.
Baran, Paul A., and Paul M. Sweezy
1966   *Monopoly Capital: An Essay on the American Economic and Social Order.* New York: Monthly Review Press.
Barkan, Joanne
1984   *Visions of Emancipation: The Italian Workers' Movement since 1945.* New York: Praeger.
Bell, Daniel
1973   *The Coming of Post-Industrial Society.* New York: Basic Books.
Bell, Wendell, and Robert V. Robinson
1980   "Cognitive maps of class and racial inequalities in England and the United States." *American Journal of Sociology* 86 (September): 320–49.
Bem, Daryl J.
1972   "Self-perception theory." In *Advances in Experimental Social Psychology*, edited by Leonard Berkowitz, 2–62. New York: Academic Press.
Bendix, Reinhard
1956   *Work and Authority in Industry.* New York: Wiley.
Benson, Susan Porter
1984   "Women in retail sales work: The continuing dilemma of service." In *My Troubles Are Going to Have Trouble with Me:*

Everyday Trials and Triumphs of Women Workers, edited by Karen Sacks and Dorothy Remy, 113–23. New Brunswick, N.J.: Rutgers University Press.

Berle, Adolf A., and Gardiner C. Means

1932   *The Modern Corporation and Private Property*. New York: Macmillan.

Bernstein, Eduard

[1899]   1961   *Evolutionary Socialism: A Criticism and Affirmation.* Translated by Edith C. Harvey. New York: Schocken Books.

Bernstein, Irving

1960   *The Lean Years, A History of the American Worker, 1920–1933.* Boston: Houghton Mifflin.

1970   *Turbulent Years: A History of the American Worker, 1933–1941.* Boston: Houghton Mifflin.

Billingsley, Andrew

1968   *Black Families in White America*. Englewood Cliffs, N.J.: Prentice-Hall.

Bing, Alexander M.

1921   *War-Time Strikes and Their Adjustment*. New York: Dutton.

Blau, Peter, and Otis Dudley Duncan

1967   *The American Occupational Structure*. New York: Wiley.

Bluestone, Barry, and Bennett Harrison

1982   *The Deindustrialization of America*. New York: Basic Books.

Blumberg, Paul

1980   *Inequality in an Age of Decline*. Oxford: Oxford University Press.

Bohrnstedt, George

1974   "Review of H. M. Blalock, *Causal Models in the Social Sciences.*" *Social Forces* 53 (September): 129–30.

Bonacich, Edna

1980   "Class approaches to ethnicity and race." *Insurgent Sociologist* 10 (Fall): 9–23.

Bookman, Ann, and Sandra Morgen

fc   *Women and the Politics of Empowerment: Perspectives from the Workplace and the Community*. Philadelphia: Temple University Press.

Bott, Elizabeth

1957   *Family and Social Network*. London: Tavistock.

Bottomore, T. B.
1966   *Classes in Modern Society.* New York: Vintage.
Braverman, Harry
1974   *Labor and Monopoly Capital: The Degradation of Work in the Twentieth Century.* New York: Monthly Review Press.
Brecher, Jeremy
1972   *Strike!* Boston: South End Press.
Breiger, Ronald L.
1981   "The social class structure of occupational mobility." *American Journal of Sociology* 87 (November): 578–611.
Broder, David
1980   "It's Ruth's Day, Too." *Washington Post* (July, 16): A19.
Brody, David
1960   *Steelworkers in America: The Nonunion Era.* Cambridge, Mass.: Harvard University Press.
1965   *Labor in Crisis: The Steel Strike of 1919.* Philadelphia: Lippincott.
1968   "The rise and decline of welfare capitalism." In *Change and Continuity in Twentieth Century America: The 1920s,* edited by John Braeman, Robert H. Bremner, and David Brody, 147–78. Columbus: Ohio State University Press.
1971   "The expansion of the American labor movement: Institutional sources of stimulus and restraint." In *The American Labor Movement,* edited by David Brody, 119–37. New York: Harper & Row.
Buchanan, William, and Hadley Cantril
1953   *How Nations See Each Other.* Urbana: University of Illinois Press.
Budge, Ian, and Dennis Fairlie
1977   *Voting and Party Competition: A Theoretical Critique and Synthesis Applied to Surveys from Ten Democracies.* London: Wiley.
Bulmer, Martin
1975   *Working Class Images of Society.* Boston: Routledge & Kegan Paul.
Burawoy, Michael
1977   "Social structure, homogenization, and the process of status attainment in the United States and Great Britain." *American Journal of Sociology* 82 (March): 1031–42.
1978   "Toward a Marxist theory of the labor process: Braverman and beyond." *Politics and Society* 8 (3–4): 247–312.

1979   *Manufacturing Consent: Changes in the Labor Process un-
         der Monopoly Capitalism.* Chicago: University of Chicago
         Press.
Burnham, Walter Dean
1970   *Critical Elections and the Mainsprings of American Politics.*
         New York: Norton.
1974   "The United States: The politics of heterogeneity." In *Elec-
         toral Behavior: A Comparative Handbook,* edited by Richard
         Rose, 653–725. New York: Free Press.
1980   "The appearance and disappearance of the American voter."
         In *Electoral Participation: A Comparative Analysis,* edited
         by Richard Rose, 35–74. Beverly Hills: Sage.
Burstein, Paul
1979   "Equal employment opportunity legislation and the income
         of women and nonwhites." *American Sociological Review* 44
         (June): 367–91.
Burton, Michael
1972   "Semantic dimensions of occupation names." In *Multidimen-
         sional Scaling: Theory and Applications in the Behavioral
         Sciences,* edited by A. K. Romney, R. N. Shepard, and S. B.
         Nerlove. New York: Seminar Press.
Butler, David, and Donald Stokes
1969   *Political Change in Britain: Forces Shaping Electoral
         Choice.* New York: St. Martin's.
1974   *Political Change in Britain: The Evolution of Electoral
         Choice.* New York: St. Martin's.
Calhoun, Craig
1982   *The Question of Class Struggle: Social Foundations of the
         Popular Radicalism during the Industrial Revolution.* Chi-
         cago: University of Chicago Press.
Campbell, Angus; Philip Converse; Warren Miller; and Donald Stokes
1960   *The American Voter.* New York: Wiley.
Cannon, Lynn Weber
1980   "On the absolute or relative basis of perception: The case for
         middle class identification." *Social Indicators Research* 8
         (September): 347–63.
1984   "Trends in class identification among Blacks from 1952 to
         1978." *Social Science Quarterly* 65 (March): 112–26.
Cannon, Lynn Weber, and Reeve Vanneman
1986   "Class perceptions in the Black community." Manuscript,
         Center for Research on Women, Memphis State University.

Cantril, Hadley
1943 "Identification with social and economic class." *Journal of Abnormal and Social Psychology* 38 (January): 74–80.
Carchedi, Guglielmo
1977 *On the Economic Identification of Social Classes.* London: Routledge & Kegan Paul.
Carroll, J. Douglas, and Jih-Jie Chang
1970 "Analysis of individual differences in multidimensional scaling via an n-way generalization of 'Eckart-Young' decomposition." *Psychometrika* 35 (September): 283–319.
Carter, Sandy
1979 "Class conflict: The human dimension." In *Between Labor and Capital*, edited by Pat Walker, 97–120. Boston: South End Press.
Case, Herman M.
1955 "Marxian implications of Centers' interest group theory: A critical appraisal." *Social Forces* 33 (March): 254–58.
Centers, Richard
1949 *The Psychology of Social Classes.* Princeton, N.J.: Princeton University Press.
Chamberlain, Chris
1983 *Class Consciousness in Australia.* Sydney: Allen & Unwin.
Chinoy, Eli
1955 *Automobile Workers and the American Dream.* Garden City, N.Y.: Doubleday.
Chorley, Katherine
1943 *Armies and the Art of Revolution.* London: Faber & Faber.
Clawson, Dan
1980 *Bureaucracy and the Labor Process: The Transformation of U.S. Industry, 1860–1920.* New York: Monthly Review Press.
Coldrick, A. P., and Philip Jones
1979 *An International Directory of the Trade Union Movement.* New York: Facts on File.
Coleman, Richard P., and Lee Rainwater
1978 *Social Standards in America: New Dimensions of Class.* New York: Basic Books.
Collins, Patricia Hill
fc "Learning from the outsider within: The sociological significance of Black feminist thought." *Social Problems.*

Collins, Randall
1979   *The Credential Society: An Historical Sociology of Education
        and Stratification*. New York: Academic.
Collins, Sharon
1983   "The making of the black middle class." *Social Problems* 30
        (April): 369–82.
Commons, John R.
1908   "Is class conflict in America growing and is it inevitable?"
        American Journal of Sociology 13 (May): 756–66.
Converse, Philip E.
1976   *The Dynamics of Party Support: Cohort-analyzing Party
        Identification*. Beverly Hills: Sage.
Coser, Lewis A.
1956   *The Functions of Social Conflict*. New York: Free Press.
1975   "Presidential address: Two methods in search of a sub-
        stance." *American Sociological Review* 40 (December):
        691–700.
Cox, Oliver C.
1948   *Caste, Class and Race: A Study in Social Dynamics*. New
        York: Modern Reader Paperbacks.
Coxon, Anthony P. M., and Charles L. Jones
1974   "Occupational similarities: Some subjective aspects of social
        stratification." *Quality and Quantity* 8: 139–58.
1978   *The Images of Occupational Prestige*. New York: St.
        Martin's.
Crozier, Michel
1984   *The Trouble with America: Why the System Is Breaking
        Down*. Translated by Peter Heinegg. Berkeley: University of
        California Press.
Cumbler, John T.
1979   *Working-class Community in Industrial America: Work, Lei-
        sure, and Struggle in Two Industrial Cities, 1880–1930*.
        Westport, Conn.: Greenwood Press.
Curtis, Richard F., and Elton F. Jackson
1977   *Inequality in American Communities*. New York: Academic.
Dahrendorf, Ralf
1959   *Class and Class Conflict in Industrial Society*. Stanford:
        Stanford University Press.
Dalia, Joan Talbert, and Avery M. Guest
1975   "Embourgeoisement among blue-collar workers?" *Sociologi-
        cal Quarterly* 16 (Summer): 291–304.

Davis, Angela
1981   *Women, Race and Class.* New York: Random House.
Davis, James Allen, and Tom W. Smith
1985   *General Social Surveys, 1972–1985: Cumulative Codebook.*
        Storrs, Conn.: Roper Public Opinion Research Center, Uni-
        versity of Connecticut.
Davis, Mike
1980   "Why the U.S. working class is different." *New Left Review*
        123 (September–October): 3–46.
1986   *Prisoners of the American Dream: Politics and Economy in
        the History of the U.S. Working Class.* London: Verso.
Dawley, Alan
1976   *Class and Community: The Industrial Revolution in Lynn.*
        Cambridge, Mass.: Harvard University Press.
Debs, Eugene V.
1948   *Writings and Speeches of Eugene V. Debs.* New York: Her-
        mitage Press.
1970   *Eugene Debs Speaks.* New York: Pathfinder Press.
Della Fave, L. Richard
1974   "On the structure of egalitarianism." *Social Problems* 22
        (December): 199–213.
Derber, Charles
1982   *Professionals as Workers: Mental Labor in Advanced Capi-
        talism.* Boston: G. K. Hall.
Dick, William M.
1972   *Labor and Socialism in America: The Gompers Era.* Port
        Washington, N.Y.: Kennikat Press.
Dill, Bonnie Thornton
1979   "Across the boundaries of race and class: An exploration of
        the relationship of work and family among Black female do-
        mestic workers." Doctoral dissertation, New York Univer-
        sity.
1982   "Survival as a form of resistance: Minority women and the
        maintenance of families." Paper presented at the annual
        meeting of American Sociological Association, San Fran-
        cisco.
1983   "Race, class and gender: Prospects for an all inclusive sister-
        hood." *Feminist Studies* 9 (1): 131–50.
Dollard, John
1937   *Caste and Class in a Southern Town.* New Haven, Conn.:
        Yale University Press.

Domhoff, G. William
  1967   *Who Rules America?* Englewood Cliffs, N.J.: Prentice-Hall.
  1972   *Fat Cats and Democrats.* Englewood Cliffs, N.J.: Prentice-Hall.
  1978   *The Powers That Be: Processes of Ruling Class Domination in America.* New York: Random House.
Drake, St. Clair, and Horace R. Cayton
  [1945]   1962   *Black Metropolis.* New York: Harper Torchbook.
Drew, Elizabeth
  1983   *Politics and Money: The New Road to Corruption.* New York: Macmillan.
Dubofsky, Melvyn
  1968   *When Workers Organize: New York City in the Progressive Era.* Amherst: University of Massachusetts Press.
  1969   *We Shall Be All: A History of the Industrial Workers of the World.* Chicago: Quadrangle.
  1974   "Socialism and syndicalism." In *Failure of a Dream: Essays in the History of Socialism,* edited by John H. M. Laslett and Seymour Martin Lipset, 252–99. Garden City, N.Y.: Anchor Books.
  1975   *Industrialism and the American Worker, 1865–1920.* New York: Crowell.
Du Bois, W. E. B.
  [1899]   1967   *The Philadelphia Negro.* New York: Schocken Books.
Duncan, Otis Dudley
  1961   "A socioeconomic index for all occupations." In *Occupations and Social Status,* edited by A. Reiss, 109–61. New York: Free Press.
  1966   "Methodological issues in the analysis of social mobility." In *Social Structure and Mobility in Economic Development,* edited by Neil J. Smelser and Seymour Martin Lipset, 51–97. Chicago: Aldine.
  1975   "Does money buy satisfaction?" *Social Indicators Research* 2: 267–74.
Duncan, Otis Dudley; D. L. Featherman; and B. Duncan
  1972   *Socioeconomic Background and Achievement.* New York: Seminar Press.
Easterlin, Richard A.
  1973   "Does money buy happiness?" *Public Interest* 30: 3–10.

1974   "Does economic growth improve the human lot? Some em-
        pirical evidence." In *Nations and Households in Economic
        Growth*, edited by Paul David and Melvin Reder, 89–125.
        New York: Academic.

Edelman, Murray
1971   *Politics as symbolic action.* New Haven, Conn.: Yale Uni-
        versity Press.

Edwards, P. K.
1981   *Strikes in the United States: 1881–1974.* New York: St.
        Martin's.

Edwards, Richard
1979   *Contested Terrain: The Transformation of the Workplace in
        the Twentieth Century.* New York: Basic Books.

Ehrenreich, Barbara, and John Ehrenreich
1979   "The professional-managerial class." In *Between Labor and
        Capital*, edited by Pat Walker, 5–45. Boston: South End
        Press.

Elder, Glen H., Jr.
1974   *Children of the Great Depression: Social Change in Life Ex-
        perience.* Chicago: University of Chicago Press.

Ellwood, David, and Glenn Fine
1983   "The impact of right-to-work laws on union organizing."
        Manuscript, National Bureau of Economic Research.

Engels, Friedrich
[1880] 1972 *Socialism: Utopian and Scientific.* New York: Path-
        finder Press.

Escoffier, Jeffrey
1986   "Socialism as ethic." *Socialist Review* 16 (January– Febru-
        ary): 117–21.

Evers, Mark
1976   "Log-linear models of change in class identification." *Public
        Data Use* 4 (September): 3–19.

Farley, Reynolds
1977   "Trends in racial inequalities: Have the gains of the 1960's
        disappeared in the 1970's?" *American Sociological Review*
        42 (April): 189–208.

Featherman, David L., and Robert M. Hauser
1976   "Prestige or socioeconomic scales in the study of occupa-
        tional achievement?" *Sociological Methods and Research* 4
        (March): 403–23.

Featherman, David L.; Michael Sobel; and David Dickens
1975 "A manual for coding occupations and industries into detailed 1970 categories and a listing of 1970-basis Duncan socioeconomic and NORC prestige scores." Manuscript, Center for Demography and Ecology, University of Wisconsin, Madison.

Felson, Marcus, and David Knoke
1974 "Social status and the married woman." *Journal of Marriage and the Family* 36 (August): 516–21.

Fine, Sidney
1969 *Sit-down: The General Motors Strike of 1936–1937.* Ann Arbor: University of Michigan Press.

Flacks, Richard
1971 *Youth and Social Change.* Chicago: Markham.

Foner, Philip S.
1980 *Women and the American Labor Movement: From World War I to the Present.* New York: Free Press.

Fortune
1940 "The people of the U.S.A.—A self-portrait." *Fortune* 21 (February): 14ff.

Foster, William Z.
1920 *The Great Steel Strike and Its Lessons.* New York: B. W. Huebsch.

Fox, William S.; David E. Payne; Thomas B. Priest; and William W. Philliber
1977 "Authority position, legitimacy of authority structure, and acquiescence to authority." *Social Forces* 55 (June): 966–73.

Frazier, E. Franklin
1939 *The Negro Family in the United States.* Chicago: University of Chicago Press.
1957 *Black Bourgeoisie.* New York: Free Press.

Free, Lloyd A., and Hadley Cantril
1967 *The Political Beliefs of Americans: A Study of Public Opinion.* New Brunswick, N.J.: Rutgers University Press.

Freeman, Richard B., and James L. Medoff
1984 *What Do Unions Do?* New York: Basic Books.

Friedheim, Robert L.
1964 *The Seattle General Strike.* Seattle: University of Washington Press.

Gagliani, Giorgio
    1981   "How many working classes?" *American Journal of Sociology* 87 (September): 259–85.
Galbraith, John Kenneth
    1958   *The Affluent Society*. Boston: Houghton Mifflin.
    1967   *The New Industrial State*. Boston: Houghton Mifflin.
Gallup, George, and Saul Forbes Rae
    1940   *The Pulse of Democracy: The Public Opinion Poll and How It Works*. New York: Simon & Schuster.
Gamson, William A.
    1975   *The Strategy of Social Protest*. Homewood, Ill.: Dorsey Press.
    1980   "Understanding the careers of challenging groups: A commentary on Goldstone." *American Journal of Sociology* 85 (March): 1043–60.
Garson, G. David
    1973   "Automobile workers and the radical dream." *Politics and Society* 3 (Winter): 163–77.
Geschwender, James A.
    1977   *Class, Race, and Worker Insurgency*. Cambridge: Cambridge University Press.
Giddens, Anthony
    1973   *The Class Structure of Advanced Societies*. New York: Harper & Row.
Gilbert, Dennis, and Joseph A. Kahl
    1987   *The American Class Structure: A New Synthesis*. Chicago: Dorsey Press.
Gilligan, Carol
    1982   *In a Different Voice: Psychological Theory and Women's Development*. Cambridge, Mass.: Harvard University Press.
Glenn, Evelyn Nakano, and Rosalyn L. Feldberg
    1977   "Degraded and deskilled: The proletarianization of clerical work." *Social Problems* 25 (October): 52–64.
Glenn, Norval
    1975   "The contribution of white collars to occupational prestige." *Sociological Quarterly* 16 (Spring): 184–89.
Goldstein, Robert Justin
    1978   *Political Repression in Modern America: From 1870 to the Present*. Cambridge, Mass.: Schenkman.

1983   *Political Repression in Nineteenth Century Europe*. London: Croom Helm.

Goldstone, Jack A.

1980   "The weakness of organization: A new look at Gamson's The Strategy of Social Protest." *American Journal of Sociology* 85 (March): 1017–42.

1980   "Mobilization and organization: Reply to Foley and Steedly and to Gamson." *American Journal of Sociology* 85 (May): 1428–32.

Goldthorpe, John H., and Keith Hope

1974   *The Social Grading of Occupations: A New Approach and Scale*. Oxford: Oxford University Press.

Goldthorpe, John H.; David Lockwood; Frank Beckhoffer; and Jennifer Platt

1969   *The Affluent Worker in the Class Structure*. Cambridge: Cambridge University Press.

Gompers, Samuel

1925   *Seventy Years of Life and Labor: An Autobiography*. New York: Dutton.

Goodman, Ellen

1979   *Turning Points*. New York: Fawcett Crest.

Gordon, Milton M.

1958   *Social Class in American Sociology*. Durham, N.C.: Duke University Press.

Gorz, André

1967   *Strategy for Labor: A Radical Proposal*. Boston: Beacon Press.

Gouldner, Alvin

1980   *The Two Marxisms: Contradictions and Anomalies in the Development of Theory*. New York: Seabury Press.

Goyder, John C., and Peter C. Pineo

1974   "Minority group status and self-evaluated class." *Sociological Quarterly* 15 (Spring): 199–211.

Gramsci, Antonio

[1948]   1971   *Selections from the Prison Notebooks of Antonio Gramsci*. Translated by Quintin Hoare and Geoffrey Nowell Smith. New York: International Publishers.

Greene, Victor S.

1968   *The Slavic Community on Strike: Immigrant Labor in Penn-*

sylvania Anthracite. South Bend, Ind.: University of Notre Dame Press.

Gross, Neal
  1953   "Social class identification in the urban community." *American Sociological Review* 18 (August): 398–404.
Guest, Avery
  1974   "Class consciousness and American political attitudes." *Social Forces* 52 (June): 496–509.
Gulick, Charles, and Melvin K. Bers
  1953   "Insight and illusion in Perlman's theory of the labor movement." *Industrial and Labor Relations Review* 6 (July): 510–31.
Gurin, Patricia; Arthur H. Miller; and Gerald Gurin
  1980   "Stratum identification and consciousness." *Social Psychology Quarterly* 43: 30–47.
Gurr, Ted Robert
  1970   *Why Men Rebel.* Princeton, N.J.: Princeton University Press.
Gutman, Herbert G.
  1973   "Work, culture, and society in industrializing America, 1815–1919." *American Historical Review* 78: 531–88.
  1976   *The Black Family in Slavery and Freedom.* New York: Pantheon Books.
Haer, John L.
  1957   "An empirical study of social class awareness." *Social Forces* 52 (February): 496–510.
Halle, David
  1984   *America's Working Man: Work, Home, and Politics among Blue-Collar Property Owners.* Chicago: University of Chicago Press.
Hamilton, Richard F.
  1966a   "The marginal middle class: A reconsideration." *American Sociological Review* 31 (April): 192–200.
  1966b   "Reply to Tucker." *American Sociological Review* 31 (December): 856.
  1972   *Class and Politics in the United States.* New York: Wiley.
  1975   *Restraining Myths: Critical Studies of U.S. Social Structure and Politics.* Beverly Hills, Calif.: Sage.
  1982   *Who Voted for Hilter?* Princeton, N.J.: Princeton University Press.

Hamilton, Richard F., and James D. Wright
1986   *The State of the Masses*. Hawthorne, N.Y.: Aldine.
Handlin, Oscar
1951   *The Uprooted: The Epic Story of the Great Migrations that Made the American People*. Boston: Little, Brown.
Hanushek, Eric A., and John E. Jackson
1977   *Statistical Methods for Social Scientists*. New York: Academic.
Hare, Nathan
1973   "Quoted in 'The black middle class defined.'" *Ebony* 28 (August): 44–48.
Harrington, Michael
1972   *Socialism*. New York: Saturday Review Press.
1976   "Foreword." In Werner Sombart, *Why Is There No Socialism in the United States?*, ix–xii. White Plains, N.Y.: M. E. Sharpe.
Hartz, Louis
1955   *The Liberal Tradition in America*. New York: Harcourt, Brace & World.
Hauser, Robert M.; Peter J. Dickinson; Harry P. Travis; and John N. Koffel
[1975]   1977   "Structural changes in occupational mobility among men in the United States." *American Sociological Review* 40 (October): 585–98.
Hauser, Robert M., and David L. Featherman
1977   *The Process of Stratification: Trends and Analyses*. New York: Academic.
Haywood, William D.
1929   *Bill Haywood's Book: The Autobiography of William Haywood*. New York: International Publishers.
Herberg, Will
1955   *Protestant-Catholic-Jew*. New York: Doubleday.
Hibbs, Douglas A., Jr.
1976   "Industrial conflict in advanced industrial societies." *American Political Science Review* 70: 1033–58.
Higginbotham, Elizabeth
1981   "Just who is Black and middle class?" Paper presented at the annual meeting of the Society for the Study of Social Problems, Toronto.

1985   "Race and class barriers to Black women's college atten-
        dance." *Journal of Ethnic Studies* 13 (Spring): 89–107.
fc   "Employment for professional Black women in the twentieth
        century." In *Ingredients for Women's Employment Policy*,
        edited by Christine Bose and Glenna Spitze. New York: State
        University of New York Press.
Higham, John
1955   *Strangers in the Land: Patterns of American Nativism,
        1860–1925.* New Brunswick, N.J.: Rutgers University
        Press.
Hill, Robert B.
1979   "The illusion of Black progress: A statement of the facts."
        In *The Caste and Class Controversy*, edited by Charles V.
        Willie, 76–79. Bayside, N.Y.: General Hall.
Hiller, Dana V., and William W. Philliber
1978   "The derivation of status benefits from occupational attain-
        ments of working wives." *Journal of Marriage and the Fam-
        ily* 40 (February): 63–70.
Hirschman, Albert O.
1970   *Exit, Voice, and Loyalty: Responses to Decline in Firms, Or-
        ganizations, and States.* Cambridge, Mass.: Harvard Univer-
        sity Press.
Hochschild, Jennifer L.
1981   *What's Fair: American Beliefs about Distributive Justice.*
        Cambridge, Mass.: Harvard University Press.
Hodge, Robert W.; Paul M. Siegel; and Peter H. Rossi
[1964] 1966   "Occupational prestige in the United States: 1925–
        1963." *American Journal of Sociology* 70 (November):
        286–302.
1966   "Occupational prestige in the United States, 1925–1963." In
        Class, Status, and Power, 2d edition, edited by R. Bendix
        and S. M. Lipset, 322–34. New York: Free Press.
Hodge, Robert W., and Donald J. Treiman
1968   "Class identification in the United States." *American Journal
        of Sociology* 75: 535–47.
Hodge, Robert W.; Donald J. Treiman; and Peter H. Rossi
1966   "A comparative study of occupational prestige." In *Class,
        Status, and Power*, 2d edition, edited by R. Bendix and
        S. M. Lipset, 309–21. New York: Free Press.

Hofstadter, Richard, and Seymour Martin Lipset, editors
1968   *Turner and the Sociology of the Frontier.* New York: Basic Books.
Horan, Patrick
1978   "Is status attainment research atheoretical?" *American Sociological Review* 43 (August): 534–41.
Husbands, C. T.
1976   "Editor's introductory essay." In Werner Sombart, *Why Is There no Socialism in the United States?*, xv–xxxvii. White Plains, N.Y.: M. E. Sharpe.
ICPSR
1968   *The SRC 1966 American Election Study.* Ann Arbor, Mich.: Inter-University Consortium for Political and Social Research.
1972   *Study of Political Change in Britain: 1963–1970.* Ann Arbor, Mich.: Inter-University Consortium for Political and Social Research.
1975   *The CPS 1972 American National Election Study.* Ann Arbor, Mich.: Inter-University Consortium for Political and Social Research.
1983   *ABC News/Washington Post Poll of Public Opinion on Current Social and Political Issues, January 1982.* Ann Arbor, Mich.: Inter-University Consortium for Political and Social Research.
ILO
1982   *Yearbook of International Labour Statistics.* Geneva: International Labour Organization.
Inglehart, Ronald
1977   *The Silent Revolution: Changing Values and Political Styles among Western Publics.* Princeton, N.J.: Princeton University Press.
Inkeles, Alex, and Peter H. Rossi
1956   "National comparisons of occupational prestige." *American Journal of Sociology* 61 (January): 329–39.
Interchurch World Movement
1920   *Report on the Steel Strike of 1919.* New York: Harcourt, Brace and Rowe.
Jackman, Mary R., and Robert W. Jackman
1973   "An interpretation of the relation between objective and sub-

jective social status." *Americal Sociological Review* 38 (October): 569–82.

1983   *Class Awareness in the United States*. Berkeley: University of California Press.

James, David R., and Michael Soref

1981   "Profit constraints on managerial autonomy: Managerial theory and the unmaking of the corporation president." *American Sociological Review* 46 (February): 1–18.

Janda, Kenneth

1970   *A Conceptual Framework for the Comparative Analysis of Political Parties*. Beverly Hills, Calif.: Sage.

Jencks, Christopher

1979   *Who Gets Ahead?: The Determinants of Economic Success in America*. New York: Basic Books.

Jensen, Vernon H.

1950   *Heritage of Conflict: Labor Relations in the Nonferrous Metals Industry up to 1930*. Ithaca, N.Y.: Cornell University Press.

Jessop, Bob

1985   *Nicos Poulantzas: Marxist Theory and Political Strategy*. New York: St. Martin's.

Jones, Mary Harris "Mother"

1925   *Autobiography of Mother Jones*. Chicago: Charles H. Kerr.

Kahl, Joseph A.

1957   *The American Class Structure*. New York: Holt, Rinehart & Winston.

Kahl, Joseph A., and James A. Davis

1955   "A comparison of indexes of socio-economic status." *American Sociological Review* 20 (June): 317–25.

Kalleberg, Arne, and Larry J. Griffin

1980   "Class, occupation, and inequality in job rewards." *American Journal of Sociology* 85 (January): 731–68.

Karabel, Jerome

1979   "The failure of American socialism reconsidered." *Socialist Register* 16: 204–27.

Katz, Naomi, and David S. Kemnitzer

1984   "Women and work in Silicon Valley: Options and futures." In *My Troubles Are Going to Have Trouble with Me: Everyday Trials and Triumphs of Women Workers*, edited by Karen

Sacks and Dorothy Remy, 209–18. New Brunswick, N.J.: Rutgers University Press.

Katznelson, Ira
1981   *City Trenches: Urban Politics and the Patterning of Class in the United States*. Chicago: University of Chicago Press.

Kautsky, Karl
1905–6   "Der amerikanische Arbeiter." *Die Neue Zeit* 24: 678–83, 717–27, 740–52, 773–87.

Kennedy, Ruby Jo Reeves
1944   "Single or triple melting-pot? Intermarriage trends in New Haven, 1870–1940." *American Journal of Sociology* 49 (January): 331–39.

Kerbo, Harold R.
1983   *Social Stratification and Inequality*. New York: McGraw-Hill.

Kerckhoff, Alan C.; Richard T. Campbell; and Jerry M. Trott
1982   "Dimensions of educational and occupational attainment in Great Britain." *American Sociological Review* 47 (June): 347–64.

Kerckhoff, Alan C., and Robert Nash Parker
1979   "Comment on equality, success and social justice in England and the United States." *American Sociological Review* 44 (April): 328–34.

Kerr, Clark; John T. Dunlop; Frederick H. Harbison; and Charles A. Meyers
1960   *Industrialism and Industrial Man: The Problems of Labor and Management in Economic Growth*. Cambridge, Mass.: Harvard University Press.

Keyfitz, Nathan
1976   "World resources and the world middle class." *Scientific American* 235 (July): 28–35.

Kluegel, James R., and Eliot Smith
1981   "Beliefs about stratification." *Annual Review of Sociology* 7: 29–56.

Kluegel, James R.; Royce Singleton, Jr.; and Charles E. Starnes
1977   "Subjective class identification: A multiple indicator approach." *American Sociological Review* 42 (August): 599–611.

Knoke, David, and Michael Hout
1974   "Social and demographic factors in American political party

affiliations, 1952–72." *American Sociological Review* 39 (October): 700–13.

Kohn, Melvin L., and Carmi Schooler
1969 "Class occupation and orientation." *American Sociological Review* 34 (October): 659–78.

Kornblum, William
1974 *Blue Collar Community*. Chicago: University of Chicago Press.

Korpi, Walter
1978 *The Working Class in Welfare Capitalism: Work, Unions, and Politics in Sweden*. London: Routledge & Kegan Paul.

Korpi, Walter, and Michael Shalev
1979 "Strikes, industrial relations and class conflict in capitalist societies." *British Journal of Sociology* 30 (June): 164–87.
1980 "Strikes, power and politics in the western nations, 1900–1976." In *Political Power and Social Theory: A Research Annual*, Volume 1, edited by Maurice Zeitlin, 301–34. Greenwich, Conn.: JAI Press.

Kraus, Richard
1981 *Class Conflict in Chinese Socialism*. New York: Columbia University Press.
1983 "Bureaucratic privilege as an issue in Chinese politics." *World Development* 11 (8): 673–82.

Kraus, Richard, and Reeve Vanneman
1985 "Bureaucrats versus the state in capitalist and socialist regimes." *Comparative Studies in Society and History* 27 (January): 111–22.

Landecker, Werner S.
1960 "Class boundaries." *American Sociological Review* 25 (December): 868–77.
1963 "Class crystallization and class consciousness." *American Sociological Review* 28 (April): 219–29.

Lane, Robert
1962 *Political Ideology*. New York: Free Press.

Laslett, John H. M.
1970 *Labor and the Left: A Study of Socialist and Radical Influences in the American Labor Movement, 1881–1924*. New York: Basic Books.

Laslett, John, and S. M. Lipset, eds.
1974   *Failure of a Dream? Essays in the History of American So-cialism.* Garden City, N.Y.: Anchor Books.
1984   *Failure of a Dream? Essays in the History of American So-cialism.* Berkeley: University of California Press.

Laumann, Edward O.
1966   *Prestige and Association in an Urban Community.* Indianap-olis, Ind.: Bobbs-Merrill.
1973   *Bonds of Pluralism: The Form and Substance of Urban So-cial Networks.* New York: Wiley.

Laumann, Edward O., and Richard Senter
1976   "Subjective social distance, occupational stratification, and forms of status and class consciousness: A cross-national rep-lication and extension." *American Journal of Sociology* 81 (May): 1304–38.

Lebergott, Stanley
1964   *Manpower in Economic Growth: The American Record since 1800.* New York: McGraw-Hill.

Lee, Everett S.
[1961]   1968 "The Turner thesis re-examined." *American Quarterly* 13 (Spring): 77–83.

Leggett, John C.
1968   *Class, Race, and Labor: Working-Class Consciousness in Detroit.* New York: Oxford University Press.

Lenin, V. I.
[1920]   1975 "'Left-Wing' Communism—An Infantile Disor-der." In V. I. Lenin, *Selected Works*, volume 3: 291–369. Moscow: Progress.

Lenski, Gerhard
1952   "American social classes: Statistical strata or social groups?" *American Journal of Sociology* 58 (September): 139–44.

Levine, Louis
1924   *The Women's Garment Workers: A History of the Interna-tional Ladies Garment Workers Union.* New York: B. W. Huebsch.

Levison, Andrew
1974   *The Working-Class Majority.* New York: Coward, McCann & Geoghegan.

Liebknecht, Wilhelm
1887   *Ein Blick in die Neue Welt.* Stuttgart: J. H. W. Dietz.

Lipset, Seymour Martin
[1960] 1963   *Political Man: The Social Bases of Politics*. Garden City, N.Y.: Doubleday.
        1963   *The First New Nation: The United States in Historical and Comparative Perspective*. New York: Basic Books.
        1974   "Social scientists view the problem." In *Failure of a Dream? Essays in the History of American Socialism*, edited by John H. M. Laslett and Seymour Martin Lipset, 25–82. Garden City, N.Y.: Doubleday.
        1977   "Why no socialism in the United States?" In *Sources of Contemporary Radicalism*, edited by Serwyn Bialer and Sophia Sluzar, 31–149. Boulder, Colo.: Westview Press.
        1979   "Predicting the future of post-industrial society." In *America as a Post-Industrial Society*, edited by Seymour Martin Lipset, 1–36. Stanford, Calif.: Hoover Institute Press.
        1981   "Whatever happened to the proletariat? An historic mission unfulfilled." *Encounter* 56 (June): 18–34.
        1983   "Radicalism or reformism: The sources of working-class politics." *American Political Science Review* 77 (March): 1–18.
Lipset, Seymour Martin, and Reinhard Bendix
        1967   *Social Mobility in Industrial Society*. Berkeley: University of California Press.
Lipsky, Michael
        1980   *Street Level Bureaucracy*. New York: Russell Sage Foundation.
Lockwood, David
        1958   *The Blackcoated Worker*. London: Allen & Unwin.
Lopreato, Joseph
        1968   "Authority relations and class conflict." *Social Forces* 47 (September): 70–79.
Lopreato, Joseph, and Lawrence Hazelrigg
        1972   *Class Conflict and Mobility*. San Francisco: Chandler.
Low-Beer, John R.
        1978   *Protest and Participation: The New Working Class in Italy*. Cambridge: Cambridge University Press.
Lukács, Georg
[1922] 1971   *History and Class Consciousness*. Translated by Rodney Livingstone. Cambridge, Mass.: MIT Press.

Lukes, Steven
1974   *Power: A Radical View*. London: Macmillan.
Luxemburg, Rosa
[1904]   1961   "Organizational questions of the Russian Social Democracy or Leninism or Marxism?" In *The Russian Revolution and Leninism or Marxism?* edited by Bertram D.
Wolfe, 81–108. Ann Arbor: University of Michigan Press.
[1906]   1970   "The mass strike, the political party, and the trade
unions." In *Rosa Luxemburg Speaks*, edited by Mary-Alice
Waters, 155–218. New York: Pathfinder Press.
Lynd, Robert S., and Helen Merrell Lynd
1929   *Middletown: A Study in Contemporary American Culture*.
New York: Harcourt, Brace.
1937   *Middletown in Transition: A Study in Cultural Conflicts*.
New York: Harcourt, Brace & World.
Mallet, Serge
[1963]   1975   *The New Working Class*. Nottingham: Spokesman
Books.
Mann, Michael
1970   "The social cohesion of liberal democracy." *American Sociological Review* 35 (June): 423–39.
1973   *Consciousness and Action among the Western Working
Class*. London: Macmillan.
Marcuse, Herbert
1964   *One-Dimensional Man*. Boston: Beacon Press.
Marglin, Stephen A.
1974   "What do bosses do? The origins and functions of hierarchy
in capitalist production." *Review of Radical Political Economics* 6 (Summer): 60–113.
Marwick, Arthur
1980   *Class: Image and Reality in Britain, France, and the U.S.A.
since 1930*. New York: Oxford University Press.
Marx, Karl
[1852]   1974   "The Eighteenth Brumaire of Louis Bonaparte." In
Surveys from Exile: Political Writings, volume 2, edited by
David Fernbach, 143–249. New York: Vintage.
[1859]   1970   *A Contribution to the Critique of Political Economy*.
Translated by S. W. Ryazanskaya. New York: International
Publishers.

[1867]   1976   *Capital*. Translated by Ben Fowkes. New York: Vintage.

Marx, Karl, and Friedrich Engels

[1848]   1976   "Manifesto of the Communist Party." In Karl Marx and Frederick Engels, *Collected Works*, Volume 6, *Marx and Engels: 1845–48*, 477–519. New York: International Publishers.

1953   *Letters to Americans, 1848–1895: A Selection*. Translated by Leonard E. Mens. New York: International Publishers.

Mason, Karen O.; William M. Mason; Harold H. Winsborough; and W. K. Poole

1973   "Some methodological issues in cohort analysis of archival data." *American Sociological Review* 38 (April): 242–58.

McNamee, Stephen, and Reeve Vanneman

1983   "The perception of class: The social and technical relations of production." *Work and Occupations* 10 (November): 437–69.

McNaught, Kenneth

1966   "American progressives and the Great Society." *Journal of American History* 53 (December): 504–20.

Mead, George Herbert

1962   *Mind, Self, and Society*. Chicago: University of Chicago Press.

Miller, Ann R.

1971   *Occupations of the Labor Force According to the Dictionary of Occupational Titles*. Washington, D.C.: Office of Management and Budget.

Miller, Jean B.

1976   *Toward a New Psychology of Women*. Boston: Beacon Press.

Mills, C. Wright

1956   *The Power Elite*. New York: Oxford University Press.

[1960]   1963 "The new left." *New Left Review* 5 (September–October): 18–23.

1963   *Power, Politics and People: The Collected Essays of C. Wright Mills*. New York: Oxford University Press.

Monsen, R. Joseph, and Kenneth D. Walters

1983   *Nationalized Companies: A Threat to American Business*. New York: McGraw-Hill.

Montgomery, David
  1979   *Workers' Control in America: Studies in the History of Work,
          Technology, and Labor Struggles.* Cambridge: Cambridge
          University Press.
Moore, Barrington, Jr.
  1966   *Social Origins of Dictatorship and Democracy: Lord and
          Peasant in the Making of the Modern World.* Boston: Beacon
          Press.
Moore, R. Laurence
  1970   *European Socialists and the American Promised Land.* New
          York: Oxford University Press.
Moore, Thomas S.
  1982   "The structure of work life 'ordeal': An empirical assessment
          of class criteria." *Insurgent Sociologist* 11 (Spring): 73–
          84.
Moore, Wilbert E.
  1954   "Occupational structure and industrial conflict." In *Industrial
          Conflict,* edited by Arthur Kornhauser, Robert Dubin, and
          Arthur M. Ross, 221–31. New York: McGraw-Hill.
Moorhouse, H. F.
  1976   "Attitudes to class and class relationships in Britain." *Sociol-
          ogy* 10 (September): 469–96.
Murphy, George G. S., and Arnold Zellner
  [1959] 1968 "Sequential Growth, the Labor Safety Valve Doctrine
          and the Development of American Unionism." *Journal of
          Economic History* 19 (September): 402–21.
Naisbitt, John
  1982   *Megatrends: Ten New Directions Transforming Our Lives.*
          New York: Warner Books.
Newby, Robert G.
  1981   "The political economy of the Black middle class: Trends
          from 1960 to 1980." Paper presented at the annual meeting of
          the Society for the Study of Social Problems, Toronto.
Newman, Dorothy K.; Nancy J. Amidei; Barbara L. Carter; Dawn Day;
William J. Krunant; and Jack S. Russell
  1978   *Protest, Politics, Prosperity: Black Americans and White In-
          stitutions, 1940–75.* New York: Pantheon Books.
Newman, Dorothy K.
  1979   "Underclass: An appraisal." In *The Caste and Class Contro-*

versy, edited by Charles V. Willie, 92–97. Bayside, N.Y.: General Hall.

Nisbet, Robert
    1959   "The decline and fall of social class." *Pacific Sociological Review* 2 (Spring): 11–17.

OECD
    1983   *Historical Statistics: 1960–1981.* Paris: Organisation for Economic Cooperation and Development.

Ogmundson, Rick
    1975   "Party images and the class vote in Canada." *American Sociological Review* 40 (August): 506–12.

Oppenheim, Karen
    1970   "Voting in recent American presidential elections." Doctoral dissertation, University of Chicago.

Oppenheimer, Valerie K.
    1970   *The Female Labor Force in the United States.* Berkeley: University of California Press.

Ossowski, Stanislaw
    1963   *Class Structure in the Social Consciousness.* Translated by Sheila Patterson. New York: Free Press.

Paige, Jeffrey
    1975   *Agrarian Revolution: Social Movements and Export Agriculture in the Underdeveloped World.* New York: Free Press.

Parenti, Michael
    1978   *Power and the Powerless.* New York: St. Martin's.

Parkin, Frank
    1971   *Class Inequality and Political Order: Social Stratification in Capitalist and Communist Societies.* New York: Praeger.

    1979   *Marxism and Class Theory: A Bourgeois Critique.* New York: Columbia University Press.

Parsons, Talcott
    1943   "The kinship system of the contemporary United States." *American Anthropologist* 45 (January): 22–38.

Penn, Roger
    1975   "Occupational prestige hierarchies: A great empirical invariant?" *Social Forces* 54 (December): 352–64.

Perlman, Selig
    1922   *A History of Trade Unionism in the United States.* New York: Macmillan.

    1928   *A Theory of the Labor Movement.* New York: Macmillan.

Perlman, Selig, and Philip Taft
  1935   *Labor Movements*. New York: Macmillan.
Pettigrew, Thomas F.
  1967   "Social evaluation theory: Convergences and applications."
          In *Nebraska Symposium on Motivation, 1967*, edited by D.
          Levine. Lincoln: University of Nebraska Press.
  1979   "The changing-not declining-significance of race." In *The
          Caste and Class Controversy*, edited by Charles V. Willie,
          111–16. Bayside, N.Y.: General Hall.
Phelps-Brown, E. H., with Sheila V. Hopkins
  1950   "The course of wage-rates in five countries, 1860–1939."
          Oxford Economic Papers, n.s. 2 (June): 226–96.
Pineo, Peter C., and John C. Goyder
  1973   "Social class identification of national sub-groups." In *Social
          Stratification: Canada*, edited by James E. Curtis and Wil-
          liam G. Scott, 187–96. Scarborough, Ont.: Prentice-Hall of
          Canada.
Piven, Frances Fox, and Richard A. Cloward
  1971   *Regulating the Poor: The Functions of Public Welfare*. New
          York: Pantheon Books.
  1977   *Poor People's Movements: Why They Succeed, How They
          Fail*. New York: Pantheon Books.
Pomer, Marshall I.
  1981   *Intergenerational Mobility in the United States: A Segmenta-
          tion Perspective*. Gainesville: University Presses of Florida.
Popitz, H.; H. P. Bahrdt; E. A. Jueres; and A. Kesting
  [1957] 1969   "The worker's image of society." In *Industrial Man*,
          edited by Tom Burns, 281–330. Baltimore: Penguin
          Books.
Portes, Alejandro
  1971a   "A note on the interpretation of class consciousness." *Ameri-
          can Journal of Sociology* 77 (September): 228–44.
  1971b   "Political primitivism, differential socialization, and lower
          class left radicalism." *American Sociological Review* 36 (Oc-
          tober): 820–35.
Potter, David
  1954   *People of Plenty*. Chicago: University of Chicago Press.
Poulantzas, Nicos
  1968   *Political Power and Social Classes*. London: New Left
          Books.

1974   *Classes in Contemporary Capitalism*. London: New Left Books.
1977   "The new petty bourgeoisie." In *Class and Class Structure*, edited by Alan Hunt, 113–24. London: Lawrence & Wishart.
1978   *State, Power, Socialism*. London: New Left Books.

Rainwater, Lee
1974   *What Money Buys: Inequality and the Social Meanings of Income*. New York: Basic Books.

Rainwater, Lee, and William Yancey
1967   *The Moynihan Report and the Politics of Controversy*. Cambridge, Mass.: MIT Press.

Reich, Michael
1978   "The development of the wage-labor force." In *The Capitalist System*, edited by Richard C. Edwards, Michael Reich, and Thomas E. Weisskopf, 179–85. Englewood Cliffs, N.J.: Prentice-Hall.

Reiss, Albert J., Jr.; with Otis Dudley Duncan; Paul K. Hatt; and Cecil C. North
1961   *Occupations and Social Status*. New York: Free Press.

Ritter, Kathleen V., and Lowell L. Hargens
1975   "Occupational positions and class identifications of married working women: A test of the asymmetry hypothesis." *American Journal of Sociology* 80 (January): 934–48.

Robinson, Robert V., and Wendell Bell
1978   "Equality, success, and social justice in England and the United States." *American Sociological Review* 43 (April): 125–43.

Robinson, Robert V., and Jonathan Kelley
1979   "Class as conceived by Marx and Dahrendorf; effects on income inequality and politics in the United States and Great Britain." *American Sociological Review* 43 (December): 813–28.

Roemer, John A.
1982   *A General Theory of Exploitation and Class*. Cambridge, Mass.: Harvard University Press.

Rollins, Judith
1985   *Between Women: Domestics and Their Employers*. Philadelphia: Temple University Press.

Rosenblum, Gerald
1973   *Immigrant Workers: Their Impact on American Labor Radicalism.* New York: Basic Books.
Ross, Arthur M., and Paul T. Hartman
1960   *Changing Patterns of Industrial Conflict.* New York: Wiley.
Rossi, Peter H.
1976   "Conventional wisdom, common sense, and empirical knowledge: The case of stratification research and views of American society." In *The Uses of Controversy in Sociology,* edited by Lewis A. Coser and Otto N. Larsen, 30–47. New York: Free Press.
Rossi, Peter H., and Steven L. Nock, eds.
1982   *Measuring Social Judgments: The Factorial Survey Approach.* Beverly Hills, Calif.: Sage.
Rothschild, Emma
1973   *Paradise Lost: The Decline of the Auto-Industrial Age.* New York: Random House.
Rubin, Lillian B.
1976   *Worlds of Pain: Life in the Working-Class Family.* New York: Basic Books.
Rudolph, Lloyd L., and Susanne Hoeber Rudolph
1967   *The Modernity of Tradition: Political Development in India.* Chicago: University of Chicago Press.
Runciman, W. G.
1966   *Relative Deprivation and Social Justice.* Berkeley: University of California Press.
Ryan, William
1971   *Blaming the Victim.* New York: Pantheon Books.
Sacks, Karen Brodkin
1984   "Computers, ward secretaries, and a walkout in a Southern hospital." In *My Troubles Are Going to Have Trouble with Me: Everyday Trials and Triumphs of Women Workers,* edited by Karen Sacks and Dorothy Remy, 173–90. New Brunswick, N.J.: Rutgers University Press.
Sacks, Karen, and Dorothy Remy, editors
1984   *My Troubles Are Going to Have Trouble with Me: Everyday Trials and Triumphs of Women Workers.* New Brunswick, N.J.: Rutgers University Press.

Sampson, William
    1980   "What is wrong with the debate over race and class?" Paper
            presented at the annual meeting of the American Sociological
            Association, New York.
Schecter, Susan
    1982   *Women and Male Violence: The Visions and Struggles of the
            Battered Women's Movement.* Boston: South End Press.
Schlozman, Kay Lehman, and Sidney Verba
    1979   *Injury to Insult: Unemployment, Class, and Political Re-
            sponse.* Cambridge, Mass.: Harvard University Press.
Schrieber, E. M., and G. T. Nygreen
    1970   "Subjective social class in America, 1945–1968." *Social
            Forces* 48 (March): 348–56.
Schulman, Michael; Linda Reif; and Rhonda Zingraff
    1983   "Race, gender, class consciousness and union support: An
            analysis of southern textile workers." Paper presented at the
            annual meeting of the American Sociological Association,
            Detroit.
Schuman, Howard, and Michael P. Johnson
    1976   "Attitudes and behavior." In *Annual Review of Sociology,
            1972,* volume 2, edited by Alex Inkeles, James Coleman,
            and Neil Smelser, 161–207. Palo Alto, Calif.: Annual Re-
            views.
Schuman, Howard, and Stanley Presser
    1979   "The open and closed question." *American Sociological Re-
            view* 44 (October): 692–712.
Seifer, Nancy
    1973   *Absent from the Majority.* New York: National Project on
            Ethnic America of the American Jewish Committee.
Sennett, Richard, and Jonathan Cobb
    1972   *The Hidden Injuries of Class.* New York: Knopf.
Sewell, William H.; Robert M. Hauser; and David L. Featherman
    1976   *Schooling and Achievement in American Society.* New York:
            Academic.
Shalev, Michael
    1980   "Trade unions and economic analysis: The case of industrial
            conflict." *Journal of Labor Research* 1 (Spring): 133–74.
Shalev, Michael, and Walter Korpi
    1980   "Working class mobilization and American exceptionalism."
            Economic and Industrial Democracy 1 (February): 31–61.

Shannon, Fred A.
    [1945]   1968   "A post-mortem on the labor-safety-valve theory."
                     Agricultural History 19 (January): 31–37.
Shapiro-Perl, Nina
    1984   "Resistance strategies: The routine struggle for bread and
              roses." In *My Troubles Are Going to Have Trouble with Me:
              Everyday Trials and Triumphs of Women Workers*, edited by
              Karen Sacks and Dorothy Remy, 193–208. New Brunswick,
              N.J.: Rutgers University Press.
Shorter, Edward, and Charles Tilly
    1974   *Strikes in France, 1830–1968*. London: Cambridge Univer-
              sity Press.
Shostak, Arthur
    1969   *Blue-Collar Life*. New York: Random House.
Shryock, Henry, and Jacob S. Siegel
    1975   *The Methods and Materials of Demography*. Washington,
              D.C.: Government Printing Office.
Siegel, Paul
    1971   "Prestige in the American occupational structure." Doctoral
              dissertation, University of Chicago.
Simler, Norman J.
    [1958]   1968   "The safety-valve doctrine re-evaluated." *Agricul-
                     tural History* 32 (October): 250–57.
Skocpol, Theda
    1979   *States and Social Revolutions*. New York: Cambridge Uni-
              versity Press.
Smith, Barbara
    1983   *Home Girls: A Black Feminist Anthology*. New York: Kit-
              chen Table, Women of Color Press.
Sombart, Werner
    [1906]   1976   *Why Is There No Socialism in the United States?*
              Translated by Patricia M. Hocking and C. T. Husbands.
              White Plains, N.Y.: M. E. Sharpe.
Stallard, Karen; Barbara Ehrenreich; and Holly Sklar
    1983   *Poverty in the American Dream*. Boston: South End Press.
Steedly, Homer R., Jr., and John W. Foley
    1979   "The success of protest groups: Multivariate analyses." *So-
              cial Science Research* 8 (March): 1–15.
Stephens, John D.
    1979   "Class formation and class consciousness: A theoretical and

empirical analysis with reference to Britain and Sweden."
British Journal of Sociology 30 (December): 389–414.

1980   *The Transition from Capitalism to Socialism.* Atlantic Highlands, N.J.: Humanities Press.

1981   "The changing Swedish electorate, class voting contextual effects, and voter volatility." *Comparative Political Studies* 14 (July): 163–204.

Stone, Katherine

1975   "The origins of job structures in the steel industry." In *Labor Market Segmentation*, edited by Richard C. Edwards, Michael Reich, and David M. Gordon, 27–84. Lexington, Mass.: Heath.

Sweezy, Paul M.

[1967]   1972   "Marx and the proletariat." *Monthly Review* 19 (December): 25–43.

Taft, Philip, and Philip Ross

1969   "American labor violence: Its causes, character, and outcome." In *Violence in America: Historical and Comparative Perspectives: A Report to the National Commission on the Causes and Prevention of Violence, June 1969*, edited by Hugh Davis Graham and Ted Robert Gurr, 270–376. New York: New American Library.

Tawney, R. H.

1979   "The American labour movement." In *The American Labour Movement and Other Essays*, edited by J. M. Winter, 1–110. New York: St. Martin's.

Tax, Meredith

1980   *The Rising of the Women: Feminist Solidarity and Class Conflict, 1880–1917.* New York: Monthly Review Press.

Taylor, Frederick Winslow

1903   *Shop Management.* New York: Harper Bros.

1911   *The Principles of Scientific Management.* New York: Harper Bros.

Terkel, Studs

1974   *Working: People Talking about What They Do All Day and How They Feel about What They Do.* New York: Pantheon Books.

1980   *American Dreams: Lost and Found.* New York: Pantheon Books.

Therborn, Goran
  1977   "The rule of capital and the rise of democracy." *New Left Review* 103 (May–June): 3–42.
  1982   "Review of Nicos Poulantzas, Classes in Contemporary Capitalism." *Contemporary Sociology* 11 (January): 34–35.
Thernstrom, Stephan
  1964   *Poverty and Progress: Social Mobility in a Nineteenth-Century City.* Cambridge, Mass.: Harvard University Press.
  1973   *The Other Bostonians: Poverty and Progress in the American Metropolis.* Cambridge, Mass.: Harvard University Press.
Thomas, William I., and Florian Znaniecki
  1927   *The Polish Peasant in Europe and America.* New York: Knopf.
Thompson, E. P.
  1963   *The Making of the English Working Class.* New York: Pantheon Books.
Tilly, Louise A., and Charles Tilly
  1981   *Class Conflict and Collective Action.* Beverly Hills, Calif.: Sage.
de Tocqueville, Alexis
  [1835,   1954 *Democracy in America.* Translated by Henry Reeve,
  1840]   revised by Francis Bowen. New York: Vintage.
Traugott, Mark
  1985   *Armies of the Poor: Determinants of Working-Class Participation in the Parisian Insurrection of June 1848.* Princeton, N.J.: Princeton University Press.
Treiman, Donald J.
  1977   *Occupational Prestige in Comparative Perspective.* New York: Academic.
Treiman, Donald J., and Kermit Terrell
  1975   "The process of status attainment in the United States and Great Britain." *American Journal of Sociology* 81 (November): 563–83.
Tronti, Mario
  1976   "The labour process and class strategies." *Conference of Socialist Economists* 1 (1): 92–129.
Tucker, Charles W.
  1966   "On working class identification." *American Sociological Review* 31 (December): 855–65.

1968   "A comparative analysis of subjective social class: 1945–
        1963." *Social Forces* 46 (June): 508–14.
Turner, Frederick Jackson
1920   *The Frontier in American History*. New York: Holt.
Tyree, Andrea; Moshe Semyonov; and Robert W. Hodge
1979   "Gaps and glissandos: Inequality, economic development
        and social mobility." *American Sociological Review* 44
        (June): 410–24.
U.S. Bureau of the Census
1963   *U.S. Census of Population: 1960. Subject Reports: Occu-
        pational Characteristics*. Washington, D.C.: Government
        Printing Office.
1972   *Money Income in 1971 of Families and Persons in the United
        States*. Washington, D.C.: Government Printing Office.
1973a   *Historical Statistics of the United States: Colonial Times to
        1970*. Washington, D.C.: Government Printing Office.
1973b   *U.S. Census of Population: 1970. Subject Reports: Occupa-
        tional Characteristics*. Washington, D.C.: Government
        Printing Office.
1979   *The Social and Economic Status of the Black Population in
        the United States: An Historical View, 1790–1978*. Wash-
        ington, D.C.: Government Printing Office.
1980   *U.S. Census of Population: 1980. Detailed Characteristics
        of the Population*. Washington, D.C.: Government Printing
        Office.
1983   *Statistical Abstract of the United States: 1982–83*. Washing-
        ton, D.C.: Government Printing Office.
U.S. Bureau of Labor Statistics
1986   *Employment and Earnings, January*. Washington, D.C.:
        Government Printing Office.
U.S. Department of Labor
1965   *Dictionary of Occupation Titles*, 3d edition. Washington,
        D.C.: U.S. Government Printing Office.
Vanneman, Reeve
1977   "The occupational composition of American classes." *Ameri-
        can Journal of Sociology* 83 (January): 783–807.
1980   "U.S. and British perceptions of class." *American Journal of
        Sociology* 85 (January): 769–90.
Vanneman, Reeve D., and Fred C. Pampel
1977   "The American perception of class and status." *American So-
        ciological Review* 42 (June): 422–37.

Vanneman, Reeve D., and Thomas F. Pettigrew
    1972   "Race and relative deprivation in the urban United States."
            Race 13 (4): 461–86.
Van Velsor, Ellen, and Leonard Beeghley
    1979   "The process of class identification among employed married
            women: A replication and reanalysis." *Journal of Marriage
            and the Family* 41 (November): 771–78.
Wachtel, Howard M.
    1974   "Class consciousness and stratification in the labor process."
            Review of Radical Political Economics 6 (Spring): 1–31.
Walker, Charles R.
    1937   *American City: A Rank-and-File History*. New York: Farrar
            & Rinehart.
Wattenberg, Ben J.
    1974   *The Real America*. Garden City, N.Y.: Doubleday.
Weber, Max
    [1915] 1946 "The social psychology of the world religions." In
            From Max Weber: Essays in Sociology, edited by Hans H.
            Gerth and C. Wright Mills, 267–302. New York: Oxford
            University Press.
    [1921] 1978 *Economy and Society*. Translated by Guenther Roth
            and Claus Wittich. Berkeley: University of California
            Press.
Weinstein, James A.
    1967   *The Decline of Socialism in America, 1912–1925*. New
            York: Monthly Review Press.
Welch, John
    1979   "New Left knots." In *Between Labor and Capital*, edited by
            Pat Walker, 173–90. Boston: South End Press.
Wells, H. G.
    1906   *The Future in America*. New York: Harper and Brothers.
Westcott, Diane N.
    1982   "Blacks in the 1970's: Did they scale the job ladder?"
            Monthly Labor Review 105 (June): 29–38.
Wilensky, Harold L.
    1966   "Class, class consciousness, and American workers." In *La-
            bor in a Changing America*, edited by William Haber, 12–
            28. New York: Basic Books.
Will, George
    1985   "Rosemary's Restaurant." *Washington Post*, December 1,
            p. C7.

Willener, Alfred
  1957   *Images de la Societe et Classes Sociales.* Bern: Imprimerier Staempfli.
  1975   "Images, action, 'us,' and 'them.'" In *Working-Class Images of Society*, edited by Martin Bulmer, 180–91. London: Routledge & Kegan Paul.
Willie, Charles V.
  1976   *A New Look at Black Families.* Bayside, N.Y.: General Hall.
  1979   *The Caste and Class Controversy.* Bayside, N.Y.: General Hall.
Wilson, William J.
  1978   *The Declining Significance of Race: Blacks and Changing American Institutions.* Chicago: University of Chicago Press.
Winer, B. J.
  1971   *Statistical Principle in Experimental Design.* New York: McGraw-Hill.
Wolf, Wendy C., and Neil D. Fligstein
  1979   "Sex and authority in the workplace: The causes of sexual inequality." *American Sociological Review* 44 (April): 235–53.
Wolff, Leon
  1965   *Lockout: The Story of the Homestead Strike of 1892: A Study of Violence, Unionism, and the Carnegie Steel Empire.* New York: Harper & Row.
Wright, Erik Olin
  1976   "Class boundaries in advanced capitalist societies." *New Left Review* 98 (July–August): 3–41.
  1979   *Class Structure and Income Determination.* New York: Academic.
  1980   "Varieties of Marxist conceptions of class structure." *Politics & Society* 9 (3): 323–70.
  1983   "A conceptual framework for the comparative analysis of class structure." Paper presented at the annual meeting of the Council for European Studies, Washington, D.C.
  1985   *Classes.* London: Verso.
Wright, Erik Olin; Cynthia Costello; David Hachen; and Joey Sprague
  1982   "The American class structure." *American Sociological Review* 47 (December): 709–26.

Wright, Erik Olin, and Luca Perrone
    1977   "Marxist class categories and income inequality." *American Sociological Review* 42 (February): 32–55.

Yanowitch, Murray
    1977   *Social and Economic Inequality in the Soviet Union.* White Plains, N.Y.: M. E. Sharpe.

Zeitlin, Maurice
    1974   "Corporate ownership and control: The large corporation and the capitalist class." *American Journal of Sociology* 79 (March): 1073–1119.

INDEX